Everyday Miracles of Lourdes

Marlene F. Watkins

Everyday Miracles of Lourdes

Twenty Extraordinary Experiences Along the Way to the Grotto

Second edition

EWTN Publishing, Inc.
Irondale, Alabama

Cover design: LUCAS Art & Design, Jenison, MI

Cover art: Front cover (Phewa Lake, Pokhara, Nepal by Kartabya Aryal on Unsplash); back cover (Heilige Lourdes Grotte in Lourdes Frankreich Europa_AdobeStock_278393469).

Nihil Obstat:
Rev. Christopher R. Seibt, S.T.L.

Imprimatur:
Most Rev. Douglas J. Lucia, Bishop of Syracuse

October 7, 2022
Memorial of Our Lady of the Rosary

EWTN Publishing, Inc.
5817 Old Leeds Road, Irondale, AL 35210

Distributed by Sophia Institute Press, Box 5284, Manchester, NH 03108.

paperback ISBN 978-1-68278-375-7

ebook ISBN 978-1-68278-376-4

Library of Congress Control Number: 2024951839

First printing

Dedication

This book is dedicated with a grateful heart and all my love to:

My Sacramental Spouse (My Handsome Prince, "Honey Luv") and to our beloved five sons, their beautiful wives, and each of our grandchildren, in thanksgiving for the many sacrifices they have made over the years for Our Lady of Lourdes Hospitality North American Volunteers and for this book—first to be lived and loved—so it could then be written here.

***

With eternal gratitude and loving memory for:

† Paul David Braden: Our Chairman of the Board of Directors in this world and the other world; husband, father, grandfather, son, brother, uncle, godfather, and friend; colonel, pilot, leader, logistician, faithful Catholic, veteran, and volunteer; for his humble example teaching us how to live a holy life and how to die a holy death; for catechizing us in his witness to the profound redemptive value of suffering; for teaching us to learn to share the extraordinary grace of an Apostolic Pardon; and for his holy wisdom and insight to keep us ever mindful of the true reality that *Heaven is the goal.*

I am not made to make you believe, but to say it to you.

—St. Bernadette Soubirous

A Special Invitation to the Reader:

In the spirit of St. Bernadette,
you are kindly requested to pass along this book to
anyone who might read it—not to try to make them
believe it, but just to share this with them.

Contents

Meet most of the people written about and pictured in these chapters through episodes of *My Lourdes Faith Journey*, the popular series filmed and produced by Our Lady of Lourdes Hospitality North American Volunteers and aired on EWTN. Use your smart device to click the QR code below or visit: https://lourdesvolunteers.org/my-lourdes-faith-journey/.

Foreword

The *Catechism of the Catholic Church* (*CCC* 972) teaches us that Mary, assumed into Heaven, is an icon of both what the Church is now "in her mystery on her own 'pilgrimage of faith,' and what she will be in the homeland at the end of her journey." Citing a passage from the Dogmatic Constitution of the Church *Lumen Gentium* (68) of the Second Vatican Council, the *Catechism* continues:

> In the meantime, the Mother of Jesus, in the glory which she possesses in body and soul in heaven, is the image and beginning of the Church as it is to be perfected in the world to come. Likewise, she shines forth on earth until the day of the Lord shall come, a sign of certain hope and comfort to the pilgrim People of God.

Mary's apparition to the young maiden Bernadette Soubirous at Lourdes in 1858 has been and still is for millions of people throughout the world "a sign of certain hope and comfort" as they make their pilgrim way "mourning and weeping in this valley of tears," awaiting that glorious day of the Lord when He "will wipe away every tear from their eyes, and death shall be no more, [and] neither shall there be mourning nor crying nor pain any more" (Rev. 21:4).

In addition to the seventy official, authenticated miracles of Lourdes, there have been and continue to be what Marlene Watkins, the author of this captivating book, calls "mini-miraculous 'Lourdesian' events." Her use of the qualifying prefix *mini* to distinguish this latter class of miracles from the former does not imply that they are less than authentic because not authenticated. They also, she notes, are "miraculous," but as privately experienced, despite not being publicly proclaimed as such by the Church; they also are works of Heaven, believed with certainty to be such by their beneficiaries, works that show evidence of exceeding in whole or in part what earthly power could obtain. Granted by God, Whom Jesus revealed to be the mystery of Trinitarian Love (see 1 John 4:8, 16) "an eternal exchange of love, Father, Son, and Holy Spirit" (*CCC* 221), these signs, these outpourings of God's love, when they become known to us in the telling, become stories of hope and comfort for us, too, as we all make our journey together in Holy Mother Church to our homeland in Heaven.

My thanks to Marlene Watkins for her inspiring account of twenty of these beautiful stories, ones made known to her and her fellow Our Lady of Lourdes Hospitality North American Volunteers. May your reading of them be occasions for the Lord to deepen your faith, embolden your hope, and fan the flames of His love within you.

—Raymond Leo Cardinal Burke

Acknowledgments

"I will forget no one."

—St. Bernadette Soubirous

St. Bernadette advised us to leave the room before being thanked—yet she never said not to thank others! Each of these amazing people is deeply imprinted discreetly "behind the door" of this book for his or her contribution of talents, skills, support, and prayers, and so we kindly thank them.

With heartfelt gratitude and love:
To the people in the chapters of this book and their families and friends, along with all those who made their pilgrimages for extraordinary experiences possible.

For it is through the Church that all graces flow:
With humble thanksgiving to the Most Reverend Douglas Lucia for his continued support and his *imprimatur* and the Reverend Christopher Seibt, J.C.L., for his *nihil obstat*, and the Syracuse Diocese (New York, United States).

With humble thanksgiving to the Guardian of the Grotto, Monseigneur Jean-Marc Micas, and Recteur Père Michel Daubanes, and the Diocese of Tarbes et Lourdes (France).

Special thanks to "The Pub Club!" for the selfless hours of collaborating with Our Lady of Lourdes Hospitality North American Volunteers Publications Committee.

With indebted thanks to those who collaborated to make this book:
Theresa Stiner (author wrangler), Teresa Lewis (prayer anchor), Marianne Fischer (wisdom-well resource and storyteller confidant), Belen Tan (book guardian), Majel Braden (book cheerleader and traveling proofreader), Mary (comma queen and proofreader) and Charlie Copeland, Jim Barton (photo finisher), Alexandria Marrow (writer extraordinaire), Sean Martin (theological steward), Jim Kernell (legal custodian), Fr. Robert Hyde Jr., J.C.L. (publication spiritual director), Tom Buchanan, Esq. (an ultimate editor-proofreader), Toni Colella (book champion and super editor-proofreader), Barry Vaughn (gentleman editor and heroic publication shepherd), and Bill Watkins (first listener).

With kind thankfulness to our pre-readers and fact-checkers:
Deanna, Aggie, Pat and Melissa, Colonel Diana, Dr. Belen, Dr. Mary Jo, Dr. Linda, Nurse Mary, Rena, Noah, Fr. Sean, Deacon Dan and Vickie, Courtney, Ashley, Duckie, Pam, and Erika.

Avec remerciements respectuex (with respectful thanks):
Lourdes Chaplain Père Régis-Marie de La Teyssonnière, Sanctuary Archivist Nicolas Dargegen, Lourdes Bureau Medical Director Dr. Alessandro de Franciscis, and Sanctuary Resources Director Stephanie Shaw.

Lourdes Sanctuary Communications Team, especially David Torchala and Marie Dorot, Pierre Vincent, photographer-drone pilot.

French familial friends:
My "Lourdes Godfather" Jean Buscail, and my Lourdes BFF Domi, our "French family" Jean et Gwen, and our historical treasure Thérèse.

And Congrégation des Sœurs de la Charité de Nevers:
Sr. Margaret Mary Homan and Sr. Marie Ange Mesclon.

With respectful appreciation to the Hospitalité Notre-Dame de Lourdes:
From Président Gabriel Barbrey to Président Daniel Pezet; from Piscine Vice Presidents Mme. Marisette Goisneau to Mariarita Ferri and to all the dedicated women in St. Jean Baptiste; to the tireless gentlemen of St. Joseph and the selfless ladies of the Accueil Notre-Dame and Accueil Marie-Saint-Frai, the knowledgeable formaters of Ste. Bernadette, and the St. Michel Service.

With thanks on the ground and in the air to:
Air France, especially the extraordinary Heftzi Kaplan, NY-JFK T1, Delta Airlines, especially the SYR Airport team (Merci, Terri Dupra!), and the Pau Airport ground staff led by Chantel and former Group Desk "Missou" Elsie Fidelia-Air France.

With continued international thanks to:
Collette Powers, Norman Servais, Jeffrey Lange, Maeve and Ishy Boyle, Gabriel McGuigan and Ita Renaghan, Aidan Gallagher and Campbell Miller, Fr. John McEvoy, and Ma Michelle Charles.

With respect and thanks to:
Our Lady of Lourdes Hospitality North American Volunteers Board of Directors: Barry, Teresa, Jim, Belen, Pam, Erika, Theresa, Jim and Pam, Tonja, Majel, Melinde, Nancy, Brian, Edwin and Charo, Linda, Kathy, and Dr. Dave.

With eternal thanks to:
Generous Belen (and Melinde) and Nancy (and Kevin) for editorial hospitality; gracious Tom (and Marie) and Toni (and Luke) for sublime edit-proofreading, meticulous Mary (and Charlie) for detailed review, Super Barry (and Marianne) for everything, and always Bill.

With indebted thanks to those who made this manuscript into a published book:
Devin Jones and Taylor Wilson at EWTN Publishing and Sophia Institute Press: Anna Maria, Sarah, Mary Beth, Molly and Molly, John (cover design), and to Ramona Rosales (providential editorial bookologist) and Nora Malone (editor supreme).

Pope Francis about Stories[1]

That you may tell your children and grandchildren. (Exod. 10:2, NIV)

Sacred Scripture is a *Story of stories*. . . . The Bible is thus the great love story between God and humanity. At its centre stands Jesus, whose own story brings to fulfillment both God's love for us and our love for God. . . . The history of Christ is not a legacy from the past; it is our story, and always timely. It shows us that God was so deeply concerned for mankind, for our flesh and our history, to the point that He became man, flesh and history. It also tells us that no human stories are insignificant or paltry. Since God became story, every human story is, in a certain sense, a divine story. Every human story has an irrepressible dignity. Consequently, humanity deserves stories that are worthy of it, worthy of that dizzying and fascinating height to which Jesus elevated it. . . .

Amid the cacophony of voices and messages that surround us, we need a human story that can speak of ourselves and of the beauty all

[1] Excerpts from the Holy Father in Rome, Pope Francis, Message for the 54th World Communications Day (January 24, 2020), nos. 3–4, 1, 5.

around us. A narrative that can regard our world and its happenings with a tender gaze. A narrative that can tell us that we are part of a living and interconnected tapestry. A narrative that can reveal the interweaving of the threads which connect us to one another.... So it is not a matter of simply telling stories as such, or of advertising ourselves, but rather of remembering who and what we are in God's eyes, bearing witness to what the Spirit writes in our hearts and revealing to everyone that his or her story contains marvelous things.

In order to do this, let us entrust ourselves to a woman who knit together in her womb the humanity of God and, the Gospel tells us, wove together the events of her life. For the Virgin Mary "treasured all these things and pondered them in her heart" (Luke 2:19). Let us ask for help from her, who knew how to untie the knots of life with the gentle strength of love:

O Mary, woman and mother, you wove
the divine Word in your womb,
you recounted by your life the magnificent works of God.
Listen to our stories,
hold them in your heart and make your own
the stories that no one wants to hear.
Teach us to recognize the good thread
that runs through history.
Look at the tangled knots in our life
that paralyze our memory.
By your gentle hands, every knot can be untied.
Woman of the Spirit, mother of trust, inspire us too.
Help us build stories of peace, stories
that point to the future.
And show us the way to live them together.

FRANCISCUS

Preface

We are a society accustomed to a sophisticated norm of "techie miracles" with smartphones, voice-activated GPS gadgets, drone digital imagery, laser microsurgery, and advanced molecular nanotechnologies. With this increasing multitude of tantalizing advancements, it could be easy to forget that "every good idea comes from God" (paraphrasing James 1:17, NIV)! It could be easier to forget or not to know that a miracle is of divine intervention and not just an extraordinary happening of luck or chance, modern intellect, or third-millennium brilliance.

The word *miracle*, from the Latin *miraculum*, from *mirari*, "to wonder," is a supernatural sign brought about by God, signifying His glory and the salvation of mankind. Only an infinite God can perform miracles—we limited humans cannot. A miracle is an occurrence above nature and beyond man. God performs miracles for our salvation so that we can know that HE IS WHO IS. As Fr. John Paul Mary Zeller, M.F.V.A., reminds us, "God IS God—*and we are just us*."

The same God Who performed the multitude of miracles in the Gospels two thousand years ago so the people of that time could know HE IS GOD performing miracles at Lourdes today so that we can know HE IS GOD! "Jesus Christ is the same yesterday and today and for ever" (Heb. 13:8). Lourdes is like the Gospel present for us now, so we can know and witness God today in His supernatural signs for His glory and for our salvation.

The Lourdes Grotto is renowned, both as a place of miracles *publicly* proclaimed and miracles *privately* experienced. Thus, the word *miracle* is often associated with Lourdes. Today, we are graced to witness Church-authenticated miracles as well as undocumented "miraculous" events at Lourdes. For a week at a time, some of us are privileged to journey to a little "global city-state of miracles" in charming southwestern France. Along our way, we often encounter mini-miraculous "Lourdesian" events. These are not to be confused with the seventy official miracles pronounced by the Catholic Church. Documented inexplicable cures pass through exhaustive scientific examination by the Bureau des Constatations Médicales de Lourdes and intense scrutiny by the Catholic Church before they can be formally proclaimed as a miracle by a bishop. Unofficial supposed, proposed, or believed works of God may still be called *miraculous* or *miracles*, but these should not be confused with official pronouncements made at Lourdes or by a bishop. And so it is for the "everyday miracles" written about in this book.

At the very beginning of Our Lady of Lourdes Hospitality North American Volunteers (most often called Lourdes Volunteers), at St. Gildard Convent, the former motherhouse of the religious order of Bernadette Soubirous, Sr. Margaret Mary of the Sisters of Charity of Christian Instruction at Nevers advised us to follow the holy example of St. Bernadette when sharing the graces of Lourdes. Bernadette said:

> *Je ne suis pas chargée de vous le faire croire mais de vous le dire.*
> *I am not made to make you believe, but to say it to you.*

Bernadette didn't add her own stitch to the simply exquisite embroidery of the Marian apparitions, nor did she need to remove a stitch to leave behind a hole in the fabric of simple truth. Her accurate telling of the apparitions was never embellished. Bernadette simply told it as it was, and we should try to do the same. Sr. Margaret Mary instructed, "It's a beautiful handiwork of God; don't try to improve on it"—*as if we could!* This sounds so obvious, yet it can be challenging as our life journeys inevitably color the lenses through which we view our experiences. It is only with the grace of God, with Our Lady as our model, and with St. Bernadette as our example that we dare to tell you the most amazing and wondrous events we have witnessed in and through Lourdes.

The Gospels are timeless, and the Gospel Message of Lourdes remains relevant today. Jesus came to save not only those He personally met or those for whom He performed miracles or those who were alive at that time. Rather, He came for all humanity and for all eternity. Similarly, the Mother of God came down from Heaven not solely for Bernadette or the people of France or those living back in the nineteenth century. Her message was meant for each of us, then, now, and long into the future. Her message is quite simple: prayer, penance, and procession, with a discreetly gentle Heavenly reminder that her Son is Our Lord and Savior; that He performed miracles during His earthly life, and He still does so today.

From 2004 until his death in 2016, Lourdes Volunteers Spiritual Director, Rev. Jeffrey Keefe, O.F.M. Conv., a Franciscan friar, priest, and psychologist, requested that the extraordinary events that took place on the way to Lourdes be written down. We pray for Father to be in the "happiness of the other world" and have not forgotten his repeated requests. Since that time, there are more stories to tell. Hopefully, he will be well pleased and will accept our sincere apologies for this lengthy wait.

Some of the many "Lourdesian" miracles, both big and small, in the founding of this humble little apostolate are so incredible, they are *almost* unbelievable. Even those of us who had the privilege to be witnesses wouldn't have believed them if we hadn't, like doubting Thomases, been present to place our hands on them to believe (see John 20:27). Hopefully, within the following pages of experiences of Lourdes, *you* will come to recognize some real-life current evidence of God on which to confidently rest *your hand* in knowing we are children of an awesome and loving triune God: Father, Son, and Holy Spirit. The God of the miracles of the Gospels is the same God of *official miracles* and *everyday miracles* today.

> *But there are also many other things which Jesus did; were every one of them to be written, I suppose that the world itself could not contain the books that would be written.* (John 21:25)

Following are true stories that happened along the way to the Grotto while we were on the way to becoming the first American Lourdes Hospitality.

Everyday Miracles of Lourdes

Introduction to Lourdes

The Grotto in 1858

In 1858, Heaven touched Earth eighteen times. . . .

On the edge of a small Pyrénéan crossroads village in February of 1858, the Mother of God appeared to a local young girl, Bernadette Soubirous. Miracles happened. Inexplicable cures began to occur—and continue to this day. Tucked away by terrain and time, little-known Lourdes became renowned for healing of both body and soul. Since then, thousands of people per day make a physical and spiritual journey, known as a pilgrimage, to this beloved holy site.

The old mass of rock that was called *Massabielle* in the local dialect is known today as *The Grotto*. Snuggled within the steep

French misty mountains near the border of Spain, the Grotto is a shallow indentation on the side of a massive hill with a trout-filled river running directly in front of it. The cave itself was a natural hollowing of igneous rock etched within the slope in such a way that sunlight never penetrated the depth of the interior. A small, indented niche was naturally carved into the surface just diagonally above the larger opening facing the meadow across the river called Gave de Pau.

Bernadette had just turned fourteen when she went in search of firewood along the riverbank and came to the grotto for the first time. She had never been there before because she was a nice girl and Massabielle was known as not a nice place. Legends report that locals went there to buy and sell what they shouldn't and to do what they should not. Wild pigs would gather in the shallow cave for shelter and to scavenge the waste and garbage discarded there. This formerly unsavory place of Lourdes unexpectedly became a Catholic sanctuary of peace and prayer for millions of people from around the world. How did this complete transformation come about? These majestic mountains are one of God's beautiful creations of nature. It was our human fallen nature that changed this place of beauty into the "bad corner" outside Lourdes. Then the holiest creation of God, the Immaculate Conception, and a holy girl, Bernadette, came together in this disfavored place—and by their presence made it holy and beautiful once again. (*So if you know or love someone who has fallen into disrepair or disgrace like the Grotto, ask our Heavenly Mother to come and be near that person—because where our Heavenly Mother is, there is certain to be holiness!*)

Bernadette was the firstborn daughter in a working family who had fallen on hard times. They were poor, illiterate, and descending into homelessness. They moved into the recently vacated jail deemed unfit for criminals by government order. They lost everything—except their simple faith and steadfast devotion to daily prayer. It was from this humble home that Bernadette would depart to fetch driftwood during the week before Ash Wednesday. On a cold, wet winter Thursday—February 11, 1858—Bernadette experienced a supernatural encounter with "the most beautiful lady formed out of a brilliant light" in the niche above the grotto.

Bernadette was frightened. After making the Sign of the Cross, following the same gestures as the illuminated figure, Bernadette was at peace and no longer afraid. *(So, if we are ever scared, for any reason, we can do the same!*) Later in her brief life, Bernadette was known to say that we can go to Heaven by praying the Sign of the Cross well, calling upon the Blessed Trinity. Bernadette described the most beautiful lady as "the same size as me, the same age as me." Bernadette was a petite, four-foot-six-inch fourteen-year-old during the time of these extraordinary meetings.

The first two times they met, they did not speak; they prayed together—in silence. The second time, plied with holy water from the parish font, Bernadette threw the blessed water on her mysterious visitor. Bernadette told her to go away if she was from the devil and to come closer if she was from God. The beautiful young lady smiled and leaned forward toward Bernadette, but still she said nothing.

During their third meeting, she spoke to Bernadette graciously, in a lovely voice:

"Would you want the grace to come here during fifteen days?" Kind, yet direct, she added, "We are not promised the happiness of this world, but of the other."

Is this not true for all of us? We are not promised constant happiness here; we are instead invited to pick up our crosses and unite them with the Cross of Jesus Christ, and in doing so, we can someday be forever in the joy of Heaven.

This does not imply that Bernadette never experienced happiness in this world. An insightful St. Bernadette follower and theologian believes she surely experienced a taste of "the happiness of the other world" in the Grotto with the Mother of God and soon after, when she was finally able to receive Holy Communion. Through her faith, her understanding of the value of her sufferings, and her prayers offered for sinners, Bernadette must have glimpsed genuine joy here—as a foretaste of Heaven, where her happiness would be constant and eternal.

The ninth time they met, the most beautiful lady appeared somber to Bernadette. Pointing to a specific area in the rear of the grotto, she said, "Go drink of the fountain and you wash there." (*Or, go drink of the fountain and wash yourself there.*) Bernadette scratched the muddy surface and uncovered what was to become a flowing spring of water. It took her three attempts to get enough moisture to drink and wash.

Miracles quickly began to happen. There were biblical-like cures of paralysis and blindness through drinking and washing with the newly flowing fountain inside the shallow cave.

Still, Bernadette never called the most beautiful lady the Blessed Virgin, Mary, or the Mother of God. She referred to her as *Aqueró*, meaning "that one" in the dialect of her valley. Bernadette was the only one who could see or hear the lady in the niche. Not everyone believed Bernadette initially, including the formidable pastor of the local parish. Her family was poor and not well respected. Bernadette was illiterate, as were her parents. It was a tumultuous time in France amid the upheaval after the French Revolution and the pain caused by the separation of Church and state. The government looked unfavorably upon religious practices, discouraging devotions and spiritual gatherings. Many French were disillusioned as they were increasingly distanced from their Faith, both spiritually and culturally.

The grotto encounters continued. Aqueró requested that a chapel be built and that the priests have people come in procession (or pilgrimage—both the same word in Bernadette's dialect). The skeptical yet wise pastor asked to know who the lady was making such bold requests. On March 25, 1858, a month after the fulfillment of her fifteen-day-meeting promise, Bernadette again felt a mysterious pull to return to the grotto. She arrived to find Aqueró within the illuminated niche. Bernadette kindly asked the beautiful lady who she was. The most beautiful lady smiled, without response. Bernadette asked yet another time. Again, a divine smile appeared on her silent lips. The third time, Bernadette pleaded with her to know who she is. Bernadette said the most beautiful lady then became serious as she slid her rosary beads from within her fingers onto her arm. She bowed her head with her hands together, trembling. She raised her arms toward Heaven, saying:

Què soy éra Immaculada Councepciou.

Bernadette had never heard such a name. So as not to forget, she repeated it over and over while running from the grotto to the parish rectory where the pastor lived in the upper town. Bernadette burst through the open garden gate to find the exceptionally tall and intimidating priest, Abbé Marie-Dominique Peyramale, towering before her. Breathless, Bernadette repeated the unique name with the gestures of the most beautiful lady she had been meeting with in the grotto called Massabielle:

I am the Immaculate Conception.

Père Peyramale was stunned. How could this uneducated, simple mountain girl, who could not read or write French or Latin, possibly know this profound theological truth? The third Marian dogma had been only recently proclaimed in 1854 as a truth revealed by God that Catholics must believe. This clarified to the world what had been known since the early Church: Mary was conceived without sin in the womb of her mother. Mary, the Immaculate Conception, was preserved from the stain of Original Sin so as to be born a perfectly pure woman to give birth to Christ, to be the Mother of God. Mary was preserved from the moment of her natural conception in a sole and unique supernatural grace. She was born perfectly disposed with free will to say *yes* to God the Father, *yes* to being overshadowed by the Holy Spirit, and *yes* to being the Mother of Our Lord in the Incarnation of the Son of God, Jesus Christ! This is Mary's fiat, her filial "Yes!" (see Luke 1:38). There is only one created Immaculate Conception in all time, for all eternity. This is how the pastor immediately knew who was appearing in the grotto to Bernadette. No other human being had this privilege or favor, this title or name. Only the Mother of God was immaculately conceived.

Père Peyramale became Bernadette's defender.

Bernadette was an accurate messenger; she never wavered in her account of each of the Heavenly encounters. Following the apparitions, the local bishop prudently conducted an extensive and thorough four-year investigation into the extraordinary appearances in the grotto of Massabielle. On January 18, 1862, the Most Rev. Bertrand-Sévère Mascarou Laurence, Bishop of the Diocese of Tarbes, declared:

> *We judge that the Immaculate Mary, Mother of God, really appeared to Bernadette Soubirous, on 11th February 1858 and the following days, eighteen times, in the Grotto of Massabielle, near the city of Lourdes; that this apparition assumes all the characteristics of the truth, and that the faithful have reason to believe it beyond doubt.*

Further, Bishop Laurence officially proclaimed seven cures attributed to the fountain spring of water as miracles. This solemn proclamation is carved in stone and remains affixed in the Immaculate Conception Basilica in the front right and to the far left of the Grotto below, on the basilica foundation near the old water taps. Lourdes truly was a holy place, worthy of pilgrimage. The grotto of Massabielle then became known simply as THE "Grotto."

When miracles began to happen at Lourdes in the mid-nineteenth century, people who had been homebound with illness or disability ventured out of their houses to travel to the holy site. The train tracks into Lourdes were laid in 1866. When the whistle would blow, signaling the arrival of a train at the station, the hearty faithful mountain residents of Lourdes would go to kindly greet arriving pilgrims and to carry them on stretchers or push them in wheelchairs to the Grotto. Seeing this, the bishop requested that they become a Public Association of the Christian Faithful, formally and legitimately of and within the Catholic Church. This would ensure that this grace would flow beyond them. He cautioned that if they did not, the grace could die when they did. In this grace, a Lourdes Hospitality was born of charity in the Diocese of Tarbes.

In 1885, the Hospitalité Notre-Dame de Lourdes was canonically erected as a Public Association by Bishop Laurence and is now the mother hospitality to more than 240 aggregated Lourdes hospitalities throughout Europe. Almost 120 years later, Our Lady of Lourdes Hospitality North American Volunteers was founded in 2002 as the first Lourdes Hospitality outside Europe, and the first in and of the Americas with a threefold charism: to share the Gospel Message of Lourdes, to assist the sick and the suffering to and while in Lourdes and at home, and to serve the sick from around the world in Lourdes, France.

Just as with the Heavenly Lourdes meetings of 1858, much *good news* is present for us today. The *Gospel Message of Lourdes* is a teaching treasury that can help us on our personal journey, especially during difficult or trying times. If we follow humble St. Bernadette to the Grotto, we can discover or deepen our faith through an encounter with the Mother of God, who always brings us to her Son, Jesus Christ, uniting us with the Father and the Holy Spirit. In the Grotto, which popes have called "the School of Mary," we learn to live the Gospel in love. Away from the busyness of everyday life, we can remember to pray—childlike, with all our hearts—and to offer the value of our personal sufferings as a prayer for others.

Nobody is getting out of this life alive. Where are we going when we leave this world? How are we going to get from here to there? Lourdes brings us to this reality in a loving way. There are no parades in Lourdes, but there are two holy processions each day. The Eucharistic Procession brings us into the Church to adore the Real Presence of Jesus in the Most Holy Eucharist. Jesus said, "This is my body which is given for you. Do this in remembrance of me" (Luke 22:19). The Candlelight Rosary Procession helps us to meditate prayerfully on significant moments in the life of Christ and brings us to the doors of the Church. There we conclude our pilgrimage day blessed by deacons, priests, and bishops, and sometimes cardinals. We are each and all proceeding somewhere in this life, into the other. A pilgrimage to the Grotto can help us to find or reset our holy compass. What is the best way to get from the here and now to eternity in Heaven? Lourdes draws us back or closer to the sacraments and the Church with St. Bernadette as a good example for us to follow. After the first apparition, Bernadette reconciled herself to God by making her First Confession. Before the last apparition, she made her First Holy Communion, receiving Jesus Christ in the Most Holy Eucharist.

Many who make a pilgrimage to Lourdes come for the miraculous water from the natural spring within the Grotto that Bernadette uncovered when directed by "the most beautiful lady" to "go drink and wash." Lourdes Water is mountain spring water, yet amazing biblical-like miracles, including physically organic cures, continually happen from this liquid source of grace. More than 7,800 cases of inexplicable cures are on file in the Medical Bureau in the Lourdes Sanctuary. The process devoted to the study and ultimate announcement of the inexplicable cures is purely scientific and extensive. There must be no doubt or dispute, according to the Lourdes Medical Bureau. These modern-day cures (the blind see, the lame walk, and the dying are restored to life) are absolutely astounding and could easily be taken from the pages of the New Testament. These cures and miracles have occurred in Lourdes since 1858 and continue to this day. In much the same miraculous way, the spring uncovered by Bernadette at the request of Aqueró, the Immaculate Conception, continues to flow thousands of gallons of fresh spring water daily.

Why do we need to see miracles in the flesh? Is it because we are much like the doubting apostle? Although the other apostles told Thomas, "We have seen the Lord," he needed to have Jesus Christ right in front of him—to touch His wounds to be sure. Thomas said, "Unless I see in his hands the print of the nails and place my finger in the mark of the nails, and place my hand in his side, I will not believe" (John 20:25). *Do you need to see, meet, and touch a real person, and not just read something?* If you have ever doubted about this or wanted to know for sure—you might be the next modern-day apostle—a doubting Thomas turned believer! Just come to Lourdes to meet a proclaimed genuine miracle, such as Vittorio Micheli, Lourdes Miracle #63, or Sr. Bernadette Moriau, Lourdes

Miracle #70, to witness the reality of miraculous faith present for us in our modern time.

Only seventy of the almost eight thousand alleged cures have been officially proclaimed miracles by the Catholic Church. After the proclamation of the first miracles, it did not seem necessary for ecclesial officials to continue to pronounce more. Yet many people continue to come forward as witnesses to their miraculous experiences. This is not for them—but for us—so we can know that the same awesome God of the Gospels is still our God today. The gift of faith for the doubting nearing the end of their lives in this world is possibly the healing grace most needed. People claim they receive the grace they most need in the form of a healing of mind, soul, or body, or in the gift of peace or faith. Not everyone is cured at Lourdes, but nobody departs empty-handed.

Popes and presidents have made pilgrimages to Lourdes, providing a beautiful example for us to follow. It is usually the sick and the suffering who want to go to the Grotto for relief, for respite, or in search of grace or healing. Volunteer helpers, including medical professionals, clergy, and youth, make the journey possible. Or, more likely, it is the sick who bring the able-bodied helpers to Lourdes for healing of their unseen inner brokenness. The dedicated, selfless volunteers are the discreet, miraculous, hidden grace of Lourdes. They claim that they receive much more than they could ever give. Possibly at this time in our history, for reasons we do not yet know or understand, we might need this grace more than ever before.

God is unmistakably evident in the following true stories of Our Lady of Lourdes Hospitality North American Volunteers. These amazing, real-life events are important to share for the benefit of those who may come to know God or come closer to Him. As this book was being written, the Holy Father highlighted the significance of sharing stories. This may have been a providential sign that current Lourdes stories are worth publishing and reading.

Pope Francis said:

> Each of us knows different stories that have the fragrance of the Gospel that have borne witness to the Love that transforms life. These stories cry out to be shared, recounted and brought to life in every age, in every language, in every medium.[1]

The Grotto Today

[1] Pope Francis, Message for the 54th World Communications Day, no. 4.

Declaration

The people are real, and their stories are true in every chapter of this book.

Each person written about has attested to the accuracy of his or her personal experience.

In the few chapters where the person is no longer living or cannot be located, firsthand witnesses corroborated the accuracy of that story.

Our Lady of Lourdes Hospitality North American Volunteers will receive all proceeds from the sale of this book. The author will not receive any money, having freely donated and assigned all rights to the Association.

Chapter 1

Greatest Grace Needed

Forgiving Marlene

Agoraphobia can set in slowly over time or develop quickly from a trauma. For me, my world swiftly became smaller and smaller, reduced to the fenced-in boundary of our postage-stamp lot in our standard suburban neighborhood. My life suddenly became small and then smaller. Friends and places dissipated, eventually evaporating. I could no longer leave the security of our house unaccompanied or go anywhere anyone could approach me. Classified as an anxiety disorder, agoraphobia is a fear of specific situations or places perceived as difficult to avoid or escape. Perception became my reality.

Nobody aspires to be an agoraphobic. I was stunned to slide down the slippery slope to debilitating dysfunction. Tightening its grip, agoraphobia choked my contact with the outside world. Disconnected, my ability to function halted, along with my career. The more isolated I became, the more everything seemed to encroach on my self-imposed confinement. The more I stayed in, the more impossible it seemed ever to get out.

My mother always said I was outgoing and vivacious. She used to tell me that I was her dimpled, "effervescent daughter." When I was young, she feared that someone might try to steal my bright interior light. She said it was her nervous mother's intuition—and she was right, as mothers usually are. It just took decades and a couple of stealth blows to knock the light out of me. The last strike was a shocking physical assault at work. Nobody helped. Everyone froze. Physical violence was unexpected in the headquarters of a multibillion-dollar corporation with business-suited employees in professional offices. After that attack, nowhere felt safe anymore. My backyard became my entire outside world. Our tiny garden turned into a teeny Eden, with hours of my laborious over-tending, filling every inch with flowers and obsessive landscaping until our privacy fence restricted my one-and-only outdoor activity. Before I knew it, I had nowhere else I felt safe to go.

Fear is a cruel dictator. Living in fright manifests itself as a treacherous obstacle course of constant maneuvering. The lists of ifs were overwhelming: if I could get to the store, if I could go in, if I could gather what was on the painstakingly rewritten list, if I could make it to the cash register, if I remembered my checkbook, if I could find my car in the parking lot afterward . . . if, if, if exhaustingly became too many ifs. Shopping trips dwindled from iffy to not likely to not going. In the beginning, I tried repeatedly to venture out. It took forever to convince myself that I was able to get out of the car. Too often, I turned around and drove home. If I made it into the store, when I set down my list to put an item into the cart, the list was then lost. Without it, I was hopelessly panicked as to what else I was there to buy. Unable to hold on to lists past the produce department, I started writing them on my hand, jokingly referred to as my Palm Pilot. The problem was that the ink would smear from profuse stress sweating and wringing my nervous hands.

Next, I resorted to writing on my forearm, adding fear of ink poisoning to the growing justification for my crippling anxiety. Grocery shopping was thereafter limited to the middle of the night and only with my best friend. Luckily, competing grocery-store chains were vying for customers around that time. They ramped up, extending their hours until they finally remained open around the clock. This made middle-of-the-night shopping possible. Nobody was in the store at three in the morning. It soon became my private pantry with only an occasional stock clerk and a sleepy cashier, both too tired to be confrontational toward a broken housewife. Only rarely—almost never—could I go out alone or during the day when other people dared to shop.

No hairdresser, post office, bank, mall, restaurant, or outside appointment. Less-and-less became more-and-more of how my life distilled itself, dwindling down to the small sanctuary of my house. Worst of all, our sons suffered more than I, with a disastrous impact, later afflicting each of them in dangerously destructive ways. The guilt I felt compounded my fear and anxiety. There were no graduation or birthday parties, school sports, or family events.

Agoraphobia twisted our normal daily life into a perverted existence. It distorts the natural roles, with the parent forced to rely on the children, instead of the other way around. If a mother is suffering, her children suffer more. My sons were forced to do for themselves and their brothers what I had always done for them. The older boys took on parental responsibilities for their newly incapable mother.

Midnight grocery runs turned into consistently parking by the far-flung "Aisle 9" sign. Set back from the store, it was sure to have an empty space. I could always find my car in the same desolate spot after stressed shopping. My family and friends ran most of my errands in the busy daytime. Too bad they couldn't go to the dentist or the hairdresser for me. I looked like I felt—a harried shadow of the woman I once was.

The final blow came one day in the worst panic attack. I could not find my way home. I knew where we lived, but I was too distraught to figure out how to get there. It took an agonizing hour in my car to quell my anxiety enough to go back to the store and ask a clerk to call my husband. My handsome prince came to the rescue. Depleted, I followed him home, shaken from the distress. We both knew that it had become too exhausting and difficult for me to go out alone anymore. There just wasn't enough air for me to breathe outside the security of my safe house and secure yard. It's too bad cell phones, GPS, and shopping delivery were not yet widely available. It might have helped, a little.

Church was a real problem. Other people kept showing up. I confessed my panic and inability to attend Sunday Mass when it was so crowded. An older priest with an accent from an old country yelled at me in the confessional. He scolded me, saying that I was going to Hell and taking my kids with me. I was beyond devastated. Inconsolable at this eternal fiery thought, a Mass-less year ensued. My sons were condemned because of me. My best friend came to the rescue. She dragged me to confession in a safely empty parish church. The gentle priest asked me if I went to the mall, parties, or other places. "NO!" I said too loudly. I wondered if he could smell the fear through the confessional screen. He gave me a dispensation from my Sunday obligation. I did not know what that was, but I felt relieved. We were given a legitimate excuse not to attend Mass on Sundays with a pastoral "Get-Out-of-Hell-Free" card canceling the perdition prediction from the year before. The good Father made it clear that when I was able to reenter the world, I must return to Mass. "When you can go out for other things," and he assured me I would someday, "you can also go to

Mass." I believed everything he said, except I knew I would never be my old self or go out again as I used to. Even my doctor said post-traumatic stress disorder, PTSD, the serious capital-lettered psycho-acronym, was incurable. Through my limited worldview, obscured by the increasing cracks of confinement, I never considered that Our Lord, the Divine Physician, was not bound to modern medical diagnostic prognoses.

At the turn of the new century, a spunky cloistered nun came into my family room through the television screen. She and I would spend rerun hours together late at night, privately. Mother Angelica, the unlikely founder of the largest Catholic television network in the world, hosted a show interviewing insightful guests, interspersed with her humor and witty quips. Like me, she loved the Polish pope. For some weird reason, while praying the Rosary with Mother and her sisters, I would feel a strong desire to see Pope John Paul II — *with my own eyes*. That was crazy! Unless the Holy Father was planning to step into my family room, my laying eyes on him was not happening. Yet I had a consistent, irrational, and intense desire to see him. Embarrassed, I kept this ridiculous fantasy to myself.

In the Jubilee Year 2000, a plenary indulgence was granted for entering through specific "holy doors" at St. Peter's in the Vatican and designated doors in every diocese throughout the world. I made an efficient list of everyone I knew who needed this extraordinary grace for the remission of temporal punishment due for sins already forgiven. (It wasn't until years later that I learned that a plenary indulgence can be granted only to the individual or applied to deceased souls, not to another living person.) Receiving the Holy Eucharist was required as a conditional norm for gaining an indulgence; it was part of the deal. It was my incentive to return to Mass, but I still could not go on Sundays, when there were people seated in every pew. Instead, I went to weekday early-morning Mass, usually attended by only eight to eleven regulars. With the typical Catholic self-assigned pew formation, I felt safe hidden in the far back.

Catholics usually don't talk at Mass, and nobody noticed me in the nearly empty church at weekday Mass. Pretty soon, I was going to Mass six days a week and confessing before Mass every Monday that I had missed Mass the day before. Then someone told me that our Catholic hospital had Sunday afternoon Mass broadcast into each room for the patients. Actual attendees in the few pews of the tiny hospital chapel were rare. So I decided to try going there. Most Sundays, I was the only person present with a rotating new priest I did not know. For an agoraphobic, it was the best way to fulfill the weekly obligation. These were the extreme measures of my anxiety-controlled lifestyle. I had become cleverly adept at finding ways to avoid people outside my trusted circle.

Then my best friend had her business card plucked out of a fishbowl and won two roundtrip tickets to Europe! People saw the Holy Father with their own eyes all the time in Italy, I thought. We started planning. She wanted to see incorrupt saints. My husband, the convert, laughingly dubbed it "The Catholic Dead Body Tour" and thought we should get matching sweatshirts made with a city saint roster imprinted on the back, like the cheap commemorative T-shirts sold at rock concerts. My faithful friend ordered books about shrines and sanctuaries to be delivered to my door so we could plan out a route map for our once-in-a-lifetime holy pilgrimage extravaganza. The ultimate American crazy-Catholic tourists, we decided to cram twenty-three holy places into twenty-one days, or the other way around. She wanted to go to Lourdes. I told her I loved that place with the three little kids. But that's Fátima, Portugal, a different country, different century, and different message—but the same Lady in a different dress!

It did not occur to me until much later that my friend chose Lourdes with the hope that I would be healed. My second-oldest son started a betting pool with imaginary squares, such as "never leaves the house" or "stays in the driveway" or "refuses to go into the airport" or "runs off the airplane onto the runway before takeoff" because it seemed unbelievable that I would actually leave home or really go there or anywhere normally ever again. My brother said that possibly the planning was the vicarious adventure, and others agreed. Still, I had a strong desire—*an inexplicable yearning*—to see Pope John Paul II, so Rome was added to the unrealistic-dream travel itinerary.

Fearful that I would get lost or separated from my trusted friend, I laid out index recipe cards and wrote my name and home phone number on them. A string was attached through two scissor-punched holes. The details of where we were staying and the shrine we intended to visit were written on the reverse side of the cards with the planned date. Carefully, I created a stringed card to wear around my neck each day, like a lost-child tag at the state fair. Years later, I came across one of them with the string still half attached, dangling with a long-lost intended purpose. Just the sight of it made me cry to remember what needing that desperate lost tag felt like.

Ingeniously, my friend brought prayer cards with pictures of the saints and shrines we intended to visit. If we were lost or up against a language barrier without an interpreter, we could just hold up the saint card, and hopefully, someone would point us in the right direction to their famous nearby holy place, certainly known to locals. Thankfully, this worked on a few occasions when desperately needed.

The departure date neared. We completed detailed plans and paid our nonrefundable deposits. I was going with my trustworthy best friend and reasoned that I would not know anybody over there.

My greater fear was running into people confronting me around my hometown than of being around people an ocean away whom I would not know. I rationalized that I had learned how to find creative ways to avoid people where I lived. Surely, with the protection of a best friend, we could find ways for me to avoid people I didn't know, in a different time zone in Europe. Somehow, the idea seemed increasingly possible, because I inexplicably needed to see the Holy Father with my own eyes.

Departure day arrived. It was then or never. We made it onto the aircraft for our transatlantic flight. I was trembling, seated securely next to my trusty friend in the last two-seat row. I clung to her so tightly that she probably still has my finger marks embedded in her forearm. Observing my anxiety, the flight attendant jokingly wanted to refuse to serve me coffee or tea. She said she feared that with added caffeine, I might look for an eject button. (She had no idea!) There was no escaping; plane windows don't open. Nobody won the imaginary pool. Not one person in my family believed I would ever make it onto a plane and fly away over the Atlantic. It was possible only with grace.

We went first to the convent in Nevers to meet St. Bernadette. Still now, I believe this to be the best way to know Lourdes—to first know Bernadette. Père Régis-Marie de La Teyssonière, a French priest, chaplain of the Sanctuary at Lourdes and considered by many to be the living authority on St. Bernadette Soubirous, would later confirm: "To know Bernadette is to know Lourdes."

My best friend, Theresa, had a best-ever friend in St. Thérèse of Lisieux. Her namesake confidant and intercessor was very real to her; she just happened to be in Heaven. I was almost jealous. It was not because she had another best friend. It was just that there was, and still is, no St. Marlene. "That's for sure!" my husband always adds, with a laugh. I did not have a holy super-friend I was named after who was dedicated to watching over me throughout my ups and downs in life. I wanted a personal patron with Heavenly intercessory pull, a saintly friend I could lean on, heavily. St. Bernadette became that dependable friend for me. From the instant I saw her, I was smitten by my holy super-duper-friend find! She was practical, humble, close to the Blessed Mother, and French — like my treasured Ma Grandmère. This little powerhouse of a saint was my new and eternal bestie! I couldn't wait to get to Lourdes, although I was becoming increasingly fearful of the consistent rumors of large crowds known to gather there.

Before we realized it, we arrived in Lourdes. Extended waiting amid throngs of ladies was required for women to enter the *Piscines* to bathe in the water famous for miraculous healings. The plateau of people outside anticipating entry was tense with anxiety. My friend and I were separated into different Baths. Exactly as forewarned, nobody spoke English. Shaking uncontrollably, I was entrusted with a small statue of Our Lady of Lourdes. It took two women to help me to the top step that led down into the bath. While entering the tub, I motioned a request for Lourdes Water for my head. Gingerly, the ladies poured a small amount of the liquid grace into their hands, tenderly allowing it to seep over my head and the brokenness within. A few years later, I learned that not everyone is handed a statue. The little Lourdes Lady is given not only for the comfort and protection of the person holding it but as a silent indicator to the helpers: this pilgrim is at risk of falling, or this woman is amiss (or a mess, in my case). Pay attention, the little Mary statue signals. More years later, I learned that excessive shaking is not always from the cold, as the pilgrim has not yet entered the chilly underground spring water. Exceptional full-body shaking, if not from a medical condition, could be an indicator of an impending spiritual grace about to happen in the form of either a healing or a conversion.

This is rare. Of the thousands of women I have had the privilege to bathe in my service over two decades, I have seen this uncontrollable shaking only twice.

After gently being lowered into the bath, I surprisingly emerged dry and warm. Floating out of the Piscines, I felt as if I glided out comfortably wrapped in a cashmere blanket of grace. My fear and anxiety had inexplicably washed off in the water. Standing peacefully by the river outside the Baths, I thanked God and told Him that I was full. If I never returned to Europe or went anywhere ever again, I was completely full. Although I never expected to go back and was still in disbelief that I was even standing there, I asked that if it was His will for me ever to make another pilgrimage in my lifetime, I asked that it be to this holy place. There was something special there.

That day, I realized that peace is not the absence of evil. Peace is a gift only Jesus Christ can give. My friend could see the calm and change in me. We prayed together in the Grotto, close to a crowd. Although I still do not like crowds, I could tolerate them after my bath. I was not expecting a healing or a profound deepening of my faith, but God is generous, and Our Lady is gracious—this is how I am confident that anyone who goes to Lourdes never leaves empty-handed.

The remarkable change in me was noticeable. My husband said it was as if he took a broken wife to the airport and picked up a new-and-improved wife upon my return, like a free upgrade! He joked that many husbands would be thrilled to pick up a new wife at the airport. The Franciscan sister at daily Mass asked if I had a nose job! She knew something was remarkably different about me. I added early Sunday Mass to my spiritual repertoire, finally fulfilling my weekly obligation, just as the priest had predicted a few years earlier. After three agonizing years, I was functional again. Almost everyone thought it was a passing excitement or religious fanaticism that would fade over time. Instead, it was truly a genuine and lasting grace. My doctors insisted there was no cure and refused to accept a holy healing. I was permanently labeled PTSD dysfunctional, likely with an added concern of religiosity.

Much to my surprise, the following year I returned to Lourdes, again with a ticket I didn't buy. Two women I love were desperate and in need of a miraculous healing like the one I had received. The planning and travel were filled with challenges. Looking back, I thought of this week in Lourdes to be the holiest week of my life. (*Surely, God laughed at this!*)

Somehow, we made it all the way to Lourdes, which was somewhat miraculous in itself. Again, it was an extremely crowded May. Skipping all of the Sanctuary activities and places of Bernadette, the three of us went straight to the Baths. We dutifully waited in line, in faithful anticipation. Just as we were about to enter, the Baths shut down. The same disappointing near miss happened the next day. Twice a day, we did not make it in—until the last afternoon before our impending departure.

Desperate, I forfeited my place in line to go beg the man in charge to let us inside. In my best high school French, I tried to explain how we had flown so far, flapping my arms like bird wings, displaying "5,000 km" written in ink on the palm of my hand. My avian frantic flailing and ballpoint-penned pretend Palm Pilot must have been a comical sight. That tough bouncer was guarding the Piscine entry like Fort Knox. Communications were strained, until I realized he was from Ireland and didn't speak French! Negotiating in English, I explained our situation.

Sympathetic to our dilemma, he interceded for us, enlisting a woman to help. Pleading in his charming Irish brogue, he said, "Listen to the plight of this poor American girl, come so far." The reluctant woman gave me a scrutinizing once-over. "Can you touch your toes?" she asked. I obediently bent over in my denim jumper, pleased to be able to reach my sneakered feet at forty-five years old. She resolutely said, "Come with me to bathe the sick and dying, and I give you my word, those you love will come in."

At that moment, as strange as it was, why she asked me to bend over did not matter to me. Since then, I have come to understand that she wanted to know two things: Was I physically capable of helping inside, and would I do whatever was asked without hesitation?

"DO NOT GET OUT OF THIS LINE!" I insisted to the two women I loved. Whispering, I confided to them that I was going to pull them into the Baths from the other side. I made them promise me that they would stay in line. They did.

Following closely behind the toe-touching-requesting woman, I realized we were sneaking around a rule I didn't want to know. Hushed, I was secretly led up a narrow, turning staircase. A damp cloth apron was wrapped around me, and I was hidden among an international lineup of women with a conspiratorial shush. We prayed together. Important ladies entered to officially assign a number to direct each woman to her duty station. I noticed that the numbers posted above each curtained bath corresponded to the assignments. Fearful of being exposed, I hid behind the others. As each woman was assigned, I was eventually left alone, the last one, painfully exposed, to be chosen or declined. Curiously, the woman in charge tilted her head as she studied me momentarily. She hesitated before saying, "Quatre" and motioned toward Piscine Four. I must have looked out of place or unfamiliar. Amazingly, in a moment of grace, although seemingly doubtful and reluctant, she did not dismiss me but assigned me instead.

Usually, each woman on a bath team speaks a different language, with French as the common language for shared communication.

Instead, all beautiful Italian women were on the team that shift in Piscine Four. Exceptionally, that day the Piscine Madams must have arranged a few baths exclusively by language in an effort to expedite the large crowds for the busy Ascension Thursday feast day. I did not speak any Italian, so my on-the-job training was only to watch their example, without verbal explanation or guidance. It was like being trained by old-fashioned nuns with an accent—they were loving, but strictly tough! Fifty percent of the pilgrims coming in to bathe spoke English, yet less than ten percent of the "staff" spoke English. I did not yet know they were unpaid volunteers. Clearly, my value was to assist the English-speaking pilgrims. My disadvantage was that I could not understand Italian instructions. At one point, the leader tried to coax some Italian out of me. I desperately tried, offering the only two words I knew: "Pizza! Pasta!" Incredulous, she dismissed me away, rolling her eyes while shaking her head.

Then I spilled precious Lourdes Water onto the floor. Even if you don't speak Italian, if you are getting chewed out in Italian, you will surely know it! Tears stung my freckled cheeks. I was exhausted and desperate to spew excuses such as "I want to go home," "I didn't ask to do this," "I was trying my best," and "I don't understand Italian"—whining and "weeping in this valley of tears," as in the Hail Holy Queen prayer, but not holy. Instead, thankfully, I could not reply. The one Italian word I had learned that day was *grazie*. All the little old Italian ladies would kindly kiss us to thank us after helping them into their bath. Saying their triple thanks with tears, they would sweetly cry, "Grazie-grazie-grazie!"

Tearfully, I looked up at the woman in charge of the bath and whispered the new Italian word I had learned: "*Grazie*." She said, "Finally! Your first Italian word is the best word!" Somehow, I knew what she was saying as she softly placed her hands to cup my face, tenderly wiping away my tears.

Then, as promised, the two women waiting in line came in to be bathed, separately. The unlikely statistical odds of both of them individually and randomly entering Piscine Four were incredible. They did not know I would be there to bathe them. What a blessing! Tears transcended language. As they each entered, both times, the woman in charge graciously allowed me to bathe the women I loved. It was like a tender kiss, softly blown to us from Our Lady in the Grotto so nearby. Unknowingly, that day was to become the record number of women bathed in the recorded history of Lourdes, Ascension Thursday 2001.

It was the conclusion of an exceptional extended seven-hour afternoon shift. The time flew by, but our aching backs grounded us to the reality of how long we had been bending and lifting. As the Baths were closing, a worker walked by sporting a United Nations–like badge with a litany of flags to indicate the many languages she spoke. I reached out to gently grasp her wrist and asked if she spoke Italian and English. Yes, she did. Kindly, I asked her to translate.

"Please forgive me for the many mistakes I made here today. Thank you for all you patiently showed me." They all seemed surprised. "Wear your badge tomorrow," they replied in unison. I explained that I did not work there. They chuckled and smiled. Neither did they! They were volunteers in service. They said I looked familiar and asked how I got in. I explained as they graciously smiled. It took me years to realize that in that moment, so tired, they could have told me that I did not belong there. I was not officially registered in service; I had no training; I was not formed in the spirituality of service; and I did not have a recommendation letter from a priest assuring them that I was trustworthy to care for the sick. Obviously, they understood I had sneaked in. They had good reason to chastise me. Instead, they thanked me and invited me back the next day.

After I told them we were leaving in the morning, they asked me if I had a bath. When I told them no, they immediately halted the closing procedure and prepared me for a bath. They must have been exhausted. Thoughtful and considerate, their tremendous charity overruled their fatigue.

For days waiting in line, I had been making a mental "Santa Claus list" for everything I and others needed and wanted in this holy place of healing. Standing at the top step of the bath, I suddenly couldn't think of a thing. When they told me to close my eyes to pray, I thanked God and apologized for not remembering what I had wanted for myself and others. Instead, *I prayed for whatever grace I was in greatest need of.*

Only women are allowed in the women's baths and only men in the men's baths. The Piscines are divided separately for males and females, both out front for waiting and inside for bathing. Standing on the top step of the women-only bath in Piscine Four, after praying, when I opened my eyes, I was in total shock to see a man standing perfectly still in the middle of the tub. I recognized him immediately. Staring up at me was the man who had broken into the apartment where I was babysitting two small children many years before. He didn't break in that night for a good reason. Before he fled, he threatened to murder my family if I spoke to the police about what he'd done to me. I believed him. I was terrified for my parents, brothers, and sisters. He left me damaged, feeling unworthy of a good husband and unable to wear a white wedding dress. The police said they knew this twisted child molester. His victims were always like me, preteen or very young teenagers. My life spiraled out of control, but I eventually married a good man, wearing a lace-layered white wedding gown with a long white veil.

Thirty-one years later, I was astonished to see my violator standing before me, motionless in knee-deep water—in Lourdes, France!

I was calm and not at all afraid of him. A tremendous outpouring of the purest love came flooding out of me with a powerful force to wash over him. I was in *awe* of this grace flowing through my chest and onto him. My intense thought was how much I wanted this man to go to Heaven! As the ladies walked me down toward him, just as I was close enough to reach him—he disappeared. Later, I came to realize I must have experienced *the grace I was most in need of*—it must have been total forgiveness through a holy love for a poor lost soul to someday be in Heaven.

After dressing, I tried to imitate the prayers we prayed before the Piscine service. As we did earlier, I knelt down to kiss the floor, as young Bernadette kissed the ground in the Grotto. Just as my lips touched the cold stone, I felt a whoosh deeply breathed into me, filling and expanding my heart and chest. Spontaneously, I promised Our Lady that I would return in one year with ten good, holy, Catholic American women to help. That promise, made on Ascension Thursday in Piscine Four, was the Heavenly inspiration for the first Lourdes Hospitality of the Americas.

Returning from Lourdes, I arrived home spiritually upgraded, for a second time. Again, and undeservedly. Most of us associate Lourdes with the physical cures and official miracles we have heard about or read in books. From my experience, the sweetest miracles are mysterious unofficial cures of the soul and conversions of the heart. Scientists cannot confirm these miraculous happenings, but that does not mean they did not occur or that they are not real. They are genuine and authentic gifts from God—I am personally sure of this.

> *My sacrifice, O God, is a broken spirit, a broken and contrite heart, You, God, will not despise.* (Ps. 51:17, NIV)

Ascension Thursday 2001

The author was the first Our Lady of Lourdes Hospitality North American Volunteer. Marlene is a wife, the mother of five sons, a grandmother, and a Secular Franciscan dedicated to sharing the Message of Lourdes. She serves the sick and the suffering at Lourdes and at home, whenever possible.

Following are twenty true stories of "everyday miracles" personally encountered over twenty years, from the beginnings of Our Lady of Lourdes Hospitality North American Volunteers along the way to the Grotto, forever changing lives both in this world and the other world.

Chapter 2

Under Her Mantle

Changed Claudette

Claudette lived an erratic life, most often on the edge. She was a straight-A student and could have been the first in her family to go on to college. Instead, she hustled pool games for quick money and tended bar for big tips to drive fast and live faster. Ultimately, she hooked up with a slick guy before settling down to a reliable union factory job. Abuse of many kinds dragged Claudette down throughout her teen and early-adult years. By the time she was diagnosed as manic-depressive, she had alienated most of her family and friends with her swinging outbursts, violent tirades, and severe melancholy episodes. If anyone thought being around her was hard, being Claudette must have been much harder. She would often say she did not have to worry about wrinkles or gray hair. She was sure she would die young enough to leave a good-looking corpse. On her fiftieth birthday, celebrating her survival thus far, she was thrilled to pop open a gifted bottle of Dom Pérignon even though she was unable to pay her rent. Because, she said, that was how she did it.

Everything was louder, larger, and more dramatic to Claudette and soon became so to everyone around her. She loved deeply, fought fiercely, and lived compassionately. She was either model-thin or solidly overweight, completely put-together or all natural. There was never an in-between for Claudette, which is typical with bipolar personalities. She struggled and suffered. Most of her relationships were strained or estranged, off and on again. She managed to remain close to only a select few who were able to see past her illness and tolerate her exasperating symptoms.

Claudette trudged from doctor to doctor for relief and prescription drugs. Two physicians gave her multiple diagnoses, including a previously undiscovered seizure disorder. Heavy medications were prescribed in attempts to control the seizures and her uncontrollable life. Sadly, instead of helping, the medications seemed to spiral her further out of control. Where all of this might end was a scary thought for those who loved her. She would frequently sleep for days. Her speech was often slurred, or she talked so loudly and fast that it was nearly impossible to follow her disjointed thoughts. She was never able to take the many medications exactly as prescribed. There were too many to keep track of or to coordinate with food and the time of day to be taken. Different dosages, variations, and combinations were tried and retried. Her routine became a revolving door in and out of medical offices, emergency rooms, and pharmacies. Doctor appointments dominated her days the way barhopping and thrilling adventures used to fill her evenings. Finding her dead was a realistic fear, and over time, it escalated into a consistent worry for her sisters.

As a child, Claudette had a nun doll that she was convinced was Bernadette of Lourdes. She loved both the story and the old movie. There was a replica Lourdes Grotto in the basement of the Franciscan Church where she made her First Holy Communion and where her parents were married almost exactly one year to the day before she was born. Half a century later, her mother agreed to send Claudette to Lourdes in the hope of helping her to find some healing or at least to slow down the craziness and constant out-of-control spirals in her scattered life. The thoughts of a flight over the ocean were more frightening to Claudette than her serious everyday problems. She said she believed in miracles and knew Lourdes was legit for scientific cures. She didn't doubt that. It was getting there and going there that was beyond her belief.

Crippled at the thought of being away from home and packing for the trip became overwhelming, disintegrating into impossible. On the morning of departure, when she was expected to be ready for international travel, Claudette answered the door fully unprepared—and totally naked. She did not know what to wear. Her speech was slurred. Swaying, it was clear she had taken her nightly pills late, and she had just swallowed her morning pills too early. Trying to be ready at dawn, her night and day dosages were colliding together.

In desperation, her things were thrown into a suitcase as she was cajoled into the car to go to the airport. She snored during the drive as her lipstick smeared onto the rear side window and back across her face while she slept. She was awakened to be dragged from the ticket counter to the flight. Groggy and scared to enter the plane, she tripped down the stairs and landed face down on the tarmac. She was splayed out at the base of the jet bridge while two airline personnel stood over her, debating whether they should deny her boarding. Her travel wranglers scrambled to scoop her up as they lovingly pleaded for her to board the plane. The reluctant gate agent finally acquiesced to let her go in their sober company and compassionate care.

Travel proved to be harrowing for her and exhausting for everyone around her, like everything else in her life. After takeoff, Claudette was gripping a small statue of Our Lady of Lourdes while loudly reciting the Hail Mary in audible fear. In a heated exchange that did not end friendly, the flight attendant asked Claudette to lower her voice and raise her tray table. Claudette strongly defended the Blessed Mother and her right to be on the not-so-upright airline tray table. She was, after all, THE MOTHER OF GOD!

In all of the hyper-hysteria (wherever hyper Claudette was, hysteria often ensued), her bag overflowing with prescription pill bottles was somehow lost in the busy terminal while she was changing planes. Without her medication, vomiting from withdrawal soon followed. Between the airport and Lourdes, the taxi driver had to pull over three times for her to throw up on the side of the road. Trying to mask his displeasure, the driver attempted to handle the messy interruption in a polite and gentlemanly French way. Encouragingly, he explained that many sick people go to Lourdes, but that many return better than they arrived! He consoled his passenger, suffering from embarrassment and discomfort, and refused a generous tip for his gracious kindness.

Lourdes was crowded, so Claudette decided to go to the Piscines first, as getting a bath was the entire reason she was there. The other pilgrimage activities could happen after she dried off from the holy experience. There is a special entrance to the Piscines for the sick to enter the Baths, but it was written in French and went unnoticed amid the rambunctious crowds vying to get in. Evidently, vomiting did not qualify for special entry, which must have been only for people in wheelchairs, Claudette later deciphered. She arrived in the afternoon without sleep from the overnight transatlantic flight. She was fatigued and nauseated. Still, she dutifully waited in line, hopeful for a miraculous healing, but she could not get into the Baths with such huge crowds pressing to enter. Disappointed, jet-lagged, tired, and hungry, she left to rest and try again in the morning.

After she didn't make it into the Baths, Claudette's intention was to shop in the little gift stores outside the Sanctuary. It was a nice plan that soon proved impossible. She tried to eat, but the rich French food did not stay long in her empty stomach. Claudette was literally gutting out her medication withdrawal at every trash receptacle. Replacing her lost medications, let alone so many serious prescriptions, proved impossible in France for a non–French speaker. The next day, although she arrived before the Piscines opened, the line was still incredibly long. After waiting all morning, she did not make it inside again. Just as she neared the entry, the Baths closed for lunch. Claudette needed to eat. She was weak from the vomiting. She ate a little bit and returned early, before the European two-hour midday meal break was over. She was shocked to discover the line was even longer than it had been at the start of the morning!

Hours later, though the line moved painfully slower, Claudette was getting close enough to tease her that she might finally get in. Just before she reached the entrance, a metal chained *Fermé* sign was latched right in front of her. Closed again! The same thing happened the next day. Claudette's vomiting became less violent and not quite as frequent, but her stomach continued to attempt revolt. She came to understand prayer and penance, the Message of Lourdes, not on a pleasant guided tour, as most pilgrims experienced, but rather, through detoxing in line at the Piscines. She never saw much of anything in the Sanctuary or the surrounding town other than the evening Candlelight Rosary Processions, and that was only because the Baths were closed for dinner and at night.

Lourdes is truly a holy place. Yet pilgrims in the lengthy lines for the Baths can become less than holy when vying for a desperately needed miracle. Pushing, shoving, and shady maneuvers can lead to unpleasant exchanges between pilgrims and tourists. That is French for outright shouting matches. Although *extremely rare*, screaming and yelling can erupt to disrupt the prayerful presence at the Piscines. This does not happen often. When it does, faithful volunteers quickly quell the anxious pilgrims with kindness, chanted singing, and soothing recited prayer. Claudette was not going to put up with any of the unholy antics, unfairness, or cheating to get a blessing. She appointed herself the Piscine Police—a fairness cop for those waiting in a line that had grown so long that people were queued up almost to the Grotto. No cutting the line, unless you were dying—and some were. Claudette placed them up front, assuring them that they would get in. She was not to be challenged, and everyone waiting understood this, no matter what language they spoke. Claudette did not know vague ambiguity. No translations were needed.

On the last day before her return flight to Paris, she stayed in line through lunch, but the closed sign was put up again—directly in front of Claudette! She just missed her once-in-a-lifetime holy opportunity for a miracle *by just one place in line.* The person in front of her was the last woman to be allowed in the Baths that day. Then the other women in line secretly pushed Claudette over the entry chain to thank her for maintaining fairness and blocking the bickering for the past few days. *Claudette was in!*

Like millions of women and pilgrims before her, Claudette had a holy experience while submerged in the bath. She came to Lourdes with childlike confidence, knowing she would receive the miracle God wanted for her. She was sure that if she came that far, the Mother of God would be obliged to deliver what was best for her. It wasn't presumption. It was the faith of a child who believed her Mother knew what was best. Claudette needed that confidence in her Heavenly Mother. She was not disappointed. After her bath, she matter-of-factly announced she was the recipient of a special grace—just for her and exactly what she needed. Further, it was her choice and responsibility to honor that grace or to dishonor it with her free will. She was determined to live a better life and to hold on to the personal spiritual gift she had been granted.

There was little time for the liquid grace to sink in fully at Lourdes, as she left early the next morning. But the grace of the Lourdes Water from her bath was about to penetrate Claudette.

To include St. Bernadette for a full-impact Lourdes extravaganza experience, Claudette's private pilgrimage continued on to Nevers. St. Gildard is where Bernadette lived her religious life after leaving Lourdes. The convent chapel now houses her incorrupt body in an elegantly adorned crystal casket. It is a favored retreat destination for many. The sisters offer their former religious convent cells as modest respite accommodations to pilgrims, mostly arriving before or after visiting Lourdes. But they were full, actually overbooked, when Claudette arrived. There was not enough room to accommodate the large number of pilgrims in the pleasant May weather. Through a last-minute room switch a few hours later, a bed suddenly became available, making a way for Claudette to extend her Lourdes pilgrimage to include a few overnights to honor St. Bernadette.

Meals were included, and the table conversations in the refectory were lively but exclusively in French. Seated across from Claudette were two attractive yet mysteriously silent young men. Once it was discovered they were both Americans and did not speak French, the English-speaking conversation quickly became as animated as at the French-speaking table. Claudette, holding court, told sensational tales of her recent Lourdes adventures. Both men, one an ordained priest, were fascinated by the experiences she described in detail, with dramatic flair and laughter—from vomiting and policing the rowdy international pilgrims to secretly jumping the Piscine chain barrier and receiving a special grace. She was quite a character! Her enthusiastic description had everyone at the table laughing loudly enough to dismay the competing conversationalists at the French-speaking table. It was the first time Claudette interacted with a priest outside of the sacraments or a church building. She had not been to Mass in more than twenty-five years, except to sob, totally devastated, through the funeral of her beloved father five years earlier.

The priest was a soft-spoken gentleman, making everyone around him comfortable, especially Claudette. They were seated together again for lunch and dinner the next day. She was surprised to discover that it was the kind Father who had switched rooms, creating the bed opening that allowed them to stay in the convent. Claudette saw that as a Heavenly sign, a signal of grace. She announced that she wanted to go to the Sacrament of Reconciliation as the holy follow-up to her bath at Lourdes. The Lourdes Water had indeed soaked in. Laughing, she warned the young priest that he was about to hear an earful and should expect to be rocked and shocked by her lengthy confession. She asked if he had a weak heart or if she should find him some smelling salts in preparation for listening to decades of her extravagant, Augustinian-style sins. Her natural sense of humor and good nature floated up within her in the spiritual buoyancy of her Lourdes bath. She was delightful in anticipation of receiving the sacraments and more like her authentic self than she had been in many years.

Claudette said she had not had a good night's sleep in more than two decades. Amazingly, she was able to sleep soundly and rest fully after receiving the Sacrament of Reconciliation. She was calmer and said that it was as if a deep, ugly weight had been removed from her. She no longer felt heavily burdened. Claudette wanted to stay in France to be sure she wouldn't lose her newly found peace. She loved France—except for the French fries. Shockingly, she preferred McDonald's American-style fries and loudly said so. That was Claudette! She was still as lively as ever, but without hostile negativity or anxiety. It was ironic that she seemed so much better without all the prescription medications she had been taking for years.

Before flying home from Paris, Claudette made one last quick stop to the Miraculous Medal Chapel. It proved to be providential.

In 1830, the Mother of God appeared to Catherine Labouré of St. Vincent de Paul's order, the Daughters of Charity, in the motherhouse novitiate of the postulant and novice sisters. These were the same "flying nuns" as at the hospital where Claudette was born and where her mother studied nursing. Claudette knew the story well. The Blessed Virgin requested a medal be struck with the words "O Mary, conceived without sin, pray for us who have recourse to thee," with the promise that those who wore the medal would receive generous graces. So many conversions and miracles happened that the medal quickly became known as the Miraculous Medal. This apparition was so closely linked to Lourdes that the Vatican struck a commemorative centennial medal of the Immaculate Conception Marian dogma in 1954 with the Miraculous Medal image on the front and a Grotto image of Our Lady with Bernadette on the back. While Claudette was praying at the shrine, a Miraculous Medal was gifted to her, pinned over her heart. She promised to wear it every day afterward, the medal seeming to protectively shield her newfound gift of healing and peace. Claudette was returning home chemically and spiritually cleansed, ready to face life refreshed and renewed, she said.

Back at home, through a series of doctor appointments to obtain new prescriptions, a pharmacist discovered that Claudette had been prescribed ten times the dosage of one of her new seizure medications. He told Claudette that the dosage error could have killed her had she had the pills with her in Europe and taken them every day. Losing the pill bottles on the way over seemed providential, like a back-door miracle with the fingerprints of Our Lady of Lourdes allowing the "accidental mistake" to preserve her life! Soon after, one of her physicians was stripped of his medical license and sentenced to prison. The other physician was allowed to practice only under the supervision of another doctor.

Although she was still bipolar, life was better for Claudette. Her renewed faith, healing, new doctors, and different medications made it easier to live with her difficult disorder. Claudette said it was a daily task to hold on to the grace she received in Lourdes and experienced in Nevers. She knew she had to honor the grace and the healing, to respect the gift given to her. Yet, at the same time, like any valuable treasure, it could be lost. She said sometimes she didn't hold on tight enough. It was a struggle, but she held on as best as she could. Claudette was always in awe of the graces she received through her pilgrimage to Lourdes, always trying to return to the grace after failing or falling.

Claudette had changed, even though her life continued to be a struggle. In a series of difficult situations, she survived various serious challenges. Five years after her Lourdes pilgrimage, she was hospitalized with a life-threatening reaction to a correctly prescribed drug combined with a simple over-the-counter sinus medication. She was in a coma in intensive care with a Miraculous Medal pinned over her heart on her hospital gown. When she awoke, she had a serious desire to live a good life, with a rekindled thankfulness for her Lourdes pilgrimage. She made plans to return to the Grotto, both in thanksgiving and for renewal. She said she needed another visit, like a holy refill.

Claudette was healthier and more subdued, careful not to mingle any substances prescribed with any over-the-counter remedy to prevent any possible chemical conflict. It was difficult.

Claudette died unexpectedly just two months later. The autopsy revealed no apparent cause of death. There were no drugs in her system, no allergic reactions or major organ problems. She simply died with a Miraculous Medal pinned over her heart.

Lourdes made Claudette different, renewed in her childhood and childlike faith. The sacraments and the grace she received continued to help her. Going to Lourdes did not cure her, but the grace of Lourdes gave her the strength to endure the challenges and difficulties in her life. She died under the protective medal shield of the Immaculate Conception, made possible by her pilgrimage and the peace she found in the sacraments in France.

Claudette continued to wear her Miraculous Medal every day of her remaining life, which was a comfort and consolation to her family of her safekeeping since Lourdes.

Under Mary's protection you have nothing to fear. (St. Bernard)

Happy in France

Before she died, Claudette was registered on the October pilgrimage with Lourdes Volunteers. The Immaculate Conception was surely waiting for Claudette to return to the Grotto, and therefore, must have been waiting for her in "the happiness of the other world." Claudette was buried wearing a Miraculous Medal from Lourdes.

Chapter 3

Crossing the Mary Bridge

Texas Pancho

Waymon Howard was named after his daddy, so it was planned that the son being the junior would be called by their middle name, Howard. Instead, his pals called him Pancho, after the devoted bumbling buddy to Cisco in the popular television series. It wasn't long before his family and close childhood friends called him Pancho. It was the perfect nickname befitting a little boy with his oversized cowboy hat growing up in big Texas.

It is surprising how many people we know by names other than the legal given names on their birth certificates. When Lourdes Volunteers began, the office team had to create and design everything. There were no applications or brochures or an existing website to copy. In developing the registration form, a space was provided for a nickname so that name tags would display the familiar name the new volunteer in France was used to hearing back home. When Howard filled out his application, he hesitated at the nickname. This was a Catholic Association. He wanted to be completely truthful. He decided to err on the side of honesty and wrote "Pancho" in the space provided, although only a very few people closest to him since childhood and fewer Spanish-speaking co-workers ever called him Pancho. Everybody in France would surely call him by his proper baptismal name; nobody else would call him Pancho, he thought.

Lourdes Volunteers was growing. It was exciting to see volunteers coming from all over. Most were from the United States, some from Canada, and a few were from Mexico and South America. When an application from a Texan called Pancho arrived in the office, it was as if a real-life cowboy jumped out of a Western movie—yes, ma'am. The New York staff wondered if he really wore a cowboy hat and boots. Were his spurs *a-jangling?* Was he *a-fixin'* to come to Lourdes? *Yes-siree, yee-ha,* and *howdy, pardner* were the staff's responses to each other about his file in the office. He was endearingly known as "Texas Pancho" in meetings for planning and pilgrimage preparation. When the group met in Lourdes and received their name tags, everyone shockingly called him Pancho, as typed on his badge. A surprised Howard kindly accepted it. To Lourdes Volunteers, Howard will always be Pancho—like Elvis, with no last name needed. You just can't forget a big Texan who is as kind as he is tall, a genteel gentleman of faith who is comfortable enough to sport a traditional Stetson and genuine leather cowboy boots.

Pancho was a convert to Catholicism not only out of love for his wife (the love of his life) or to be united in the same Faith, but mostly as a result of his prayerful discernment. He entered the Catholic Church through the Rite of Christian Initiation of Adults (RCIA), which is an instructional program to learn all things needed to become a Catholic. Converts often confess that an obstacle to entering the Church is the Catholic tradition of honoring Mary, the Mother of Jesus. Many find this devotion unnecessary and even offensive—a personal relationship with Our Lord being the only spiritual connection needed.

As some converts do, Pancho found a way around this problem by deeply immersing himself in the rich history and teachings of the Catholic Faith—except anything about the Blessed Virgin Mary. Excluding the Mother of God, it is still quite an ambitious undertaking to study the treasury of two millennia of Church Tradition of Sacred Scripture, dogma and doctrine, theology and spirituality, sacraments and sacred music—to put it more directly, to be so preoccupied with the Faith and the Church as to discreetly avoid Mother Mary.

Pancho was an enthusiastic convert. He eagerly enrolled in a new course on mystagogy offered by his pastor. This fourth step in RCIA comes from the Greek word meaning "to interpret mystery." It is an ancient way to lead new converts through the Mysteries of Faith. This follow-through instruction supports neophytes (those "newly planted") as they steadily mature in the growth and practice of their recently professed Catholic Faith. Mystagogy is heavily influenced by and grounded in the very early Church, when the Mother of Jesus was strongly revered. Throughout the series, Pancho realized that the same Mary he had so cleverly avoided before entering the Catholic Faith was now present everywhere he turned, and specifically in these classes. Her role in the life of Jesus Christ was more than just mentioned; it was significant. While in class one day, Pancho prayed in earnest:

> *Lord, if Your Mother is truly that important to You, if YOU truly want me to know and honor her, please make it unmistakable to me.*

After the class concluded, Pancho didn't give his sincere prayer request much more thought.

Vicki and Pancho were wed as teenagers. Their marriage is one of those high school sweetheart stories in which "happily ever after" actually happened. Being such young newlyweds, they somewhat grew up together. As their family nest filled and emptied, they preferred not to be apart from each other. When Vicki went to Albuquerque to visit her sister, Pancho knew he would not be able to fall asleep in their bed without his wife beside him. Fatigued from lack of sleep, he thought that if he watched television or read long enough on the oversized lounger in front of the TV, he might finally drift off. He was tired enough to try both.

Pancho was rudely awakened by a violent tug on his arm at two o'clock in the morning. He was startled into consciousness as if being urged forward to pay attention. The grasp was real, strong, and firm, yet not threatening. Still, Pancho jolted upright, vaulting straight out of the lounger and whirling around, only to confirm that he was alone. Nobody was there. Nothing was out of place. If a big, strong Texan is surprisingly awakened by a stronger hand put upon him — it doesn't matter how tall or tough a man he is — that grasp is sure to wake him up rattlesnake fast! This startling and inexplicable touch snapped Pancho into full attention. He was wide awake.

The television was on, and a woman he did not recognize was being interviewed on some show. Startled, Pancho focused on the lighted screen which was glaring at him in the completely darkened room. A priest and his guest were talking about Our Lady of Lourdes. Deep down, he knew it immediately. Pancho recalled his heartfelt prayer from Mystagogy class a while back. He thought how ironic it was. "Be careful what you pray for," he chastised himself.

Lourdes Volunteers was seeking English-speaking volunteers to serve in France. An invitation was extended to be the "hands and feet of Christ" to the sick and the suffering from around the world, to animate the charity of Jesus Christ to others. Why would Pancho need to go all the way to France to find out if Jesus wanted him to know His Mother? Besides, for practical reasons, it was illogical for him to travel to Europe. Still astounded by his nerve-wracking awakening, Pancho wrote down the number to request an application. Another rude late-night wake-up call would not be necessary to get his attention a second time. Pancho clearly got the message. He just didn't believe he would ever really go to Lourdes.

He somehow made it to France despite the obstacles and impracticality of spending two weeks abroad. Howard was as surprised to find himself in Lourdes as he was to be called Pancho by foreigners and strangers who had not known him since childhood. A mismatched group of first-time volunteers from around the United States arrived together along with a pilgrimage leader and a Canadian priest for spiritual support. In the opening welcome and orientation meeting, each new Lourdes Volunteer explained how and why he or she joined. Pancho entered the room and sat in the back corner, at the furthest amen-end of the bench in the last row. He was humbled to listen to the deep faith, selflessness, and lifelong Marian devotion in the unique stories of each first-time volunteer.

In the company of such good and seemingly holy people, Pancho felt obligated to tell the whole truth when it came to his turn. He revealed his mysterious late-night experience, his heartfelt prayer, and, truthfully, his disbelief that he was actually present in Lourdes. He confessed that he came to see whether Mary was truly that significant to Our Lord Jesus, although he couldn't see how. He said that if it was going to be necessary for him to get to know the Mother of God, he thought he had come to the right place for an introduction. Besides, as the week wore on, they would quickly learn that he did not hold Mary in the same high regard they had all just professed. He reckoned it was best for him to "fess up" right up front. He felt relieved that the truth was out in the open like a Texas tall tale. Pancho wanted them all to be sure to know that he was absolutely pleased to be the "hands and feet of Christ" to anyone who needed him during his week in service — because, after all, he was all about Jesus.

To serve with the Hospitalité Notre-Dame de Lourdes (Hospitalité or HNDL), a volunteer must do the following: pay for his or her travel, accommodations, and meals; be a person of goodwill; be physically capable of offering service for a minimum of one week; and provide a letter from their pastor attesting to his or her trustworthiness to care for vulnerable people. Service includes practical training and schooling in the Message of Lourdes, with its history and spirituality, in addition to familiarization with the extensive Domain of the Sanctuary. A volunteer, after completing four separate weeks of service, can choose to engage in a lifetime commitment to serve annually, whenever possible.

More than eight thousand committed members of the Hospitalité make it possible for the Sanctuary to welcome millions of pilgrims each year. There is only a small paid year-round staff that maintains the administrative and technical needs of the Sanctuary. The bishop is the head, his rector is the voice, the chaplains are the heart, and the employees are the bones. Together, they form a "skeleton crew" that keeps the gates open yearly for tens of thousands to enter the Grotto of Lourdes each day of the pilgrimage season. The members of the Hospitalité are the flesh on the bones of the hands and feet of Christ to animate the welcome and the experience of all the pilgrims and tourists visiting the Sanctuary. Hospitalité members assist the sick and the disabled arriving and departing from the train station and the airport, help in the two hospital-bed facilities, bathe pilgrims in the Piscines, and facilitate the twice-daily holy processions and twice-weekly International Masses, along with maintaining order and a prayerful presence throughout the Sanctuary, especially in the Grotto. Without these dedicated volunteers, it would be impossible for the most-visited Marian shrine in Europe to function. It would not be financially feasible to employ a large staff supported by the small donations given by a fraction of the pilgrims. Volunteers are crucial to the Sanctuary.

New volunteers with the HNDL are required to attend Formation which is a series of introductory classes about the history of Lourdes hospitalities, the apparitions and the Message of Lourdes, the Sanctuary, the spirituality of the Immaculate Conception, and St. Bernadette. While in service, Pancho was obliged to attend this "School of Mary," as popes have referred to the Message of Lourdes. Practical technique instruction was provided in his on-the-job training, with evening service positioning Pancho on the frontlines of the Rosary Procession. Service in the Grotto placed him beneath the statue of Our Lady, as if always under her tender yet watchful maternal gaze. Daily homilies featured Mary. The Blessed Virgin Mary was everywhere Pancho turned. There was no escaping the Mother of God in Lourdes! Pancho realized that if ever there was or is a place in the world all about Mary—this was it! Unable to avoid Mother Mary, he again prayed, reflected, and discerned. Pancho had always considered the Rosary to be a vain, repetitious prayer. Ironically, it was the Mysteries of the Rosary that led to the unexpected answer to his Mystagogy-inspired plea. He seriously contemplated the words of the angel Gabriel to Mary found in the Gospel of St. Luke:

> *Hail, full of grace.... The Lord is with you.* (Luke 1:28)

He discovered that the Hail Mary was not a misguided Catholic invention. It is taken directly from the Holy Bible. He could not argue against a biblical account. "Hail Mary!" is the angelic salutation and acclaim, followed in the prayer by the Church's proclamation of our human response:

> *Holy Mary, Mother of God.*

She is holy and, indisputably, the Mother of Jesus, Our Lord and God. Again, Pancho could not argue with "pray for us sinners" because we are all sinners who benefit from prayer. Pancho was all about praying for others and was grateful to anyone praying for him. Surprisingly, he could no longer find an argument against the very Marian Hail Mary prayer.

What about the Mysteries of the Rosary? Pancho shockingly discovered they were scripturally grounded too. Contemplating the life of Jesus Christ with our active minds and praying the words of angels—good ol' Bible quoting—in our passive minds made sense as a way to avoid distraction while in prayer. Somehow, this previously dreaded prayer was no longer vain or repetitious. It became a spiritual chant intertwined with prayerful meditations on the Gospel life of Jesus Christ. Unbelievable! How had he never known or figured this out before?

Still, why would we ask Mary and not go directly to Jesus with our prayerful wants and needs? We ask her in the same way we so often ask friends and family to pray with us and for us, in addition to our direct prayers and our personal conversations with God. We pray for others, either upon request, through inspiration, or out of love for one another. Pancho's newfound Lourdes friends were praying with and for him every day. Likewise, he was praying with and for them. The pilgrimage priest directed Pancho to the Scripture verse about the Wedding at Cana (John 2:1–12). Our Lord performed His first miracle and began His public ministry at the request of His Mother, Mary. She is a proven-effective intercessor, "for the Bible tells us so," just as Pancho sang as a little boy.

Further, upon entering through the main gate of the Sanctuary, Porte St. Michel (the Gate of St. Michael), there is a statue of the archangel Gabriel—from the "Hail, full of grace" Gospel passage—along with the other two archangels mentioned in the Bible,

Michael and Raphael. These statues are poised as visual imagery to protectively greet and guide pilgrims arriving and departing. Once a person is inside the most-visited Marian shrine in Europe, the first and most prominent statue he or she encounters is not one of Mary. It is Jesus Christ on His Cross—front and center at the entrance! This Breton Cross has a statue of Mary as one of the four faithful who remained at the foot of the Cross while He spoke His dying directive to His beloved disciple:

> *Behold, your mother!* (John 19:27)

Therefore, "We must be beholdin' to her too," Pancho realized. Jesus bequeathed His Mother to us as He was dying on the Cross. Moreover:

> *The disciple took her to his own home.* (John 19:27)

So she must be welcome in Pancho's home and in his heart. Mary *was* important to Jesus after all. It became obvious that the Message of Lourdes is a Gospel message and Christ-centered. Lourdes is a Christocentric sanctuary, and Mary has a special role in Heaven and in eternity. The Texan tearfully wondered, *Who'd a thunk it?*

Serving in the train station and looking at a statue of little St. Bernadette, Pancho dared to be like her, willing to meet the Mother of God in the Grotto. Pancho knelt down, weeping, then sobbing. Texas-size tears, as big as quarters and dimes, saturated the wooden bench and spilled onto the stone floor beneath. It was as if the Mother of God had placed her finger tenderly yet deeply in his heart, to leave her imprint profoundly within him forever. His faith was expanded to include a place of spiritual honor for the Mother of Jesus. It was as if an orphan with a deep longing to know his mother had miraculously stumbled upon the woman who had always loved him, and she was all that he could ever imagine or hope her to be—and so much more. He went from a resisting child fighting against maternal love to a docile newborn in sweet surrender. Pancho knew his Mystagogy prayer had been answered. On September 7, 2005, Pancho crossed the Mary Bridge and entered into the center of the fullness of the Catholic Faith, including honoring the Mother of God, just as Jesus taught us.

The old St. Louis de Montfort Catholic expression, "To Jesus *through* Mary," suddenly made sense to Pancho. Jesus was born into the flesh *through* Mary. So many more insights gently surfaced and became obvious each day. It was all unfolding within him, like turning the pages of the Gospel. Was it being in the company of so many people who personally clarified and expressed their loving devotion to—*not worship of*—Mary with a deep faith rightly grounded in the Blessed Trinity? Maybe it was the insightful homilies at Mass, revealing how the Virgin Mother brings everyone to her Son, not to herself. Or could it be the classes they were taking? Ultimately, the Holy Spirit was responsible. For each question Pancho had, and every argument he made, an answer was gently yet convincingly presented to him, either through the priest on the pilgrimage, a fellow volunteer, a talk given, a conversation, or a complete stranger encountered in service or in the Sanctuary. Mary was no longer important only to Jesus. She was now—and forever—unmistakably important to Pancho.

At the end of the service week, everyone came together for French wine or coffee and a luscious dessert or ice cream. It was a final celebratory gathering and a perfect pilgrimage ending. During the festivities, Pancho announced that he was going home to dispel the misunderstanding about Mary and the Rosary in Texas. He was inspired to write a small booklet that could explain what non-Catholics completely misunderstand about the Mother of God and the Rosary. He said that only those who had made this journey themselves, like him, could know what needed to be explained to build a bridge to help reunite children with their loving Mother.

> *Then He said to the disciple, "Behold, your mother!" And from that hour, the disciple took her to his own home.* (John 19:27)

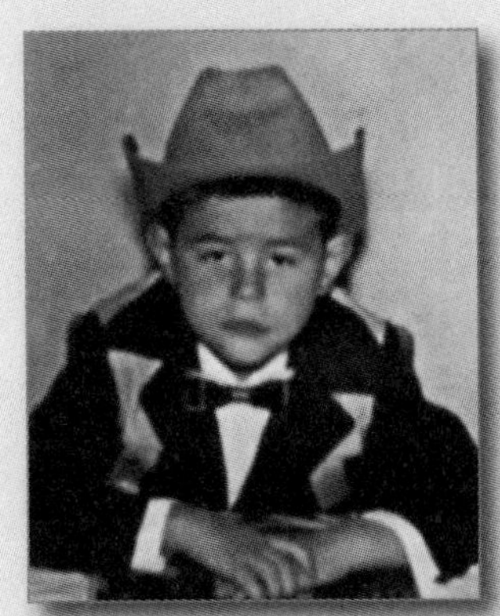

Cisco's Pal Lil' Pancho

Pancho returned to Lourdes in service and continues to be a faithful volunteer. Vicki and Pancho cared for his elderly Daddy in their home during his final years, living the mission of Lourdes Volunteers to care for the sick and the suffering at Lourdes and at home. Pancho continues to serve in whatever capacity is needed and whenever requested. All the volunteers still call him Pancho and always will.

Chapter 4

Cured to Serve

Saint-Frai Chrissy

Lourdes Volunteers was blessed to rent affordable office space in the old Franciscan Convent School on the north side of the city of Syracuse. The library was a spacious room formerly filled with students and rows of heavy oak bookcases, ideal to house a growing apostolate founded by a former student. Open cubicles connected a small team accessible to each other in what affectionately became known as "the Pit." A little room protruded as a single appendage from the larger space, providing a small private office.

The pilgrimage leader jumped out of her chair and catapulted from her office into the Pit. "Who registered someone with ALS *as a volunteer*?" she asked, clearly in distress.

"What is ALS?" asked Erika, the first employee and new office manager.

"Lou Gehrig's disease!" was the reply.

"Who is Lou Gehrig?" Erika inquired.

"One of the greatest New York Yankees who ever lived! He is famous and well loved. His amazing baseball career was tragically ended by ALS. It was a diagnosis mourned throughout the sports world. That's why it is called Lou Gehrig's disease! There is an old black-and-white movie about him and his heartbreaking farewell speech," she tried to explain, exasperated.

The airline tickets had been paid in full and printed. There was no turning back. This volunteer group was beyond the refund deadline for both airfare and accommodations. This might be the only time that Erika, the competent future Executive Director, made a costly error—or perhaps it was a hidden grace.

Amyotrophic lateral sclerosis (ALS) is a motor neuron disease. Lou Gehrig, revered as baseball's "Iron Horse" for playing the most consecutive games, brought the debilitating disease to worldwide attention with his diagnosis. When his dynamic and historic baseball career was tragically halted, the disease became known across America by his name. Lou Gehrig's disease most often strikes adults, with onset in the prime of mid-adult life. As this nerve disease of the voluntary muscles progresses, it can result in the loss of the use of limbs and the ability to talk, swallow, and breathe. This devastating diagnosis is often accompanied by a bleak prognosis of a life expectancy of two to five years. Some succumb quickly, while most deteriorate and descend over several months or a few years into complete motor dysfunction. The tragic truth is that ALS is incurable and terminal.

After her ALS diagnosis, Chrissy signed up for a volunteer Lourdes pilgrimage with a group of friends, at their urging and insistence. She was from the same area as a friend of the pilgrimage leader. A quick phone call confirmed that he knew "Chrissy-with-ALS." He had recently seen her at a gathering; she was in a wheelchair with a feeding tube. He had heard that she would be traveling with friends to Lourdes. Serving was probably the best way they could get her to go to the Grotto. He thought if her friends were always with her, she would be able to volunteer in some limited capacity with their support.

It was too late to do anything about it anyway. It was decided that "Chrissy-with-ALS" would go to Lourdes in a hopeful service capacity. If she became unable to volunteer, she would instead become a supportive needs pilgrim on a volunteer pilgrimage. Chrissy signed on for the only service possible for her with stamina limitations, in the Accueil Marie Saint-Frai. The four-hundred-hospital-bed facility houses the sick and the disabled on pilgrimage to Lourdes. The sisters who founded, owned, and operated the Accueil were strict yet kind. Most did not speak English, so explaining her ALS would not be possible anyway. If Lourdes Volunteers registered a group of eight ladies in the same type of service, Chrissy might be able to have one of her friends take her place if she was unable to fulfill her duty shifts.

The next obstacle was transporting the liquid nutrition for her feeding tube. They could not risk transporting the large cans with the checked baggage for fear they might be lost and because they needed to be in both a climate-controlled and pressure-controlled place. Each of the nutritional cans was heavy. The solution was for every volunteer to bring one can onto the plane in his or her carry-on bag. Returning home, they could bring back the same amount of space and weight in Lourdes Water. Those were the good old days when schlepping gallons of Lourdes Water onto planes was still allowed. Sometimes a drop would leak here and there from inside the overhead bins to the giggles of knowing passengers seated directly beneath the blessed drippings.

Meeting the group in the airport, the Lourdes Volunteer leader noticed that Chrissy seemed anxious both about the travel and her service. No matter what, she was determined to serve. She was insistent about not asking for help, except for the required wheelchair and special nutrition, which she accepted with reluctant resignation.

Arriving fatigued in Lourdes, almost everyone went to Mass, had dinner, and went to bed for a good sleep. Chrissy went straight to bed, weakened from the long flight. After a restful night and an orientation meeting, volunteers formed into groups to register for service.

The Accueil Marie Saint-Frai ladies began an intense exchange within the interior office. Speaking in French, a counselor asked loudly from the adjoining office, "Who was so foolish to bring a volunteer with such a disease to serve?" The Lourdes Volunteers pilgrimage leader answered that she was responsible. They were shocked at the reply from a non-French speaker who surprisingly understood the gist of their conversation. Silence halted the buzz in the room. Whether startled or embarrassed that her question had been understood, they felt obligated to process her paperwork. Chrissy was in!

Chrissy helped at meals three times each day and made it to every assigned duty. The sister on her floor was infamously particular. Everything was "nun clean" in her kitchen. She observed Chrissy, and without question or explanation, Sister provided her with a chair to sit on while drying dishes. She had never done this before for anyone else. Despite the language barrier, the religious sister and Chrissy became a dynamic duo of synchronized cleaning. They developed a rhythm and a system to accomplish tasks. They were both proficient in their responsibilities and joyful in their duties. Clearly, Sister was just as demanding about the quality and quantity of Chrissy's service, making no exceptions other than letting her use the chair. Still, everyone noticed that Sister liked and favored Chrissy.

Instead of joining her volunteer group and friends for daily Mass, Chrissy was invited to the pilgrimage Masses with the sisters, which worked within her service schedule. Being in the building, it was also easier for her to attend. Chrissy skipped meals with her friends and fellow volunteers to use her feeding tube and get much-needed rest. If she had enough energy, she caught up with them after service at a little place close to the Ave Maria volunteer accommodations. This bistro doubled as a convenient halfway rest stop between the Accueil and the Ave Maria. Her devoted friends made certain Chrissy was well enough to volunteer each day and had anything she wanted or needed. The first week of service in Lourdes is demanding even for a person without a debilitating motor neuron disease, yet Chrissy kept up—until the last day. She was just too drained and exhausted to complete her final assignment.

The pilgrimage leader was called into Chrissy's room by her concerned friends. The leader pinned Chrissy's volunteer name badge onto another woman's uniform and sent her to do Chrissy's service—as if the nun who favored Chrissy all week long would not notice the switch! Sister certainly did, but she said nothing and marked Chrissy as having completed all her required duties. Chrissy was upset at being unable to complete her last assignment. She tearfully explained that she had come to serve, not to be cured. Her prayer was only to ask Our Lord to let her live long enough to be the caregiver for her ill father-in-law back in their home in New York. As part of her plea, she came to offer service to Our Lady. She then failed on the very last shift. Chrissy was crushed.

The leader explained that missing one shift of service for a valid reason does not ruin or negate an entire week of selfless dedication for her or any volunteer. Her service was officially completed. She had fulfilled her obligation and kept her end of her holy bargain. Following her service, Chrissy returned home from Lourdes. As hoped and prayed for, she was able to continue as her father-in-law's caregiver. Surprisingly, after a bout in the hospital over the winter, Chrissy recovered well enough to return to Lourdes and serve again, in September 2008.

In honor of the Lourdes 150th Jubilee Apparitions Anniversary, Pope Benedict XVI was coming to the Grotto. Lourdes Volunteers was given a special assignment, a privileged once-in-a-lifetime service opportunity, and a great honor. At the request of Most Rev.

Jacques Perrier, the Tarbes et Lourdes Bishop, the volunteers were requested to assist the bishops and cardinals of the world around the Sanctuary throughout the three-day papal visit.

Chrissy remained dedicated to her service, rendering her unable to attend most of the scheduled events with the Holy Father. The Accueil Marie Saint-Frai needed every volunteer possible. Because of the Jubilee and the pope's visit, they were filled to capacity. The dates also coincided with the annual feast day of the religious order of the sisters who founded and ran it. The Lourdes Volunteers leader privately pleaded with Mother Superior to allow Chrissy to attend the Papal Mass being offered for the sick. Knowing she would not miss any assigned shift, exceptionally, Mother discreetly did not assign Chrissy to service during the Papal Mass.

The crowds swelled to hundreds of thousands of pilgrims. Chrissy was spotted by her pilgrimage leader amid the crushing sea of people vying to see the beloved Holy Father. "You won't believe it!" Chrissy said, beaming and overjoyed. "Mother Superior did not have me on the schedule this morning! I can't believe I am here!" In a grace received through their special service to the Holy Father, Lourdes Volunteers was able to arrange for two chairs to be squeezed into the center of the first row, directly in front of the pope, for Chrissy and a physician volunteer.

When an ordained Catholic priest holds the Host in his hands and prays the words of Christ, "Take this, all of you, and eat of it, for this is my Body, which will be given up for you" (see Matt. 26:26–28), Catholics believe the unleavened bread mystically and actually transforms into the Body of Jesus Christ, into Our Lord, sacramentally present. This power of the Word of Christ and the action of the Holy Spirit through the priest is the doctrine of transubstantiation.

At that precise moment of transubstantiation, on the feast of Our Lady of Sorrows, September 15, 2008, Chrissy said she felt a shaft of heat completely envelop her being. It moved through her entire body, from the top of her head down to the tips of her toes. In awe, she was immobilized as the warmth radiated in a mystical love. Chrissy was trembling—yet calm—and thought, "Oh! This is how we die!" She was not afraid. On the contrary, it was as if she was flooded with a profound inner peace. Instead of dying, Chrissy was fully alive—filled with the warmth and glow of a Heavenly peace-filled experience. She knew something profound had happened to her. Chrissy felt energized and no longer needed a wheelchair. She was hungry. After Mass, she discovered she was able to chew, swallow, and eat.

Suddenly, her feeding tube popped out. Chrissy was not concerned because she knew exactly how, when, and where she was healed. Her Lourdes Volunteers pilgrimage leader and a few others believed the same, but her doctors at the ALS Center were not convinced. Back home in the United States, they surgically reinserted her feeding tube. Then it popped out a second time. She returned to the doctor to have it laparoscopically reinserted again.

The third time it popped out, Chrissy again called the Lourdes Volunteers office and pleaded not to keep having the tube inserted. Must she keep doing this? How many times? Chrissy was advised to cooperate with her doctor and was referred to the Lourdes Volunteers Head Nurse. The respected registered nurse encouraged Chrissy to ask her ALS physician to consider leaving the tube out for a specific time. Any weight loss would quickly reveal whether she would require a feeding tube to be reinserted for nutrition. Chrissy pleaded with her doctors not to reinsert the tube a fourth time. They reluctantly acquiesced, insisting they would insert a feeding tube as soon as she lost one single pound. They were sure this would happen quickly—*but it never did!*

A new specialist came into the ALS Center when Chrissy's physician retired. The doctor demanded new tests. He called her in for a thorough examination and consultation. Upon meeting her, he said, "I have a real problem with you. My problem is that you are still alive!"

ALS is a progressive incurable disease. A physician is put in a difficult situation to explain why a patient does not get progressively worse or succumb to a diagnosed incurable, terminal illness. A lawsuit could be brought against a physician for the cruelty of a misdiagnosis, treatments, expenses, and psychological suffering, especially in the United States, which is well known to be medically litigious. Chrissy was not seeking a lawsuit. She was interested only in giving thanks. A trusted physician specializing in ALS privately told Chrissy, "I know you had ALS. I know you were cured at Lourdes, but as a physician I can never medically admit this to anyone."

Meanwhile, in 2009, Chrissy returned to serve in Lourdes. She presented her cure to the Bureau des Constatations Médicales, commonly called the Medical Bureau by English speakers. The scientific scrutiny to proclaim a miraculous cure is an exhaustive review over many years. This thorough process and evaluation must leave no doubt or question as to the medical condition before the alleged cure and the long-term sustained health of the person afterward.

The Lourdes Medical Director is an unusual physician because patients do not visit this good doctor when they are sick; instead, they seek an appointment only when they are cured! Therefore, the resident Lourdes Medical Director sees only healthy patients. The responsibility is to examine and explore whether the cured person was formerly genuinely sick and with valid diagnostic proof. This extensive process requires a mountain of substantiating documentation for verification.

American HIPAA regulations can present a challenge to this exhaustive process in Europe. The Health Insurance Portability and Accountability Act of 1996 (HIPAA) is a federal law requiring standards to protect sensitive health information from being disclosed without the consent or knowledge of a patient. This became a small wrinkle in a previously smoother process to obtain and share records between Lourdes and the United States. Some medical documents had to be sent directly by American physicians to France. Other documentation could only be given to Chrissy by her physicians to be hand-carried and submitted by her. An official dossier was opened at Lourdes. Chrissy was asked to write what happened to her, and she was invited to return the following year with her medical history. The Medical Bureau at Lourdes employs the Lambertini Criteria, the same strict rules the Catholic Church uses to proclaim a miracle for the canonization process of a person for sainthood. These criteria require a disease to be serious or impossible to cure, at an advanced stage, with an instantaneous, complete, total, and permanent cure that cannot be attributed to any treatment received or to natural healing. After this thorough and intensive scrutiny over several years, with a majority vote of the Association Médicale Internationale de Notre-Dame de Lourdes (AMIL), the cure being considered proceeds forward to the Comité Médicale International de Lourdes (CMIL) at their annual fall meeting, traditionally held in Paris. Another two-thirds majority vote of those medical and scientific professionals is required to continue the cure forward in the process. After the declaration of an inexplicable cure, the bishop of Tarbes et Lourdes or, preferably, the bishop where the cured person resides, can choose to proclaim the inexplicable cure an official miracle recognized by the Catholic Church.

Each year, for ten consecutive years, Chrissy went to the Medical Bureau in Lourdes during her week of annual September service. After a decade of examining hundreds of pages of documentation in her expanding file, including laboratory, radiological, and pulmonary testing results, detailed physical examinations, and physician notes, Chrissy was informed that her dossier lacked a definitive diagnosis that would be universally medically acceptable. Two significant tests needed for complete diagnostic evidence were not in her medical records.

Chrissy reported that, according to her doctors, she initially had the symptoms and progression of ALS (before Lourdes). However, the most definitive tests, including repeated electromyography (EMG) tests and a biopsy, were not in her files. Only one EMG test, not the usual required full series of three tests, is referred to in physicians' reports and notes. Further, the actual result of the single test was not present in her medical file. Complicating the need for this test result was the impact of HIPAA, which initiated the practice of destroying medical records after seven years. After ten years, finding a decade-old test result seemed nearly impossible. The definitive diagnosis was in question; it was not in consensus and lacked needed evidence.

A final review of Chrissy's extensive file was conducted again in 2018. The Medical Directors of Lourdes Volunteers reviewed the documentation. Stacked page upon page on the conference table, the file was taller in inches than the number of years of her collected scientifically recorded evidence. Two physicians spent two days organizing and reviewing the file, both chronologically and medically. It was decided that American physician specialists should conduct a blind review of the case for a final determination. Possibly the mountain of evidence was sufficient for a defensible diagnosis by American neurological standards. It was agreed that prestigious specialists from three well-known and highly respected medical facilities in the United States would be asked to conduct a blind review of the case. The final consideration would be done by asking three impartial, *non-Catholic* neurologists who specialize in ALS to conduct independent reviews.

Lourdes Volunteers arranged for Chrissy's case to be reviewed by the first of three specialists. An esteemed New England physician stated that without a biopsy and a series of three EMG test results, a scientific diagnosis of ALS would not be possible for a patient who no longer exhibited ALS symptoms.

Although a diagnosis based upon the other extensive results had been accepted as a medical diagnosis for treatment and health-insurance coverage, it would not be sufficient for a scientific diagnosis so many years later. Without the first of three physicians in agreement, Chrissy realized her case could no longer continue for consideration as an inexplicable cure. The Lourdes Medical Director kindly told her that he did not deny Chrissy experienced some kind of a blessing or a healing at Lourdes but that a pronouncement of an inexplicable cure of ALS could not be made.

Chrissy is humble about her experience at Lourdes. Humility is a known hallmark of anyone associated with a miracle. Those who have been cured do not seek attention. God has touched them in a profound and deep way. These awed souls come forward only for the benefit of others and to give glory to God.

As requested by the Medical Bureau, Chrissy did not speak publicly during the decade of scientific scrutiny of her case file at Lourdes. She did not speak privately in Lourdes either, except once. After five years, an exceptional request was made of her to speak to a small group of medical professionals in the fall of 2013.

An Engagement, a lifetime commitment to serve the Hospitalité Notre-Dame de Lourdes annually whenever possible, can be made in the fifth year of volunteer service. On September 9, 2009, Chrissy committed to serving in Lourdes every year for the rest of her unexpected life. Following this ceremony at Mass, there is a lively reception to honor all those who made their lifetime Engagement commitment. Any member of the Hospitalité in Lourdes may attend, along with family, friends, and Sanctuary dignitaries. The Lourdes Volunteers pilgrimage leader was also in service that week, serving as the English-speaking teacher for those preparing to make their Engagement. Five American physicians were students together with Chrissy. They all knew one another because they had been in classes and service at around the same time in Lourdes for the past four years.

As a gift to the students on their special day, the teacher asked Chrissy to explain to the doctors how she came to Lourdes. They politely listened but were clearly unconvinced. Their arms crossed tightly against their stark white medical coats silently signaled their scientific skepticism. The panel of doctors aggressively questioned Chrissy. One physician asked probing pulmonary questions. As he listened to her responses, his tone suddenly changed; his posture shifted. He straightened to stiff attention and became still. His lips trembled. The doctor was nearly in tears as he reached out his arm toward Chrissy and asked if he could touch her—if he could touch a living miracle. At that moment, it was as if the Bible came alive—as if St. Thomas, the doubting apostle, was reaching out to touch the wounds of Jesus Christ, to believe through his unbelief (see John 20:27). These men of medical science were visibly moved. All five doctors gently placed their hands on Chrissy. They prayed quietly, spiritually connected with Chrissy and each other. It was a profound occasion of medicine for the body meeting the faith of the soul. It was an unforgettable moment for those who witnessed this moving encounter.

Chrissy does not know why she was inexplicably given more than a decade of unexpected years with her family since the 2008 grace she received in Lourdes. She sometimes wonders if she is still alive so that others can know that we have a God Who loves and cares for each one of us, personally and individually. Chrissy does believe her added years are a blessing from God. She remains grateful to have been able to care for her father-in-law, the answer to her prayers the first time she was in Lourdes. It's possible that Chrissy was cured to serve as a witness to others, as well as to serve others at Lourdes and at home. Only God knows.

Chrissy continues to return to Lourdes in the Accueil Marie Saint-Frai service. Karin, her youngest daughter, started coming with her for a mother-daughter service week in France every September. Lourdes Volunteers requested that Chrissy formally come as a volunteer leader, something she had been informally doing for years by shepherding new volunteers along her way.

Early in 2020, Chrissy and her husband were invited to join a small contingency to Rome, Italy, for the annual Lourdes Volunteers meeting in the Vatican with the Apostolica Penitenzieria to report about the plenary indulgences granted. Chrissy and the other Lourdes Volunteers representatives requested that the Holy See continue their Apostolic Blessing for seven more years to encourage the opportunity for life-changing graces that she personally knows to be generously granted to those in service at Lourdes.

> *To one who has faith, no explanation is necessary. To one without faith, no explanation is possible.* (St. Thomas Aquinas)

Thankful Volunteers

Chrissy and Karin are a mother-daughter duo serving in Lourdes in the Accueil Marie Saint-Frai hospital bed facility. Chrissy made her lifetime commitment as a Lourdes Volunteer with the Hospitalité Notre-Dame de Lourdes in 2009. A decade later, her daughter Karin made her lifetime commitment in thanksgiving for her mother's cure at Lourdes.

Chapter 5

A Will to Live

Baby Ida-Linda

Ida entered the world weighing a scant two pounds and five ounces to unintentionally join the precarious one percent of babies delivered at such a meager birthweight. She hurriedly slipped onto the delivery table—*alive*—startling her young mother, who was left alone in the unattended maternity room. Arriving far too early to survive outside her mother's womb, she was expected to be stillborn. Ida had "blood clot boils" on her tiny left wrist, her inner thighs, her chest, and her head. Born a perilous preemie in 1955, the miracle of her survival was more about her teeny birth size than the swollen marks scattered randomly across her tiny body. Ida, called Linda since her surprising live birth, would later be taken monthly on a train to New York City for therapeutic radiation to treat the bulging boils. Yet, from the very beginning of her life, the more significant concern was her puny growth rate compounded by her lackluster developmental performance milestones. This dangerous combination soon overtook any worries about the boils and the resulting treatment burns. Ultimately, the scars became an accepted part of her, like her soft blond hair and her blue pointy-cornered glasses, which she detested having to wear. It just was what it was, or so it seemed to be.

Linda's story began before her unexpected birth survival. Her mother had grown up suffering under an abusive stepfather. Terrified and traumatized, she did what she thought would help her out of her desperate situation. In her fear and her eagerness to escape, she jumped into the arms of a tough guy she hoped could protect her. At the time, it seemed like her only way out—and anything was better than living with her cruel and alcoholic stepfather. But the haphazard escape quickly disintegrated into a doomed-to-fail teenage marriage.

Not long after rushing out of one disaster into another, ignorant of birds, bees, and babies, Linda's mother discovered she was pregnant. She had married to get out of the abusive house of her mother and stepfather, but she was not ready to take care of herself or anyone else, especially a baby. In desperation, she found herself in a bathtub with a knitting needle, frantically attempting to end her unplanned pregnancy. But God had knitted Ida-Linda tightly in her mother's womb (Ps. 139:13)—so tightly that not even her distraught mother could unknit her.

Ida was born with delicate resilience. But the blood-clot and radiation scars were not the most severe damage caused in that botched home-abortion attempt. They were just the physical evidence of the knitting-needle jabs. The emotional, spiritual, and psychological impact inflicted the worst and longest-lasting blows to both child and mother.

The hospital nurses loved nurturing the feisty two-pound survivor, but most of the medical staff had little sympathy for her mom. Although this young mother denied it, the nurses knew why her baby was born so early and what had happened. Her dysfunctional behavior was also obvious in her unnatural maternal detachment.

It was apparent that this mother could not be expected to care for a baby, especially a fragile preemie.

The Department of Social Services was called in to intervene. Ida-Linda left the hospital to enter into a foster home. A frail infant, she heroically struggled to survive, but her status eventually declined to the dismal failure to thrive in foster care. Social Services stepped in again. The social workers knew an older couple who were known for never refusing to take in troubled teens or scraggly toddlers.

For years, Mr. and Mrs. Bray had lovingly turned around every desperate child sent to them. Although they were beyond childbearing age, the social worker asked them to take Baby Ida-Linda. This baby had a strong will to survive but required attentive nurturing if she was to have any chance to make it. She immediately became the light of the Brays' lives and the forever daughter of their hearts.

Mr. and Mrs. Bray were phonetically called *Town-tea* and *Bone-key*, a bad-to-worse French-Acadian-Canadian-to-English translation mispronunciation of *Tante* (aunt) and *Oncle* (uncle). Tante was the granddaughter of a Native American. She concocted drinks made of herbs plucked fresh from her garden and the nearby woods in the Adirondack Mountains to boost the skinny, weakling baby. The combination of love, attention, and pungent drinks worked perfectly, but Tante always attributed Linda's health improvements to her consistent Rosaries and the intercession of the Blessed Virgin Mary. Fortified in faith and nurtured in love, the wispy baby grew, just as her social worker had hoped—thriving, happy, and spunky!

Although she disagreed with the radiation treatments, Tante compliantly took Linda to New York City every month on the train, healing her burned skin after each treatment once they returned home. Tante preferred to treat the birth boil wounds with her natural remedies and blessed holy water from her parish church. Medical decisions were not the choice of foster parents without legal parental rights. For a mature couple never able to have children, nurturing a fragile, extremely premature baby created a lasting bond born of protective, loving care and prayerful thanksgiving for the unexpected gift of the life of Linda to the world—and to the Brays in their later midlife years. Although they spoiled her, Linda was well behaved and undemanding. She was shy, without the need to try to be the center of attention because she was the entire world to her Tante and Bonkie, who dotingly lavished her with affection. Linda was embraced by her extended foster family, and she loved spending time with her "cousins." One of the girls was just her age; they were inseparable whenever they were together. Spending Sundays with other children was a healthy interaction for Linda, especially as the only child of older parents.

Linda's birth mother surprisingly turned her tumultuous life around. She married a professional man with the promise of stability and reliability, a seemingly solid foundation for raising a family. Social Services could not refuse to take Linda out of foster care and return her to her biological mother. Her new father-to-be arranged a formal adoption. Her name was legally changed to Linda, which is what she had always been called anyway. The adoption was not an easy transition for anyone. There was continuous crying. Linda joined a new baby sister and new parents in a new home with a new life, a new last name, and a new extended family. It was a lot of newness for one little five-year-old girl.

To an outside observer, Linda's new life might have seemed like the success story of a foster child returned to her natural parent—but that was not the reality. Linda had suffered yet another abandonment and total upheaval in her young life. Inside, she felt as if she had been ripped out of the security and comfort she knew and needed. At the same time, her mother found herself in a relationship she was ill equipped to handle. And she was unprepared to explain her suddenly present daughter to others. Linda was expected to shift instantly into the role of older sister in a young family with a drastically different life, pace, and routine. There was no time for bonding or adjustment. Further complicating the transition, Linda contracted spinal meningitis in her first year of school. It was hard to remember all the new rules, so different from her former life. Her new parents thought she was spoiled and difficult. She felt uprooted, a foreigner in a flash family switch beyond her young understanding. Visiting her foster parents only worsened the situation. Her mother had to peel Linda off Tante, kicking and screaming, after each encounter, which was emotionally draining for everyone.

It was decided that Linda needed to make a permanent transition; she just had to adjust. Her new parents cut off all contact with her foster family in hopes of forging acceptance of her new adoptive life. It seemed cruel, but it was intended for her own good—this one-time clean break to give her a promising future. After the adoption, Linda's birth and her baby, toddler, and preschool years were never discussed; any inquiry or accidental mention was abruptly dismissed. It would be decades before Linda came to know her story. She had been forcibly taken away from the only parents she had ever known—but not before she memorized their address.

Linda struggled as a child with a strict, inexperienced adoptive father. As with many families, there were good times and bad. Boisterous extended family, adventurous vacations, expansive vegetable gardens with fruit trees to climb, and traditional Italian cooking punctuated Linda's childhood years. Her family experienced the struggles and complications of blended families, sprinkled with nightly cocktails and noisy backyard parties so popular in the sixties. The years sped by, and before it seemed possible, Linda went off to college.

A statue of the Immaculate Conception of the Grotto of Lourdes was prominently positioned in front of the small Catholic campus. Linda would stop to pray before the image of "Our Lady of Whoever." She was unable to differentiate Our Lady of Fátima from Our Lady of Lourdes or other depictions of Mary. From Tante, Linda had been given a connection to the reliable Mother of God to help guide her through her rocky transition to adoption. While she was away at college, Linda secretly wrote to Tante and Bonkie.

She soon found out that she and her long-lost "cousin" were both students at the same all-girls Marian college. Linda was finally reunited with her foster family! Tante and Bonkie had prayed for more than a decade to see their little Linda again, and their prayers were answered in their senior years! Linda and her cousin became inseparable again, making up for a painful decade torn apart. Life was complicated, but life was not only good, it was better than ever.

After graduation, while pursuing a higher-level degree, Linda met and married the handsome guy from across the hall. Smart and idealistic, he looked like the academic intellectual he truly was, stylishly sporting a trendy leather vest under a corduroy blazer with suede elbow patches. Linda and Kevin were both majoring in human services. Compassionate and hopeful, bursting with helpfulness and altruistic ideals, the couple intended to embark on an earnest social mission to save the whales and the world. Their only meaningful disagreement was about religion. They were both raised as Catholics, but Kevin had stopped attending Mass as a young adult. Even so, he took issue with the non-Christian church Linda had recently joined.

They married with the agreement that he would never follow her new religion, and he never did.

The newlywed couple chose a simpler life with a single income while raising three beautiful daughters. They conscientiously made the financial sacrifice for Linda to stay home with their girls while she baked bread in her earth shoes. Linda loved to cook, and Kevin loved her cooking—no onions, please and thank you. They were the unnoticeable young couple around the corner, living everyday family life until a Friday afternoon when two policemen knocked at the door.

The officers would not tell Linda anything, but they didn't have to. She knew. She just knew in the way a wife can somehow know. There had been a horrific darkening of the sky followed by a vicious downpour in a violently fierce and fast-moving storm a few hours earlier. It was as if a wave of ferocious anger voraciously had touched down, like the tornados typical of the Midwest but unusual for New York. Her beloved husband had been broadsided in the storm and was killed on impact. His future and his dreams as a healthy young father raising his daughters died along with him. Linda faced yet another cruel and total abandonment in her life.

For Linda, the days, months, and years ahead turned into a continuous struggle to survive. Bereavement settled into deeply entrenched depression. When it became unbearable, she would confide to her best friend and cousin that she needed only to hold on until her girls were grown, as if there would be an expiration or scheduled relief for her grief. Putting a time limit on survival and suffering was intended to affix a hopeful, imaginary ray of light at the end of an unbearable, unending tunnel. When good-intentioned people said that they would all be together again in Heaven, it became a comforting thought for the young widow to hold on to during difficult times.

A few years after her husband died, steeped in the awareness of the impact of his loss on her fatherless daughters, Linda became determined to find her biological father. She was finally able to meet the man who had lost her at birth through divorce, foster care, and adoption. Amid her search, information surfaced from reluctant relatives about her unexpected birth and infant life. Linda puzzled the pieces of the scattered details together to shockingly discover that she was the survivor of a failed abortion attempt.

This must be why, after leaving foster care for adoption, Linda could never find a way to reconnect her ruptured umbilical cord back to her birth mother. It intuitively made sense to her. She had been abandoned and rejected in an ultimate maternal betrayal. She realized she had been craving a motherly connection from before her first breath and for her entire life ever since. The verification of the abortion attempt tipped a scale of trauma rippling deep within Linda. It catapulted Linda into the deepest despair and into a pit of bottomless grief. Then suddenly, her girls were grown, and Linda was an empty-nester. Just like that, her three reasons for years of survival were gone. Linda had fulfilled her commitment to raise her daughters. Then, she simply lost her desire to live.

Linda discovered that when she was born alive, her startled mother had promised God that if He would allow her unexpected baby to live, she would raise her Catholic. This explained why she had attended Catholic schools while her younger half-sister received a public school education. At a loss in her life and spiritually unfulfilled without the sacraments of her childhood, Linda left the austere church she had joined as an unsettled young adult. She considered different spiritualties and lingered in personal prayer, but the strength of her childhood Catholic Faith was no longer there to be the rock she could cling to when the waves of despair crashed against her weakening will to survive.

Linda had unraveled. She simply came undone, a stitch at a time, like knitted yarn loops slipping off slender needles. Born despite a death wish, she reluctantly resigned herself to it. She was exhausted from struggling to survive, and her will to live was sapped. Linda was depleted. Despondent thoughts culminated in an accidental overdose, which her medical-care providers and most family members suspected was a failed suicide attempt. She was hospitalized a few times for severe depression and heavily medicated. Yet again, God intervened. His Mother would help knit Linda back together again—this time in Lourdes.

The journey to France was fraught with hand-wringing anxiety and tears interspersed with laughter and the comedy of monolingual, inexperienced international travelers. The language barrier was, at times, as funny as it was frustrating and challenging. Getting to the Grotto was not easy. Once in Lourdes, getting into the Baths proved to be just as difficult. It seems anything worth having is usually not easy to obtain, sometimes even grace.

All the effort to get into the Piscines proved worthwhile. Once inside the Baths, Linda was blessed with a profound experience. The cool water in the tub was soothing. It was a maternal healing like an amniotic submersion, repairing the tragic harm caused in the womb in another tub so many years earlier. All the shards of Linda's shattered self amazingly floated back together in her bath at Lourdes. It was a mystical grace. Linda felt whole for the first time in her life. It was as if she had been reborn with a desire to live life fully. Her will to live was restored in a grace.

Although Linda had been away from the Catholic Faith for more than a decade, she never wavered in her connection to the Mother of God. Many converts to Catholicism identify Mary as their hesitation or obstacle to joining the Church because they do not know or realize that, from the Cross, Our Lord gave us His

Mother to behold (John 19:27). He gave us Mary as our mother. For Linda, reverting to Catholicism was exactly the opposite. It was the Mother of God who drew her back to her childhood Faith. It was the steadfast faith of the Mother of Christ, standing by her Son at the foot of the Cross, that brought Linda home to the Church. And Linda's once-doubted belief in the Holy Eucharist was restored in the silence of prayer before the Blessed Sacrament in the tabernacle. Where her birth mother fell tragically short, the Mother of God had picked her up to be healed of the damage inflicted before her birth and beyond. And where Mary is, we are sure to find Jesus Christ. Linda was healed of her deepest mother-wound in the Baths at Lourdes. She made a good, holy Confession, by the grace of God, through the gentle and loving intercession of her Heavenly Mother. After more than fifteen years away from the Catholic Church, Linda returned to the holy sacraments.

She came home from Lourdes to begin her life anew with the foresight of trustful abandonment. With her renewed will to live, she received counseling balanced with medications to secure the pieces of her fragmented life, which had been pulled back together in a grace received in the Baths in France. Linda realized that her abandonment at birth left her free to choose total abandonment to God. She joyfully embraced a healthy life, grateful that God had knitted her into being, to live, and to love. Her interests returned with her renewed life, filled with family, friends, career changes, ministries, and service.

As her faith deepened, she studied women who consecrated their widowhood to God. She, too, wanted to dedicate her widowed life to God. She became a Secular Franciscan, embracing a humble lifestyle and further abandoning material distractions. In thanksgiving, Linda returned to Lourdes to volunteer. The sisters at the Accueil Marie Saint-Frai were thrilled to see her arrive for her annual service because she cleaned the hospital-bed facility like one of them—nun-clean! She and the sisters laughed their way through cleaning and caring for the pilgrims in Lourdes with miming gestures and smiles for translation. Life since Lourdes was again better than ever.

Linda held no resentment against her mother, a grace she attributes to her faith. In an irony of grace, the traumatic delivery-table promise that Linda would be raised Catholic became a boomerang blessing for both mother and child. When her mother was diagnosed with terminal cancer, it was her faithful Catholic daughter, returning from Lourdes, who arranged for a priest to bring the deathbed sacraments of Anointing and Viaticum (the "Bread of Angels" or Last Holy Communion) and the holy Apostolic Pardon, which offers forgiveness for sins and temporal punishment. Linda and her mother were at peace. Together, through the intercession of Our Lady of Lourdes, they found some happiness in this world, as her mother departed for "the happiness of the other world"—a lasting gift from the Grotto. This precious time of caring for her mother was the much-needed, holy, life-bonding gift for both mother and daughter.

Until the writing of this book, Linda had never shared the story of her birth trauma and healing with anyone, aside from her family and closest friends. It was her personal and private Lourdes "miracle," restoring her desire to live—and the desire to live a holy life. Her experience of Lourdes was never reported to the Sanctuary and will never be counted as a measurable inexplicable cure by the Medical Bureau. Yet the miraculous grace of her Lourdes experience must surely be known in Heaven as the miraculous intercessory handiwork of the Immaculate Conception, ever attentive to her children in need, especially Baby Ida-Linda.

You formed my inmost being; you knit me in my mother's womb.... Your eyes saw me unformed; in your book all are written down; my days were shaped, before one came to be. (Ps.139:13, 16, NABRE)

Foster Visit with Mom

Linda is a grandmother and Accueil Marie Saint-Frai handmaid. She was the original inspiration for the first community of women to become consecrated widows in 2023 with Our Lady of Lourdes Hospitality North American Volunteers.

Chapter 6

To "Bee" in the Heavenly Procession

Floral Cora

Debbie told Cora she was too afraid of dying to fly anywhere, let alone a long-haul flight from California to Europe. Why her practical exercise partner was not at all hesitant to fly all the way to France seemed illogically mismatched with her typical sensible thinking. Cora was not crossing the Atlantic for a compelling crisis. She was only going to Lourdes for her annual volunteer service. Actually, Cora was accustomed to lengthy flights, having immigrated years earlier from the Philippines to the United States. She neither liked nor disliked spending hours on a plane to visit her family every January or to go anywhere at any time. It was just that she had a peace about dying and air travel that did not come from statistics or expressions intended to comfort reluctant travelers, such as "we are much safer in a plane than in a car." Cora was not fearless or fearful of flying. She was just a woman confidently grounded in faith.

Cora explained that God could take her home to Himself whenever He wanted; she was not afraid to die. "Are your bags packed?" Debbie asked, rolling her eyes. Cora thoughtfully considered whether her soul was as prepared to meet God as her suitcases were ready for international travel. "Yes! My white nurse volunteer uniforms are folded and packed in my luggage. I'm ready to go to Lourdes or to go with God. *I am really ready*—right now!" Cora smiled as Debbie shrugged off the spiritual sentiment. They finished up in the locker room and walked outside together. "See you next time," they said, without a thought otherwise, walking to their cars.

Cora returned home to prune her roses in the pleasant morning sun. Michael and Cora tended impressive flower beds in their backyard and across the entirety of their compact front yard. Coming from the scenic island of Cebu, Cora cherished the flowers and lush greenery typical of the tropical gardens back home. Living in California, she nurtured delicately scented floral delights interspersed amid winding stone pathways and outdoor statuary. Michael was born in Bombay while his father was heading up an American bank expansion there. He was an equally enthusiastic garden hobbyist with extensive plantings reminiscent of his childhood in fragrant India and his teen years spent living abroad in Lebanon. The couple equally enjoyed time with each other and with their extensive gardens. Cora returned from the gym intending to first prune the roses nearest the walkway by the front door. This task could be completed before she had to depart for noon Mass and to escape the crescendo of California's midday peak heat.

A bee stung Cora on her neck at about eleven forty-five that morning. It was unpleasant but not extremely painful. She had been stung by a bee only once before. Today's sting swelled quite badly, but Cora did not know that severe swelling was a potential indication of a bee-sting allergy. She felt dizzy immediately. She was puzzled about why she felt so strange, but she made no connection between the sting and her escalating wooziness. Instead of her daily routine of going inside to freshen up and grab the keys and then driving to Mass, Cora barely made her way into the house. Noticing the familiar daily show airing on the large television screen as she entered the living area, Cora knew it was after eleven thirty but before noon. She thought maybe she was hungry or thirsty—she knew something was very wrong. It was as if she were swaying on the outside and floating on the inside. She felt as though time had somehow inexplicably been suspended. The reality was that Cora was dangerously close to dying.

She began to pray the Rosary, *slowly*.

The Holy Rosary is a scriptural form of prayer favored for centuries by saints and everyday faithful alike. This powerful intercessory prayer is a meditative practice through which we deepen our relationship with Our Lord as we contemplate significant moments in His life and ministry. Rosary beads are a practical, holy tool that helps us count the individual prayers so that we can focus on our meditation and pray undistracted by the counting of individual prayers. Made of glass, stone, wood, knotted rope, or glow-in-the-dark plastic for children, rosaries have larger beads for praying the Our Father and sets of ten smaller beads for praying the Hail Marys. Recently canonized Pope St. Paul VI was known to say that when praying the Rosary, key moments of the Gospel can be experienced. Cora knew that to be true and had always loved to pray the Rosary, her favorite prayer.

She lay helplessly on the floor, motionless, her rosary beads clenched in her fist. She suddenly remembered her comment in the gym locker room. She pleaded with the Blessed Mother, crying to her as a regretful child would cry to an understanding mom: "Please forgive me; I'm not ready to die. I want to be here for my son when he returns from Iraq—and I need to go to Lourdes and volunteer for you." Cora wept softly while pleading with the Mother of God to help her. Then it was as if time remained suspended and stretched in a mystical way, allowing her to continue her prayers.

Michael did not often have time to talk to his wife during his busy workdays. Neither of their schedules was routine or predictable, especially when Mike was working a job in San Francisco proper. Traffic could easily derail his day, often delaying both his drive and his arrival home. On this day, Cora had called Michael as he was nearing the Golden Gate Bridge. Her speech sounded unusual, almost slurred. Worried, he called her back throughout the afternoon. No answer. He called two neighbors. He was unable to reach them. Mike finally dialed 911. It was just after four o'clock in the afternoon.

Friends living nearby had a key, but it was not needed. Cora had left the door unlocked as she came in from the garden. The neighbors entered with the paramedics to find her on the floor—eerily still and unnaturally blue. She was barely breathing and cool to the touch. The ambulance crew ultimately discovered her swollen neck and found the bee sting. The emergency operator instructed Mike to drive directly to the hospital. They told him there was no need to rush and cautioned him to drive slowly. No mention was made that Cora might not be alive. Cora arrived at the hospital unresponsive. She was treated for a severe allergic reaction and admitted to the intensive care unit. Cora was in a coma. Mike was told that her prognosis was not promising. As she was loved by many, her faithful family and friends stormed Heaven with prayers, pleading for her life.

Cora remained unconscious the day after the bee sting. Unaware of her coma, she instead found herself in Lourdes, France. She was somehow looking from up above at the pilgrims who were beneath her in the Grotto where they were preparing for the daily Eucharistic Procession. She could clearly see the top of the head of each person as the pilgrims turned to cross over the bridge to be near the outdoor altar. Cora followed them, joining them by floating above. She could see and sense the excitement mixed with reverent anticipation of the Blessed Sacrament's arrival to commence the regal procession. Crowds and small groups converged with stragglers while the St. Joseph's men hurriedly attempted to maintain an orderly queue in preparation for a dignified procession. Cora could see the volunteers had their hands full! Under the expert guidance of the St. Joseph *Brancardiers* (volunteer stretcher-bearers), everything and everyone eventually fell into place, as it somehow amazingly always does every time at Lourdes.

The Eucharistic Procession is a highlight of the daily pilgrimage for many in Lourdes and not to be missed. The trumpets blow in evangelical harmony, with a muted bugle sounding a royal announcement: Our Lord is coming! Catholics believe Jesus Christ is truly present in the Holy Eucharist, the Blessed Sacrament (Luke 22:19). The sick join in at the place of privilege at the very front of the procession, followed by the Blessed Sacrament under a four-corner poled canopy held by volunteers dressed in respectful uniforms. Banners precede the holy fanfare worthy of Christ the Risen King. The daily Eucharistic Procession at Lourdes might be the first or only time some people witness this magnificent historical devotion.

A procession is a holy follow-the-way proceeding and should not be confused with the pomp of a parade. Every day at Lourdes, between Holy Week and All Saints' Day, tens of thousands process with the Holy Eucharist from across the Grotto, over the bridge along the Basilica ramps and onto the Esplanade roadway following Our Lord into the St. Pius X Underground Basilica. Once inside, the twenty-five thousand or more pilgrims, on stretchers, in wheelchairs, or seated in pews, sing as hundreds of priests process to the altar. The music continues, amazingly led by pilgrims from around the globe, sounding more like a world-class professional choir than impromptu volunteers. It is an astounding, beautiful, and incomparable holy event—*every day.*

Even though she was in a deep coma, Cora experienced the procession with fervent joy. Enthralled, she followed the Holy Eucharist, continuing from above, a perfect vantage point for sound and sight without the usual obstruction of the crowds on the ground. Cora was filled with awe, content to follow Jesus to the *happiness of the other world.* In these moments, she did not realize that her body was in a California hospital bed in the United States of America, far away from Lourdes, France.

On the third day of her life-suspending coma, Cora's Lourdes Volunteers friends brought Lourdes Water to bless her. She soon surfaced from her deep sleep in the intensive care unit. She excitedly insisted that she call the office of Lourdes Volunteers. She exclaimed in a strained, groggy voice that she wanted to explain that when we go from this world to the other world, we just have to follow Jesus in the Blessed Sacrament to Heaven. It's the same way we process at Lourdes. This must be what happens when we die! It's a holy road map—*just follow Jesus in the Holy Eucharist!* Cora said if everyone just understood this, if they would only go to Lourdes, they would know the way to Heaven. Simply follow Jesus in the Holy Eucharist in the Eucharistic Procession because "He is the way!" (John 14:6).

Cora fell back into a coma for a few more days but later woke up to recover fully. The physicians said it was impossible for someone with such a severe allergic reaction to remain alive for hours after a deadly bee sting. They insisted that Cora was mistaken about the time she was stung. Cora is certain it was about eleven forty-five in the morning, the time she usually left for daily Mass. She knew because of the specific Catholic program streaming on her television when she went into her house immediately after being stung.

What Cora could not explain is why it took her more than four hours to pray one Rosary, which usually takes only fifteen to twenty minutes to pray. She said, "It was as if God slowed or suspended time while I prayed the Rosary, until help could arrive hours later to save my life."

Cora is confident that the Mother of God heard her heartfelt request, remaining with Cora and interceding for her throughout her prayerful plea to welcome her only son back from deployment. Cora is forever grateful for this favor and insists that the Blessed Mother is the best Heavenly friend to ask to pray for us when we are most in need of a seemingly impossible favor!

> *Grant us your tender devotion to Mary, the Mother of Jesus and our Mother. Accompany us on our earthly pilgrimage toward the blessed homeland, where we hope to arrive to contemplate forever the glory of the Father, the Son, and the Holy Spirit.* (St. John Paul II's Rosary prayer to St. Padre Pio)

Cora in Her Rose Garden

Cora returned to Lourdes in 2010 to make her commitment to serve in the St. Jean Baptiste Service as a Lourdes Volunteer. In thanks for her "time-suspending and lifesaving" Rosary, Cora makes and gifts hundreds of crystal rosary beads each year. She frequently hosts prayer groups in her homes in both California and Cebu.

Chapter 7

A Sign of the Cross

Joyful Jamie

Jamie was bitter. He wasn't born that way—he was born with cerebral palsy. Jamie came into the world good-natured. Turning from teen to young adult, he slowly stewed himself into sour bitterness. Resentful was his upgrade from discouraged after he left school and no longer needed to be somewhere with others every day. God was not present in Jamie's life—or so he thought. Religion was only for his sister. After their parents divorced and went their separate ways, his sister embraced a God-centered life. Jamie moved into a group home and later claimed his quadriplegic adulthood in an act of bold independence by moving into a condominium for a while with a quad friend.

Both men required full care provided by social services through governmental agencies. Jamie's roommate had a girlfriend and was financially supported by his family, who provided him with the condo and supplemental private care. Jamie was totally dependent on government services and received occasional family visits. Otherwise, he was mostly on his own in this unusual living arrangement.

Once the seeds of bitterness sprouted, they grew in Jamie like prickly weeds, deepening and expanding their ugly roots.

His sister knew God was the answer. She was praying for Jamie's conversion—for him to turn to God and to be at peace with his physical limitations for the rest of his life. She was hoping this would happen sooner rather than later, before his dwindling natural goodness totally depleted. She was confident that if she could just get him to Lourdes—the holy place of miracles and healing—the graces would overtake his bitterness and restore and renew Jamie. She wasn't praying for him to jump out of his wheelchair or suddenly be able to use his arms or legs; she was praying for his soul. The body is temporary, but the soul is forever. And as the old saying goes, *in the end nothing matters but the state of the soul.* Jamie's sister enlisted a small but powerful army of saintly religious sisters to take on praying specifically for her brother. If Hell hath no fury like a woman scorned, then Heaven has no joy like cloistered nuns praying for the conversion of a lost soul! Jamie didn't stand a chance: those persistent nuns were going to root the anger out of him prayerfully, lovingly, and quickly so that he could be reformed in faith to flourish in God's infinite love for him.

The trip to Lourdes was a near disaster. It might have been a sparkling new millennium of hope and a few decades into handicapped accessibility in both France and the United States, but accessibility advancements were mostly stationary, still on the ground. The airlines did not anticipate the necessity for serious physical-needs adaptability in economy class. That was going to take another decade. Very few quadriplegic customers flew on long-haul international flights. If they did, those passengers usually flew in upgraded business or first-class accommodations and could afford the pricy airfare. It was a challenge to get Jamie onto the plane, down the narrow aisles, and into an economy seat accessible to the non-handicapped restroom—with dignity and without incident. Every humiliating frustration along the way could have embittered anyone—*but for love*. Love made the difference and, ultimately, the transformation. Each obstacle in getting Jamie to Lourdes and back was conquered, often at thirty-five thousand feet in a plane flying five hundred miles per hour. The volunteers who traveled with Jamie and the airline personnel on his flights literally rose to the occasion. The biblical assertion "love never ends" (1 Cor. 13:8) was manifest, both in real time and in real life.

His complaining and criticizing while on four connecting flights to Lourdes, although justifiable and for valid reasons, revealed the depth of the well of anger and self-pity within Jamie. He was questioning his purpose in life, but his thoughtful pondering was soon to be answered. Jamie was unknowingly about to become a significant catechist as a fruit of his soon-to-be conversion. God could have chosen anyone; God chose Jamie.

Jamie was cared for in Lourdes by people who paid for their own pilgrimage, selflessly dedicated to helping him. Back at home, hired staff earned an honorable paycheck to care professionally for him. Each volunteer in Lourdes literally and physically became the selfless hands and feet of Jesus Christ to Jamie. Embraced in the warmth of this authentic, loving care under the gaze of the Mother of God in the Grotto, Jamie was inspired to return to his childhood faith.

Like Bernadette, after his first visit to the Grotto, Jamie went to Confession. After another visit to the Grotto, like Bernadette before the last apparition, Jamie received the Holy Eucharist. Every encounter with the light of Christ in each person sparked within Jamie a light that illuminated his heart, leaving no room for dark anger or blackened bitterness. Each volunteer, nurse, doctor, pilgrim, and priest genuinely loved Jamie. This love expanded to overpower all the darkness that had consumed him. "One person to another" is how Bernadette described her encounter with "the most beautiful lady" in the Grotto. One person to another was the love that forever changed Jamie's heart and his life. The cloistered nuns who had been praying unceasingly won! Jamie was transformed in faith.

Back at the airport, Jamie knew that the handicapped accessibility of the airlines had not changed in one week. The difficulties he experienced on the return flights were sure to be similar to those on the outbound travel. It was how Jamie responded that was so drastically different.

Aisle chairs are armless mini-wheelchair-like contraptions. They are designed to fit exactly between the narrow rows of aircraft seats to move down the aisles. It is a tight squeeze. Any protruding elbows are exposed to painful banging on stiff metal armrests. A passenger is lifted from his personal wheelchair and put into an airport wheelchair and then lifted and strapped into a transport chair, both to enter and exit the aircraft. Add to these rare encounters a language barrier, and the results of this understandable inexperience could range from precarious to almost comical contortions of theatrical air-travel gymnastics.

On the first flight of the return series of flights, the aisle chair was missing from the aircraft. It was either hidden away under the belly of the plane or inside a cabin recess or inadvertently left at the airport where it was last used. To the credit of the airlines, and Air France specifically, this particular fiasco never happened again. Sweeping changes were made in a few short years through increasing awareness and the kind yet passionate persistence of Lourdes Volunteers and compassionate Air France personnel. Meetings and on-the-fly friendly negotiations with dedicated ground and flight crews consistently came together for needed changes to develop quickly over a relatively short time. But that was a few years yet to come. Jamie and others had first to endure many turbulent exchanges necessitating the heightened attention of one of the world's largest airlines.

Jamie's return flight was held while awaiting an aisle chair to transport him safely onto the plane. The passengers, the pilot, and the crew were all increasingly anxious about missing their connecting international flights in Paris. The flight needed to take off without further delay. Leaving Jamie behind was not an option. The pilgrimage leader was pleading with the airline to negotiate a dignified solution to honor boarding for a quadriplegic passenger. The longer the delay, the more the distress mounted. Jamie finally agreed to be carried onto the aircraft, like a baby, in the arms of his adult male caregiver. Jamie could have felt humiliated, insulted, or justifiably angry. Instead, he was beaming, smiling ear to ear! The full plane erupted into spontaneous applause! It was hard to complain about the seriousness of the situation when the wronged passenger was so unmistakably happy.

Remarkably, his joyful embrace spurred airline personnel to commit to making the changes needed to welcome Jamie and the other supportive-needs passengers on future flights with fewer incidents. And there would be many more to come. Airlines needed to accommodate this unexpected new niche market of passengers with varied and serious disabilities, most of whom were previously unable or reluctant to travel to France without a Lourdes Hospitality. Love transformed Jamie—and, contagiously, the airline personnel he encountered. The graces flowed far beyond the Grotto spring in a ripple effect.

Some struggles continued for some flights, but love overcame every obstacle, each and every time. It is said that where there is love, there is suffering. For this arduous travel, it became clear that where there was suffering, there needed to be love. Moved by Jamie's conversion, a sponsor offered to fund an annual pilgrimage to Lourdes for Jamie. Like an almost-empty tank being filled with gas, Jamie returned to Lourdes the next year to be filled with the grace of the Grotto to live another year in his room in the group home he had moved into.

On each return pilgrimage, Jamie would learn more to be able to teach more. During the initial encounter between Bernadette and Our Lady in the Grotto, the first action of the two young girls was to pray, making the Sign of the Cross. Bernadette knew when the Lady lifted the crucifix of her rosary beads to her forehead that she was thinking of the God Who created them. Bernadette said later in her short life, *"If we make this one prayer well, we can go to Heaven."*

Like a holy shield, we cover ourselves with the Father, Who created us; the Son, Who died to save us; and the Holy Spirit, Who breathes life into our faith. This motion of our arm from our mind to the center of our being, and then from our left shoulder across our heart to our right shoulder, is a physical act of faith. This simple prayer covers us with the depth and breadth of the Holy Cross. Many of us are in the good habit of making the Sign of the Cross, but sometimes it slips into a habitual gesture, such as before and after we pray grace or when we join in a formal prayer or bless ourselves with holy water. Sometimes, we are not mindful of the Trinity or of authentic prayer. Rather, we distractedly lapse into a quick and thoughtless circular motion, more like the Heavenly eternity we desire than the Cross that makes our eternal entrance possible.

The authentic prayer of the Sign of the Cross profoundly struck Jamie with the example of Bernadette following the Immaculate Conception. In the Accueil Marie Saint-Frai, Jamie confided to his pilgrimage leader that he wished he could use his arm, if only once. He wanted to make the Sign of the Cross like Bernadette, like the Mother of God. When the group prayed, he imagined he would make the motions with them. Jamie could have wished to move a limb for so many other reasons that most of us take for granted in our mobile daily activities. Jamie could not scratch an itch, brush his teeth, open a door, wipe away a tear, or sign his name. Yet, if he could move his arm—only once—it would be to make and pray the Sign of the Cross.

The pilgrimage leader listened intently and tearfully. How many times had she made a poor Sign of the Cross with her capable arms before knowing about Bernadette and hearing Jamie? How did it go unnoticed that Jamie was motionless while the rest of the pilgrimage group made the movements along with this prayer? Making the Sign of the Cross over Jamie was to become a blessing and catechesis for many. Every time the pilgrimage family prayed together, the pilgrimage leader would discreetly seek out Jamie to physically make the Sign of the Cross over him.

It was said that Bernadette prayed the Sign of the Cross with all her heart. Jamie prayed the same way, sometimes with someone making the physical gestures for him. Jamie asked the volunteers at meals to make the Sign of the Cross over him before and after grace. They would make the Sign of the Cross over him and then over themselves in the same way they would put a forkful of food in his mouth at the table and then lift their own fork to take a bite from their own plate. This crucial gesture gave the magnitude of this simple yet significant prayer a deeper meaning for everyone. A profound thankfulness for the ability to pray this prayer freely and with the physical gestures of moving one arm expanded to an awareness of oppressed people who are fearful to be found out as Christians or those who risk their very lives by making the Sign of the Cross. Soon after, everyone was taking their renewed love for this prayer back home with them. One pilgrimage leader was inspired by this to invite parishes learning about Lourdes to offer a prayerful and reverent Sign of the Cross for someone who could not. Jamie had affirmed his first and primary purpose as a Lourdes Volunteers teacher and catechist, in a call to authentic prayer.

Unable to stand, walk, dress, bathe, or reach over to touch someone, Jamie could have remained steeped in resentment. Yet, in his stillness, he chose instead to follow Bernadette to the Grotto to learn more. Dying to self was the next lesson to be learned. Bernadette said, "If the Good God allows it, there must be something good in it for me." Jamie noticed that Bernadette called Him "the Good God" even when life was not always good for her. Dying to what Jamie wanted or wished to do often accumulated in a nerve-wracking and never-ending pile of daily frustrations. His situation did not change. Again, he was transformed by offering to God with joyful surrender each small thing he could not do. The penance of what he was unable to do became his humble, prayerful offering. When he was asked to teach teenage volunteers, an age notorious for selfishness, Jamie invited them to an experiment while serving in Lourdes. Simply be present—*smiling*. Be the physical feet of Christ because your feet can move. He suggested they wheel a pilgrim around town to shop for rosary beads without complaint, when they would rather go out with friends for a luscious French ice cream, and then come back to report.

The youth were amazed and returned to tell Jamie how they had received more than they had given. They were happier doing things for others than if they had done what they originally wanted to do for themselves. They were dying to themselves and their preferences. This allowed the desire of someone else to live through their sacrifices. The more you do this, the better you will be at it, Jamie told them. When you slip up or fail—and you probably will—offer the next opportunity for what someone else wants that you can help them to do, instead of what you want. Jamie quickly became the favored catechist for Dying-to-Self Day during the pilgrimage week.

Jamie continues to make the annual journey after more than a dozen years of pilgrimage. He considers his pilgrimages to be personal miracles of Lourdes for him. Once bored and bitter, Jamie became prayerful and joyful, although life isn't always easy for him. When he is alone or back in the group home, he makes the Sign of the Cross with all his heart, imagining the gestures over him. When he is on pilgrimage, a new group of sloppy Sign-of-the-Cross makers always arrives to learn unexpectedly from Jamie how to make the prayer of the Sign of the Cross well, slowly, and with reverence—*because they can*. The able-bodied pilgrims ask to wheel Jamie to the Grotto. They start out the week thinking they are taking him. By the end of the pilgrimage, they know that Jamie took them to the Grotto.

> *The life I now live in the body, I live by faith in the Son of God, who loved me and gave himself for me.* (Gal. 2:20, NIV)

Joyous Catechist

Jamie continues to live in a group home in Minneapolis. In 2022, he was featured on CBS's *60 Minutes* in a segment filmed in Lourdes. He shared his insight into the value of a pilgrimage journey and how faith has made a difference in his life. Jamie goes to Lourdes in the fall to help with Young Adult Catechesis and to refill himself with graces from the Grotto for another year.

Chapter 8

The Last Obstacle to Total Love

Wishful Andrea

Andrea was born into a loving Italian American New Jersey family who live so close to the Pennsylvania border that they jokingly claim they are from East-East Philadelphia. Andrea was more than pretty; she was noticeably beautiful. She was so attractive that she could have pursued a career on the runway or on television. As smart as she was beautiful, Andrea chose science for her education and her profession. She was kind, intelligent, and creative, she was genuinely sweet and wholesome. Any young woman would want to be Andrea—until her leukemia diagnosis.

Cancer is too often a daunting, ugly, protracted battle. Chemotherapy, failed bone-marrow transplants, and platelet infusions robbed Andrea of the years after college when she should have been sunning carefree on the Jersey Shore with her girlfriends. But instead of leisurely wasting time, Andrea was wasting away. In between her marrow transplants, a close school friend of hers was ordained a Catholic priest. Fr. Chris strongly urged (that's Italian for insisted) that Andrea and her parents make a pilgrimage to Lourdes, France. He told them that the world-famous Catholic shrine is the most renowned holy place for healing and miracles—and Andrea needed both.

As faithful Catholics, Andrea's parents committed to trying to take their dying daughter to Lourdes. It would not be simple or easy. Medically, there were serious risks for Andrea to travel. Her immune system was compromised by ongoing extensive treatments. Rare platelets would need to be arranged with the small local Lourdes hospital, tucked away by the Pyrénées Mountains in the southwest of France. Courageous physicians and nurses signed on as volunteers, paid their own expenses, and dedicated their sacrificed vacation time to providing necessary delicate supportive care for Andrea to be able to join the pilgrimage. Her Jewish doctor supported Andrea and her parents, as if prescribing a spiritual medicine for her suffering soul as he prescribed extensive treatments for her depleted body.

Andrea scientifically understood exposure risk, especially in confined spaces with crowds. Millions of pilgrims visited Lourdes each year. Although it would be a personal journey for Andrea, it would not be a private pilgrimage. She would be exposed to numerous people with incalculable germs. Any travel could shorten her life by days or weeks. She no longer had months left to forfeit in a measured risk. Andrea was a scientist. She understood. But she was not average or above average. She was extraordinary. A young woman of faith, she was wise beyond her age. According to her prognosis, time was precious. Andrea knew it. She decided to go to Lourdes.

Fr. Chris joined Andrea and her parents on the trip. At the gateway airport, they met the medical team who had carefully planned Andrea's supportive care throughout her international travel and her stay abroad. Like insurance, hoped never to be needed but smart to have, a plan was painstakingly prepared for death en route and in France. That was how critically ill Andrea was in the weeks and days prior to her anticipated departure. Lourdes Volunteers, Andrea, and her family were prepared, or as prepared as can be imagined in such a heavy-hearted situation.

Andrea was weak. Adamantly, she refused a wheelchair at JFK Airport in New York. Passengers using wheelchairs preloaded the plane for Paris. Andrea distanced herself from the visibly "sick and disabled" group, insisting on standing in line with the seemingly healthy, able-bodied passengers waiting to enter the aircraft. At first glance, this might have made sense. Passengers using wheelchairs could be sick with germs that Andrea should avoid. It was a long wait. Even the supposedly fit passengers were tired by the time the plane was fully loaded for departure.

Cancer and aggressive treatments tap into a different world of fatigue and exhaustion. It is as if the vibrant life-giving source within a soul has been sucked out, leaving behind only a wisp of the former self—like a flimsy, wobbly copy of what was once a vigorous life. Halfway down the ramp, the team halted. Andrea had become too weak to take another step without some rest. Promptly, she was perched atop a carry-on suitcase for a makeshift respite and leaned against the jet bridge enclosure. She did not protest or complain. She smiled sweetly. After a brief regrouping of her depleted strength, Andrea summoned herself and steeled her body, somehow drawing from a nearly empty reserve to will herself to her seat. Although she was fragile, she was radiant, as if exuding a deep inner grace.

Travel abroad sapped the last whisper of her remaining strength. Andrea required platelet infusions shortly after arriving in France. Totally depleted, she could no longer decline the wheelchair needed to transport her. The Lourdes Volunteers Medical Team doctor and nurse along with a Sanctuary priest accompanied the family to the small yet sophisticated local hospital. They were attentive to every preplanned detail. The sensitive transfusion went well.

Afterward, lacking the energy to put one foot in front of the other, Andrea had no choice but to be wheeled to the dining room and to all the scheduled pilgrimage events. After her French hospital adventure, the only possible way out of her hospital bed in the Accueil Notre-Dame was to be seated in a wheelchair.

Most people are hesitant to use a wheelchair, for fear it will become a permanent situation instead of a temporary solution. It was a different fear for Andrea, who was hiding an embarrassing secret. Sweet Andrea *skeeved* people in wheelchairs. *Skeeve* or to *skeeve out* (sometimes pronounced *schkeeve* or *schkeeved out*) is an American-Italian Jersey or New York slang expression of repulsion, a negative term describing an instant reaction of discomfort to a person, place, or thing.

Andrea never openly expressed her fear of people with disabilities or in wheelchairs. She was sincerely polite to everyone she encountered—wheeling or walking. People in wheelchairs just made her extremely uneasy. She didn't know why or when this came about. Maybe it was from nursing-home visits as a child or possibly from a deep intuition that she would be counted among them someday. Why or when no longer mattered. Her discomfort always seemed to be with her. She wished it were not so. It was an instinctual response she could not stop, avoid, or control. Immediately beneath her disdain, Andrea had genuine tender compassion, but she did not know how to bypass or override her instantaneous skeeving reaction.

St. Bernadette used to say that our first reaction belongs to us in our humanness and that our second reaction, in our soul, belongs to God. As we grow closer to God, the time between our human and holy reactions is reduced, and with holiness, it can disappear. Just arriving in Lourdes, Andrea had not yet learned this from Bernadette.

Somehow, she had always managed to conceal her secret skeeve throughout her entire life. Nobody knew. She was too embarrassed to admit it and too ashamed to discuss it with anyone. She had been able to discreetly avoid people in wheelchairs—until Lourdes. In Lourdes, that would prove impossible.

In Lourdes, the sick and the disabled are the Very Important Persons, the VIPs, honored everywhere—*and they are everywhere*! There is a special place of privilege for the sick and the disabled at every event and in every place in the Sanctuary and in the town. Inevitably, Andrea would be wheeled and seated next to, between, or near someone else in a wheelchair at every place in Lourdes. She could no longer avoid her secret fear.

Andrea found herself eye to eye with others in their wheelchairs. Being at eye level changed everything. Intimate seated conversations revealed a profound understanding of interior connectivity and innate wisdom. These exchanges were simple, wholly humble, and holy inspired. The wheels, and possibly Andrea's dependence on them, smoothly stripped away the façades that had protected her. Patience, humor, and gratitude were noticeably present among those in wheelchairs—and notably less amid the fast-paced walkers distracted by their constant movements of busyness. Seated stillness afforded Andrea a heightened sensitivity of thoughtfulness that led to a deep, insightful grace—like an infused spiritual wisdom. Andrea fell in love with her newfound wheeling family, especially her new Lourdes "brother," Dave. Everyone bonded and blended together in an extended pilgrimage forever family.

Individually and collectively, Andrea was fully embraced without hesitation, and she returned the love completely. It was "love without measure," as Bernadette had said. Andrea was learning—not out of sentimentality or pity but out of true love—to see Jesus Christ seated in the wheelchairs across from her, next to her, in front of her, and behind her. It was a transcending love—holy, eternal, and total. Andrea was "de-skeeved" through an unexpected life-changing grace that she never knew she needed. This was not because she was in a wheelchair herself but because she had overcome her "last obstacle to total love" through looking into the eyes of Jesus Christ.

Although Andrea was of Italian descent, she did not know the story of a radical man from Italy who changed the world: St. Francis of Assisi. In the thirteenth century, as a young man returning home broken after battle, Francis experienced an extraordinary conversion. At the onset of his conversion, Francis was growing in love, except when it came to lepers (now respectfully called Hansen's disease patients). Like everyone in his time, he feared the contagious disease. One day, Francis saw a leper on the road, alone and in need. As was customary, he quickly turned away. Suddenly, infused with a grace, he was moved with deep compassion; he stopped and dismounted his horse. Francis fully embraced the suffering leper with love. As he walked back to his horse, he turned around and found that the leper had mysteriously disappeared. Francis understood that he had embraced Jesus Christ. His heart was expanded, magnified in love, through and in Christ. Francis had overcome his "last obstacle to total love!"

Soon after his life-altering embrace of the leper, Francis "left the world" in a radical abandonment of the luxury and comfort that his family afforded him. He decided to live *in* the world but not be *of* the world. He chose to live among lepers, outcasts, and the sick to care for them selflessly. He lived in simplicity, embracing poverty amid a materialistically obsessed society. Francis detached himself from the secular world. Others soon joined him. His followers became the first Franciscans. Caring for the sick and those on the margins of life, Franciscans continue today to love the poor and the sick in the spirit of their "Seraphic Father," Francis.

Andrea had overcome her last and secret obstacle to total love. She loved her most feared untouchables, wheelchair to wheelchair. She explained that her heart had exploded, blown wide open to magnify her capacity for love by loving everyone she met in their wheelchairs, while seated in hers. When she stood up on stronger days, her expanded and magnified love extended to everyone she encountered, standing or seated. Like St. Francis, Andrea understood that she had overcome her final fear to love without boundaries. She was transformed. The story of St. Francis resonated within Andrea. Although she had never heard it before, she now had a name and explanation for her holy experience. She wanted to tell everyone about the value of a pilgrimage to Lourdes. It was the eternal healing she needed most, more than a physical cure.

After returning home, Andrea wrote a tender letter to her family and friends trying to explain the life-changing experience and great deepening of her faith she had received on her pilgrimage. She was grateful. She knew that it was not financially possible for everyone in need of healing or graces to go to Lourdes. Some families could never afford the gift of international travel that her family was blessed to afford her.

A talented amateur photographer, Andrea took her pilgrimage pictures and created artistic Lourdes note-card and prayer-card sets. Painstakingly, she printed the images, hand-cut delicate scalloped edges, and then folded and wrapped them in silk ribbon. She selflessly gave of her limited hours to design and make these cards. Like Andrea, the cards were beautiful. They were the kind of note cards she wanted to buy in Lourdes but was not able to find in the many shops surrounding the Sanctuary. She hoped that others who might want them would give a small donation for a set of her cards to help send someone to Lourdes. It was a small yet practical beginning to spur a sponsorship fund when a formalized one did not yet exist with the recently founded Lourdes Volunteers. It was about to become her gracious legacy.

Andrea died six weeks after returning from France. Her parents shared her passionate letter at her calling hours. In response to her letter, Our Lady of Lourdes Hospitality North American Volunteers received twenty-six thousand dollars in donations in honor of Andrea. The donations arrived in checks, small and large, most often with compassionate notes. There were no specific instructions received other than a few marked "Andrea's Fund," which did not yet exist but was to be born out of love for her and her wish. The fledgling apostolate had never received such a large sum of money. Andrea's Wish needed to be officially established by Lourdes Volunteers. As the Association was already a nonprofit charity, attorneys and accountants legally accomplished what was required to formally establish the designated fund within the organization. Whatever was needed to be known to administer the fund was either written in her letter or lived in her pilgrimage experience. Anyone who needed to go to Lourdes should be able to make a pilgrimage—*exactly Andrea's wish!*

All the funds were used in the first year, in time for the 2008 Lourdes 150th Jubilee, when the record number of pilgrims swelled to almost ten million! The next year, sixty-three thousand dollars was received and disbursed—more than twice the funds of the inaugural year. Doubling again the following year, Andrea's Wish went on to sponsor more than a million dollars for pilgrims in need and their family members in its first decade. There is never a surplus, only "our daily bread" needed at the moment. Andrea's Wish might seem beyond dreams or logic, but it continues through the generosity of many, mostly in small gifts, accumulating to sponsor one pilgrim at a time. Continuing to provide sponsorship to "anyone who needs to go to Lourdes" is a testament to Andrea's total love and her holy wish.

Most High, glorious God, enlighten the darkness of my heart and give me true faith, certain hope, and perfect charity, sense and knowledge. (Prayer of St. Francis of Assisi)

Wishing Total Love

Lourdes Volunteers Andrea's Wish continues to sponsor pilgrims to holy Lourdes. Andrea's parents support Lourdes Volunteers and remain active within the apostolate. In 2020, they traveled as valuable members of a Plenary Indulgence team representing multiple aspects of Lourdes Volunteers to the Vatican in Rome.

Chapter 9

A Liquid Grace Fills the Hole

Scottish Sheena

Sheena is a sweet, soft-spoken Scottish woman and the mother of seven grown children. Although she met and married a United States Marine when she was nineteen, has lived in Georgia and Virginia, and recently retired as an American citizen with her husband in Pennsylvania, her lovely Scottish accent remains delightfully unmistakable whenever she speaks. Sheena is quiet and reserved, never wanting to draw attention to herself. She would choose a seat in what was known in the American Bible Belt of the old Deep South as the "amen corner." This was the place furthest back, where someone could be intentionally unnoticed in prayer. That's why it was surprising when Sheena came forward as the first woman to officially sign up with Lourdes Volunteers to serve in France. A humble modern-day Bernadette joined the fledgling hospitality with a small group from her parish in May 2003 to serve at Lourdes. The group bonded quickly as a family in the spirit of their new hospitality. They were helpful and encouraging to each other throughout the week and would continue to be so for years, remaining bonded together as Lourdes family-friends.

The presence of English speakers was needed at the Sanctuary in Lourdes. More than half of those who made the pilgrimage to France spoke English as a first or second language. Yet fewer than ten percent of the volunteers were fluent English speakers. Language and interpretation had sometimes proven to be a challenge at the international shrine. In the Sanctuary's priorities, the ability to speak English to communicate with pilgrims began to push against the long-standing requirement to speak French to communicate with fellow volunteers. It was also exceptional for volunteers to arrive in Lourdes for the first time in service. This made for a more complex week for the new American hospitality than for Europeans coming to dedicate service after years of experience with annual diocesan pilgrimages or having grown up with family holidays or school trips to Lourdes. Without this past-pilgrimage foundation of knowledge to build upon, a more complete introduction to the Sanctuary and the different services was needed for the new American hospitality. Additionally, it was unusual to have entire groups of volunteers. Individuals or a few friends together would typically come in service but not groups of sixteen to forty first-timers. The beginning years of these introductory weeks of service were difficult, both for those trying to manage the influx of volunteer groups and for the groups of typically monolingual, non-French speakers.

Sheena was registered to serve in the Piscines (the Baths). *Piscinière* (female bath attendants) perform a demanding service of assisting women from around the world seeking the experience of being immersed in Lourdes Water from the Grotto. Some of the sick who arrive are profoundly debilitated and enter on stretchers or in wheelchairs, while others are walking wounded. Healthy tourists with no faith at all or of different religions also come, curious, or with deep longing for the unknown, generally seeking or sometimes in search of something specific. Lourdes and the spring of water from the Grotto are world-renowned for miraculous cures and conversions. When non-Catholics are asked why they visit the Catholic shrine, they often reply that they came for a cure or the peace to accept their situation—"because it works!" Sometimes, it takes a while for the "liquid grace" to sink in, but the grace of Lourdes eventually penetrates deep within to quench the parched recesses of even the weariest or driest of souls.

For an experience as physically intimate and deeply spiritual as the Baths, the Mother of God certainly chose the most suitable country. The dignity of the experience is ensured by the genteel decorum of French culture, with gracious French ladies who are sensitive to the delicate discretion needed to assist women in an intimately personal experience. The prayerful ritual is as gracious as the Mother of God. Modesty is protected for each person. Undressing, bathing, and dressing are tenderly accomplished by volunteers in the spirit of humble St. Bernadette. Sheena was grateful to be registered in the St. Jean Baptiste (St. John the Baptist) Piscine Service. She was pleased to help women from around the world get into their spiritually physical baths, and as a European American, she proved to be naturally well suited to this meaningful service.

There is continuous bending by piscinière volunteers on both the left and right sides of the tub within the Baths. In their first service week, piscinière trade between tub sides and alternate in assisting the women to dress and undress. Learning the techniques, most often by watching the example of others or being instructed in a foreign language, makes for a challenging transmission of a century and a half of expertise to first-timers. Trying to remember so many nuances of the protocol to assist a woman in her once-in-a-lifetime holy Lourdes experience can be daunting at best and easily overwhelming.

The Piscines are frequently crowded with women who must often wait for hours to enter. Inside, they are careful not to rush anyone, but the pace can still seem rather quick to a trainee. Lourdes Volunteers came to refer to the fifth day of service as "Crying Thursday," because it often proved to be the emotional breaking point for many new volunteers. For some, it is their first time witnessing physical suffering or intense pain up close or their first personal encounter with raw mortality, holding a dying woman or child before, during, or after her bath. Hearts and emotions can easily overflow, and they often do.

Sheena exited the Piscines in tears following her first Thursday afternoon service. Having been given a bath herself, she asked to meet the pilgrimage leader privately for a *cuppa* tea.

Occasionally, Piscine volunteers surface from service soaked in Lourdes Water, as if having literally immersed themselves in the figurative grace of the service. It remains a mystery how piscinière can plunge their hands, wrists, and arms into naturally chilled mountain spring water countless times throughout each shift of service without noticing the cold. It is humorously considered a "miracle" of service! Although repeatedly submerging their arms in the frigid-feeling water for hours, somehow the volunteers are always surprised at just how cold the water is when they bathe in it themselves as pilgrims.

Tearfully, Sheena shared her observation of this phenomenon of the Lourdes Water, but there was much more on her heart. She came as a volunteer and did not think of herself as a pilgrim, yet everyone who goes to Lourdes—knowingly or unknowingly—truly is on a personal holy journey. There are many graces of healing that come through Lourdes, often unexpectedly delighting volunteers. Maybe God knows it is only as a volunteer that these generous souls will go to the Grotto to receive graces for themselves.

Sheena poured out her story over a pot of tea. She was born and raised on the Scottish coast, to the far north of Edinburgh. Religion was not a part of her schooling or her family upbringing. Her parents were hardworking hotel restaurant managers. As with any small business, every family member was busy with his own duties. An oil boom in the North Sea brought an influx of tradesmen with comfortable paychecks from Aberdeen to farther up the northeast coast of the United Kingdom. This brought Sheena and her family much-needed new business. A twenty-two-year-old frequent patron occasionally offered to help out behind the bar, affording him more time with a much younger Sheena than proved prudent. With her parents preoccupied with tending to a prospering business, the inappropriate friendship went unnoticed until Sheena unexpectedly found herself pregnant at fifteen. The guy took off. It was soon discovered that he had abandoned another girl in the next town over in the same circumstance.

The 1967 Abortion Act legalized the termination of a pregnancy up to twenty-eight weeks in Scotland. Back then, early-stage abortion was touted as the removal of unwanted clumps of undeveloped tissue and cells. Abortion soon became a controversy between medical scientists and religious leaders. It was not fully exposed or understood by the general public or by the average person in the pews or on a medical examination table. For Sheena's family, without any faith or religious affiliation, abortion was not a problem; it was the solution.

As a minor, Sheena was legally subject to parental decisions. Her mother made a wrongful decision for her that was ignorantly intended to be in her best interest. An appointment was scheduled for an abortion. Although she lacked any spiritual influence or the technology of a sonogram, Sheena somehow felt inexplicably protective. Her baby was unexpected—*but it was her baby*. Unfortunately, she had no say in whether to keep or deliver the baby. Sheena was never defiant and rarely gave any trouble to her parents, teachers, or anyone else, for that matter. But in her feelings about her unplanned pregnancy, she remained defiantly and defensively strong against her parents.

Four days after her sixteenth birthday, at twelve weeks pregnant, Sheena was literally dragged from her house to the car, kicking and screaming. The struggle had become physical when Sheena realized she was being taken to the hospital for an abortion. Her mother was insistent and pulled Sheena out of the house by her hair. A fistful of Sheena's soft curls fell onto the hard pavement. Although she physically resisted, her mother's controlling forcefulness won out. Sheena was pushed into the car and then into the hospital the same way.

Sheena was chastised by the maternity-ward staff for having been with an older guy. Somehow, the adult man received no such criticism for being with someone of such a young age or for abandoning her and the baby. Sheena was hastily discharged and sent to her grandmother for one week, hidden away in shame. She felt sickly with a fever of 103 degrees, which thankfully disappeared as quickly as it came. From that dreaded day in the hospital, nothing filled the unspoken hole forcibly carved out of Sheena on that nineteenth of May in what was to have been her sweet-sixteenth year.

Three years later, in her first year of marriage, Sheena miscarried twice and secretly blamed herself. She knew nothing of the truth of God and thought a punitive omnipotent was surely punishing her for what had happened. Her first three pregnancies left Sheena childless. Years later, her last pregnancy would also end in a miscarriage at twelve weeks. The guilt of four lost lives, especially that of the first baby, aborted, was overwhelming and left Sheena deeply saddened. Her math simply did not add up. Her first baby was cruelly taken from her, and she mistakenly thought the next two were sacrificed as a punishment. Between the heavy bookends of lost lives, seven healthy babies were born, proving to Sheena that she was meant to be a mother and blessing her with the joys of motherhood.

Before her fifth baby was born, Sheena's mother-in-law made a deathbed wish for her son to return to his childhood Catholic Faith. To honor her husband and his mother, Sheena sought out a Catholic priest for counsel. Unexpectedly, she found what she had been unknowingly missing and seeking her entire life—faith and a loving, merciful God! Sheena and her five children entered the Catholic Church together. She understood that all the sins of her life, right up to the moment of her Baptism, were wiped away. Yet the kindly, helpful priest could not fill the hole left by her first baby forcibly taken from her. Being a good mother did not fill the hole created by her babies who were not with her. A busy life did not fill the hole either. Absolutely nothing filled the hole—*nothing.*

The unfillable void never decreased and continued for almost thirty years, until Sheena was immersed in the spring water at Lourdes. She had not come seeking anything for herself. She simply came to help others. At Lourdes, "miracles" often unfold and transpire in this way. Over the outpouring of tea and tears, her deeply hidden secret, steeped in shame, seeped out into the open. Sheena asked in awe, "How was it possible to fill this hole today? How did this happen? Why here? Why now?" *"A liquid grace filled the hole,"* she said in awe, answering her own question. In selflessly giving of herself, Sheena received more than she gave.

Sheena understood that her mother fully but wrongfully believed she was helping her. Having been raised in shame as an out-of-wedlock child herself, her mother did not want her daughter or grandchild to endure the same difficult upbringing that culminated in her misguided decision.

Going on to complete her schooling as a practical nurse, Sheena graduated, married, and had a wonderful family. They lived and traveled around the world as her husband advanced his impressive career, taking them to live in exciting places. Life was good—except for the hole. A gaping hole had remained in Sheena for almost three decades. Through Lourdes, she was healed of guilt, grief, and loss. She was finally whole once again.

Post-abortive women often suffer in silence with a painful and sometimes debilitating sense of loss long after a difficult decision, often made hurriedly and secretly. Many wrongly believe they are unwelcome or excommunicated by the Catholic Church, without recourse, banned forever or unworthy ever to receive Holy Communion. This is untrue. Women and men cannot physically undo what has been done, but they can spiritually right the wrong through the grace of the Sacrament of Reconciliation.

Sheena found her healing unexpectedly in the Baths at Lourdes. She says she measures her life as "before Lourdes" and "after Lourdes." Everything was different for her when her devastating grief was washed away in the Baths; the grievous void was soothed with a healing balm of grace. Her pastor sent a letter to Lourdes Volunteers after Sheena returned home. He beautifully wrote, "A light dimmed by suffering went to Lourdes in generous service, and a brilliant light returned to illuminate our parish and everyone she encountered." He was a humble priest of a modest parish. In thanksgiving, he sent a personal, significant donation to ensure that another illuminating miracle at Lourdes could be available to someone else in need.

Through another grace, Sheena held no resentment toward her mother. She and her mother had a beautiful, loving relationship. The long-ago wound was healed. Sheena lovingly cared for her mother, never speaking a harsh word of her or their past. Mother and daughter talked every day and visited together as much as possible. Neither living across the Atlantic from each other nor a painful past decision kept them apart. Sheena was able to be in Scotland with her mother as she was dying in her advanced years.

There are many women who come into the Piscines with the same hidden wound as Sheena's. They whisper their secret, weeping on their way into the water. They cry tears of joy on their way out, in awe of the mercy and goodness of God.

Interior healing cannot be examined to be pronounced an unexplained cure in the Medical Bureau at Lourdes. Forgiveness or interior peace cannot be physically examined or scrutinized, quantified or X-rayed, to be scientifically proven. Thus, these immeasurable interior healings cannot be proclaimed as official miracles. Yet miracles of the soul, miracles of the "heart," and miracles of intrinsic or interior healing are considered by many—including unofficially by physicians and bishops—to be some of the truly sweetest miracles of Lourdes. These profound cures and healings through the grace of Lourdes are not officially recognized in this world but are certainly known to many here and to many more in the other world.

> *I would now like to say a special word to women who have had an abortion. The Church is aware of the many factors which may have influenced your decision, and she does not doubt that in many cases it was a painful and even shattering decision. The wound in your heart may not yet have healed.... But do not give in to discouragement and do not lose hope.* (St. John Paul II)

Secondary School Sheena

Sheena returned to serve at Lourdes, bringing and sending four of her seven children in service. Until her mother died, Sheena spoke to her daily by phone and returned to visit her in Scotland as often as possible. Sheena and her husband are busy in retirement with their grandchildren.

Chapter 10

'Til Death Do Us Part

Dolores and Alejandro

Dolores was ninety-eight years and eight months old when she boarded the plane to France. Several things were notable upon meeting Dolores: her chic sensibility, evident in her tailored Chanel-style jacket; her silky smooth skin; her captivating smile and tasteful lipstick; her well-chosen jewelry; and the pure, sweet love of her gentle husband, devotedly attentive to her. It was delightfully charming and obvious that Alejandro was still totally smitten with Dolores after all their decades of married life. Although they had lived in Miami for years, Dolores didn't speak English, leaving her doting husband to translate and do all the talking for her.

Alejandro had been a merchant marine, traveling the world for his career. Both he and his wife had emigrated from Ecuador to the United States. They settled in southern Florida as their favored port to spend their retirement and the rest of their lives together. As faithful Catholics, they centered their lives on prayer, saintly devotionals, and the sacraments. Living in South Florida for the climate, the culture, and the language was also a blessing to them in their senior years together. The handsome couple could never have children after a tragic stillbirth. That devastating loss seemed to bring them closer together, more solely devoted to each other. Their favorite niece lived nearby. She protectively checked in on her beloved aunt and uncle in their elderly years.

Slowly after her ninety-eighth birthday, nearing a century of life, Dolores descended into a silent remote place inside herself, far away from her usual spontaneous self. She somehow lost her zest—and her zeal for everyday life along with it. Alejandro was also in his nineties but was a few years younger than his wife. He decided that a holy pilgrimage to Lourdes was the best remedy for his cherished sacramental life partner. Their beloved niece helped them to arrange their pilgrimage with Lourdes Volunteers, including a plan for her to stop by the Marian Sanctuary herself for a brief visit while she would also be nearby in Europe.

Dolores and Alejandro took surprisingly few medications for their ages and had fewer care needs than many others on the pilgrimage, even those much younger than the near-century-old spouses. The couple planned to care for each other as they always had daily at home and whenever they traveled. They lived independently in Florida and planned to do the same while in France. They said they would need no assistance, or only limited assistance, from the Lourdes Volunteers Medical Supportive Care Team.

Over the ocean, Alejandro was concerned when Dolores refused to eat or drink a thing. He worriedly hovered over her as she abruptly pushed away her airline food tray. She wouldn't take even a sip of water—nothing. She was adamant that she didn't want anything. On the way to the restroom, accompanied by Alejandro, Dolores fell to the floor of the aircraft just over an hour before landing in Paris. She went down with a loud thud.

The Lourdes Volunteers Medical Team was at her side in moments. The well-trained and competent Air France flight attendants were alert, attentive, and kind. Dolores was completely unconscious. With cold cloths placed on her head and wrists by the pilgrimage nurse, she quickly awoke, feeling groggy. The pilgrimage physician gave her water to sip through a straw. Dolores wasn't pleased to be the center of a fuss and was obviously less than thrilled to be instructed to drink fluids before trying to stand up, but she reluctantly complied.

After she recovered, the flight captain decided that Dolores needed to deplane in Paris with an ambulance transport. He prudently required that she be examined by an airline physician before being allowed to board the smaller plane to the South of France or an international return flight home. Alejandro, the pilgrimage physician, and one of the pilgrimage leaders deplaned with Dolores. The rest of the pilgrimage group traveled on to the connecting flight terminal to wait for their next plane, scheduled to depart in a few hours to Pau, near Lourdes.

An estimated ninety-two million travelers arrive and depart via the Paris Charles de Gaulle (CDG) Airport in an average year. Unknown to almost everyone bustling about in the busy airport above, there is a small but efficient urgent-care facility discreetly built underneath one of the major terminals. Dolores was swiftly moved on a stretcher from the back of the plane via airport ambulance to a hospital bed in the secluded airport emergency room. A young French doctor entered the examining room wearing a United States Navy lanyard with his official CDG Airport badge securely attached. He was surprised to meet Americans and a fellow sea-loving merchant marine. He explained that an American naval physician had gifted him the lanyard—a Lourdes Volunteers Medical Team doctor he met in Lourdes during the May International Military Pilgrimage.

What a small world and what a grace of Lourdes, they all agreed, smiling—it was surely one of those infamous Lourdes-incidences!

The young doctor conveniently spoke Spanish, making direct communication with Dolores and Alejandro comfortable and easier. Alejandro revealed that Dolores had briefly been hospitalized a few weeks before this international departure. He added that she had lost her appetite over the past few months. Dolores had not eaten before departure and nothing during travel. She wasn't drinking much of anything either. After having something to eat and drink, Dolores went through several medical tests. A normal electrocardiogram (EKG) report, blood pressure, and blood-sugar results were efficiently and swiftly presented to the medical team for evaluation.

The doctor was impressed with both of his Lourdes Volunteers Medical Team encounters—respectful of the team's care of the severely wounded veterans he had seen on their May pilgrimages and respectful of the attentive physician before him, clearly dedicated to the elderly couple. The French airport physician felt confident that Dolores was fit to travel, accompanied by the competent American doctor and the seasoned leader, familiar with travel to Lourdes. He kindly cautioned Dolores to drink more fluids. Amazingly, the newly refreshed pilgrim and her escort team were transferred by speedy ambulance to their scheduled connecting flight just in time to board the plane with their original travel group.

As the day continued, the medical team was increasingly concerned. Dolores was again refusing all food and fluids since leaving Paris. Several hours after her arrival in Lourdes, later into the night, Dolores was confused to find herself in a hospital bed in the Accueil, in France. She feared she would be hospitalized in Europe and separated from Alejandro. She was becoming uncharacteristically belligerent, which is typical of someone suffering the onset of dehydration. One of the Spanish-speaking pilgrimage priests was called to administer the Anointing of the Sick because of her illness and her age, but she rudely dismissed him from her room. Alejandro insisted this was not her usual temperament, and he was distressed by her escalating refusals, explaining that this was only recent behavior and not at all like his beautiful wife of so many years.

She became upset with her husband and blamed him for her situation. For every harsh complaint or accusation she had about him, he had a lovely compliment or comment for her. Alejandro described Dolores as a talented seamstress with fashion-designer taste. She was prayerful, cultured, gracious, kind, and smart. He was blessed to be her husband. The proof of his devotion and of the truth of all that he said was evident in her manicured nails, her elegant clothing, her tasteful jewelry, and his loving, attentive care for her well-being. Dolores and Alejandro's niece called to ask if her aunt and uncle had safely arrived. She said her uncle was a holy and prayerful man who took wonderful care of his equally kind and faithful wife. She said her uncle was worried about her aunt and hoped the pilgrimage to the healing shrine of Lourdes would restore her appetite and good nature, as well as dispel her recent melancholy.

Alejandro requested that Dolores receive a blessing; he was increasingly worried about his beloved. A second Spanish-speaking priest was called in to offer an anointing. Dolores threw him out—at the door—faster than he could enter her room. Dolores had all the classic symptoms of dehydration. The medical team called her primary-care family practitioner in Florida and spoke to Alejandro. He confirmed that dehydration was the cause of her recent hospitalization but insisted that Dolores wasn't herself and needed a blessing as much as she needed fluids and food.

A third priest, although not a fluent Spanish speaker, came to bless Dolores. He was a tall, dignified, elegant man blessed with an operatic tenor voice. Father graciously gestured a large Sign of the Cross in the air, singing the prayer as he entered the room. Gently taking Dolores's arm and drawing it toward him to kiss her hand in a formal and enchanting gentlemanly greeting, Father softly traced the Sign of the Cross on her delicate hand and then again on her forehead, singing and signing with each blessing. Everything changed in a mystical moment. Through Alejandro interpreting, Dolores agreed to receive the Sacrament of Anointing with holy oils with the Sacrament of Reconciliation. She joked that not only could Alejandro translate her Confession, but he could easily make an accurate list of all of her sins for her! The kind young Spanish-speaking priest returned to hear her Confession and was welcome to enter this time. Dolores agreed that she needed intravenous fluids and some supper.

Dolores explained that she was afraid to outlive Alejandro. She could not bear the thought of living in this world without him. She was always certain over the years that she would die before him because she was four years older. Then Alejandro became sick. Nearing one hundred years, she began to worry she might outlive him! Although Alejandro recovered, he said he knew that she had become distressed over the past few months about her age, death, and dying. Her fear had somehow begun to outweigh her lifelong faith and her trust in what God had in store for them both. She seemed to give up on life, a little at a time. Then, suddenly, she lost interest in her favorite devotions, lively dinner conversations, and the meals themselves—refusing to cook, eat, drink, or pray. Alejandro believed Dolores was suffering both physically and spiritually. Hydrated and anointed, her shining personality and faith were quickly restored, proving Alejandro right. They prayed together as they had for years, holding hands intertwined with their shared rosary beads and their stack of favored holy cards with devotional sayings.

As the week continued with the Message of Lourdes, prayer in the Grotto, and a visit to the Baths, Dolores was renewed in her trust for whatever God knew was best for her and her husband. Like a wilted flower soaking up the refreshing moisture of a soft rain, Dolores perked up and blossomed with the grace received from the sacraments. Being in a holy place surrounded by prayerful young university volunteers and faithful experienced helpers rejuvenated Dolores. Her appetite returned along with her interest in life with Alejandro, in the present, without so much fear for the near or extended future. She knew that God had a plan for her, and she announced that she would once again trust in Him. Surely, what God planned for her was better than whatever she could imagine for herself, she said.

The young-adult students and volunteers loved caring for Dolores and Alejandro. All the other married couples on the pilgrimage were grateful for the holy, loving example of the elderly husband and wife — models of what they could aspire to in their later years. One of the nurses caring for Dolores and Alejandro said that she learned what authentic, selfless love was — both when Dolores was ill and when she had recovered — because God is truly the silent third partner in a sacramental holy marriage. Dolores and Alejandro returned home to Miami filled with faith, living in the confidence of God for however many days they would have together, happily ever after in this world, on their way to the happiness of the other world.

So I will bless you as long as I live; I will lift up my hands and call on your name. (Ps. 63:4)

Happily Married Forever

Alejandro and Dolores remain the oldest pilgrims to have made a pilgrimage to France with Our Lady of Lourdes Hospitality North American Volunteers. Dolores died before Alejandro. He remained faithfully by her side until the time came when they would both be in the happiness of the other world.

Chapter 11

Blessed Daughter and Mother

Awesome Alley

Preteens tend to be sulky and moody, or erratic at best. Alexandria was no exception. Turning *tumultuous twelve,* she was crossing the tender terrain from little girl to close in on the dreaded emotional gap years of early adolescence. Petulant, insolent, and downright angry, she stormed into the terrible teens with gusto. Known as Alley, she was born an all-in kinda gal and would directly tell you so, if she thought you needed to know—or not. Her Russian-royalty bone structure and name, along with her fiery disposition, were inherited from her biological father. Alley saw him only occasionally during the first four years of her life and did not reconnect with him again until she went away to university as a young adult. Her delicate features and sensitive heart were gifts from her attractive mother. Although twelve is not always a pretty age, the desirable traits from both her parents made Alley a beautiful, bright, and intelligent girl, even when she was brooding.

Alley knew she was adopted. She was four years old at her mother's wedding, when "mom and me" changed into "we three." Alley's dad, the stepfather who was to raise her, loved her from their first meeting. When he had moved into the same apartment complex as the mother-daughter duo, Alley's mom presented them as a package deal, which appealed to the smitten military officer. He was instantly charmed by his new neighbors, who delightfully made him a husband and a father all in one day. Both his brother and his uncle were Catholic priests, so faith was important to him although he was never overt with his personal spirituality. Soon after marriage, Alley's mother converted. As they had always done everything together, Alley entered the Church alongside her mom. Four babies soon followed, one after another, propelling the happy trio into a hectic, Catholic-size family of seven.

Throughout Alley's upbringing, her mother increasingly struggled with depression, which affected her marriage and her motherly duties. She suffered sporadic bouts of melancholy and anxiety, which she likely would have experienced regardless of her family size. Back then, postpartum depression was called the "baby blues" and was considered a natural and eventual self-correcting occurrence for a small percentage of new mothers. But as a woman with a history of depression before childbirth, she was left grappling with mounting feelings of intense anxiety and insecurity that she did not know how to escape. Her depression was likely exacerbated by the adjustment to the constant uprooting of a military-spouse life when she was moved often and far away from her friends and family support.

Alley was a sweet, sensitive child who was easy to care for and love. Everyone was happy to be around her because she was such a lovely little girl. At seven years old, that all changed when a neighbor sexually abused her, robbing her innocence. She did not understand what was happening, though she knew it was wrong. Afterward, she was terrified that her parents would find out. As is typical with sexual abuse victims and children, Alley felt it was her fault. She convinced herself that she was responsible. She felt guilty, damaged, and unworthy of love.

The experience of shame wrapped in guilt is typical of victims of sexual abuse, especially children. Tragically, the extensive psychological and emotional damage caused by the trauma of a sexual violation reverberates deeply within a victim for years, often for decades, most often for an entire lifetime. Moreover, Alley was extremely worried about adding to her mother's problems. Without consistent emotional stability at home, she felt unable to confide her devastating experience to her mother. Alley loved her mom and was afraid to do anything that would disappoint her or add to her anxiety and depression or anger her. Alley said nothing. Ashamed, Alley held the abuse she suffered as a dark secret: a heavy burden for a seven-year-old.

She did not tell anyone about her suffering—instead, stuffing it down, where it festered for more than a decade. Throughout this time, her mother's depressive episodes progressed in both intensity and frequency, making her behavior sometimes erratic and unpredictable. As a survival mechanism, Alley instinctively grew a thick, protective skin, making herself resilient. But, deep down, this caused anger and resentment. Alley felt that no one understood her. She had to be strong all the time to hold in her pain and to hide her burdensome, festering, dirty secret. Nowhere and nobody was safe or trustworthy.

Family life became more complicated for Alley and her parents. Being the oldest, Alley often took the brunt of the depressive episodes her mother suffered. She felt protective of her younger siblings, trying to shield them from seeing their mother's self-destructive behavior when she emotionally spiraled out of control. Alley felt alone as she entered into the tumultuous twelfth year of her hidden and tortured young life. She was in pain, hating herself for what had happened. She was crying inside for someone to notice, for anyone to understand. In this dark place of confusion, she was suddenly no longer thrilled to be adopted or Catholic.

Sensing turbulence ahead, Alley's Air Force dad was as prepared as possible—as a first-time father of a preteen daughter embracing her strong-willed Russian temperament. Throw in the complications of secret sexual abuse, adoption, and her mother's struggles, and it was undeniably apparent that a rough ride was ahead—or would have been, except for the unexpected grace of Lourdes.

Moving around the world had been their constant routine; it was the typical military family way of life. They eventually wound up in the exotic Azores, where they met the holy couple who were to become Alley's Godparents when she entered the Catholic Church. Years later, both families were thrilled to be stationed together again, this time in Germany. The Catholic youth leader there was planning a unique opportunity for teens to make a mission trip to Lourdes, France. It was a stretch to ask families to send a teenager such a long distance in a new program. Alley's Godmother wanted her only daughter to join, but her juvenile diabetes proved a challenge, as most overnight camps or programs refused to accept insulin-dependent teens. Working through the practicalities, it was decided that if a parent joined her, she would be welcomed to Lourdes, affirming the precedent for the new hospitality to do all possible to bring everyone to the Grotto—including volunteers with specialized needs, especially youth.

Alley's Godmother offered to be an adult chaperone with her diabetic daughter and, soon after, requested that her younger son, Stephen, also join them. He was only eleven. Figuring that her good friends and their oldest could use a one-week break, she invited her twelve-year-old Goddaughter Alley to join them. The minimum age to join the mission service pilgrimage trip was fourteen. At twelve and eleven, Alley and Stephen were too young. The youth leader called Lourdes Volunteers and appealed for the underage youth to be allowed to join the group. Pleading, she said that she just knew they should come to Lourdes. "Sometimes, *you just know*," she begged. It was impossible to refuse her passionate plea. It was agreed the two preteens could join—but only if one chaperone was solely dedicated to the oversight of the "junior youth" volunteers. It was to be an exceptional category created exclusively for the first-ever preteen Lourdes Junior Volunteers.

When the youth entered Lourdes, it was summer-hot, reminding the new arrivals that they were near the border of sweltering Spain. The group was housed at the Youth Village, which meant a tiring trek into the foothills of the Pyrénées Mountains. Though picturesque and pretty, it was an arduous climb. Since they were nearly the same age as St. Bernadette during the Heavenly apparitions, it was easy for the teens to relate to the little shepherdess with her sheep long ago as they trudged up the hill. It was charming when lambs and cowbells could be heard in the distance. Unbeknownst to them, this youth group was to be the "first ones chosen," as the first-ever youth group to serve in Lourdes with the new apostolate of Our Lady of Lourdes Hospitality North American Volunteers. If the new Lourdes Hospitality had been more experienced with teen mission programs, they possibly would not have relaxed their rule to allow two preteens. In retrospect, it is evident that it was truly Our Lady extending every invitation to Lourdes for a holy experience.

The first orientation meeting was in a large, open-sided tent pitched in the back of the Youth Village. The place was packed full. The fledgling group had been squeezed into accommodations through an extraordinary exception made to welcome them. The youth were surprised to see an American priest waiting for them, dedicated to serving for and with them the entire week ahead. Many of the priests at the American military bases and posts were deployed to the Middle East. Most of the youth on the pilgrimage had a parent stationed in harm's way. This reality was an unspoken worry just beneath the surface in these young people who were now farther away from their only parent back home. Realizing the opportunity to begin the pilgrimage with the Sacrament of Reconciliation, the American priest secured a place out of earshot, but within sight of the group. Who would go first? The youth leader jumped up and took the opportunity, leaving the volunteer leader to entertain the tired yet restless teenagers after their long travel from one side of Germany to the other end of France.

Not knowing what else to do while trying to stall for unscheduled time, the volunteer leader asked the group members to introduce themselves by stating who they were and why they came. The novice volunteer leader was curious to know what the youth wanted during the coming week so that the leaders could try to fulfill their expectations. Not knowing what they might say, she expected altruistic replies, such as wanting to push someone in their wheelchair. As she began calling on them in the order they were seated, the first girl said she did not want to stay home to babysit her little brother. Shocked, the volunteer leader asked if her little brother was in the group.

"NO!" The girl smiled and giggled, quite pleased with herself.

"Well, the Blessed Mother answered your prayer! Next!" The volunteer leader continued, thinking that first answer was a fluke.

"My sister always gets to go everywhere. I never get to go anyplace good. I wanted to come to France!" Another wish granted by the Mother of God from the Grotto.

The self-interested responses continued. French food, a travel adventure with friends, coveted international scout badges, making a grandmother happy or a grandfather proud were some of the better reasons given. When it was Alley's turn, she said, "My mother made me come here," displeased and pouting that being in Lourdes was dumb and a waste of her summer. The volunteer leader noticed there was something special about Alley, despite her snippy exterior. Children of military service members are endearingly called "military brats," and this group, Alley specifically, was proving the "brat" moniker to be true. The self-centered excuses continued. It seemed no teen had come for any selfless reason, except one girl who wanted to help people in need. Later, it was revealed that she had recently given birth at only sixteen. Her mother, hopeful for healing for the struggling teen mom, stayed home with her unexpected grandbaby, sending her daughter to the holy place of Lourdes for a special grace.

It was going to be a long pilgrimage week.

As the week unfolded, helping others surprisingly expanded the hearts of the teenagers. Spreading their arms to reach the handles of a stretcher to help someone in need left their hearts softened and wide open to receive grace. The youth had not been exposed to people with disabilities because they were stationed away from extended family while living in a world of fit-for-duty service members. It never occurred to these healthy youngsters that someone their age could depend on a wheelchair. Once they met them, they were compassionately excited to be literally the hands and feet of Jesus Christ for them.

In a healing grace, Alley stepped out of her inward pain, suffering, and anger. Being in Lourdes forced her to turn herself outward, changing and softening her in ways she did not fully understand. By helping others, she began to heal. She felt needed, loved, and safe. Alley began to realize, unmistakably, that God loved her. She knew it would be foolish to reject such incomparable love. Clinging to that pure love gave her hope, a sense of belonging, and a home in the Grotto, full of consistency and stability that she could turn to whenever she felt that things in her family home were beyond help. It was an initial seed of healing, firmly planted.

The leadership in Lourdes knew nothing of Alley's secret suffering. They could see that Alley was visibly moved with passion and compassion to help others, often an ideal antidote to preteen selfishness. The week unfolded in a deep conversion for her, the seed opening like a flower springing into the full bloom of its intended beauty. For Alley, suddenly the Church was not just a building; the words prayed together at Mass revealed the family of the universal Church. She realized that the Holy Sacrifice of the Mass transcended nationality, culture, race, and age. The sacraments were no longer an obligation; Alley genuinely wanted to receive them. The intense, selfless service was formative and helped her realize that the world was backward. In Lourdes, the suffering sick, the disabled, and the elderly, along with any struggling youth, came first. This noticeably changed Alley. It was as if she had tilted onto her correct axis, suddenly seeing the world around her aright, with new eyes. She returned to her family with a new perspective and a deepened faith, and although the crosses she bore were still present in her life, she was able to face her trials and joys with a different attitude.

After the pilgrimage, the volunteer youth leader was asked to reunite with the young volunteers and their families in hopes of inviting a group for the following summer. When she arrived on base, Alley's mother asked for a private meeting. She explained that when she was younger, she was unmarried and pregnant. Bravely, she decided to keep Alley as a single mom. A few years later, she met her future husband, and he adopted Alley after the wedding. She explained that eight years and four children later, Alley had begun to regard every parental correction as unfair, suddenly believing that she was treated differently by her adoptive dad. Her mother explained that Alley was negative, moody, and angry about everything, making family life increasingly unpleasant, and her behavior caused stress and tension in their home. At the time, her mother did not know about the hidden sexual abuse or the effect her own mental health issues were having on her daughter.

Further, she explained that after Alley went to Lourdes, she returned home helpful, happy, and prayerful. At first, her parents thought the good behavior would soon wear off, but it stayed. Her mother was surprised when Alley demanded to be included in the local Confirmation class, insistent on learning more about her Faith and the Church. She was told she was too young and needed to wait another year, just as she had been told about going to Lourdes. Shockingly, Alley appealed directly to their bishop, kindly explaining to him that he could not validly refuse her this sacrament. She had researched and read the *Catechism of the Catholic Church* (*CCC*) and discovered that the ages from seven to sixteen are allowable for the reception of the sacrament, necessary for completing baptismal grace. Alley knew she needed "a special strength of the Holy Spirit" (*CCC* 1285) so that she could spread and defend the Faith to other teens who were like her before she went to Lourdes. The bishop listened and granted Alley permission to be confirmed one year earlier than the usual requirement.

Alley's mother wanted to know what happened on the mission trip. Our Lady of Lourdes was given the credit, along with the Holy Spirit.

Alley returned to Lourdes to volunteer every summer until she was nineteen. Each year, Our Lady of Lourdes was waiting for her with a different treasure of grace to be gifted to Alley. At sixteen years old, she came to realize the motherhood of the Mother of

God. Alley realized that her Heavenly Mother was someone she could always go to, a Mother who knew every inch of her heart and her hidden suffering. Alley knew Mary could give her the love she needed when her earthly mother was too busy or stressed. This supplemental Heavenly maternal love broke down many walls of distrust for Alley, restoring and building new trust.

At eighteen, the fruit of God's full healing took place while Alley was serving in the Piscines. During her bath, the weight of her seven-year-old experience was washed away, her secret cleansed. In a healing grace, she understood that nothing that had happened or could ever happen to her had the power to steal her inherent dignity. At last, Alley no longer felt damaged, and in that moment of grace, her purity and dignity were restored. This life-changing realization was revolutionary, changing how Alley saw herself and the way she related to others, especially men. It helped her understand the power of forgiveness and opened the door to forgiving her mother, as she realized that her mom was in desperate need of healing herself. This grace gave Alley the freedom and authentic courage to let people in, instead of blocking them out. Alley returned from Lourdes and began the deep work of emotional healing through competent counseling. Soon after, in God's generous mercy, she was given the opportunity to help other women who had been through similar traumas that they, too, had kept secret. Helping others helped Alley to heal.

At Lourdes, Alley was a witness to many conversions and healings. She was moved by grown men crying because they had discovered God or reconnected with Him. Lourdes was always overflowing with grace, and indirect blessings also came to Alley. She was introduced to Franciscan University of Steubenville one summer when the young-adult volunteers inspired her to choose the school for a degree in theology and catechetics. It was also a safe and stable place where she could receive holy counseling. Her siblings followed her to both Lourdes service and the university. While at Franciscan, Alley met her future husband and made lifelong friends in faith. She always credits her Lourdes conversion for every good thing in her life and for getting her through all her difficulties, though there were still some tough times ahead.

After graduation, Alley began to teach high school theology. She was engaged to be married. Life was good. Then, shockingly, her mom was diagnosed with aggressive metastasized cancer. She fiercely fought the disease with advanced treatments, powered in faith by prayer.

Alley was devastated by her mother's prognosis, as were her dad and siblings. Only their faith firmly sustained them as a family. At one point, Alley and her mom prayed a fifty-four-day novena asking God to make a way for the entire family to go to Lourdes. Just as they pulled up to the church to pray the last day of the novena, Lourdes Volunteers called to invite them on a pilgrimage. The profound healing and transformation about to begin in the Grotto was a blessing for both mother and daughter.

Alley's mom began to heal from the root causes of her mental suffering through the debilitation of her incurable physical illness. Unable to do things for herself, she was forced to let people serve and love her. For the first time, she began to see herself in the beautiful way her family saw her, a way she could never see herself before. Her cancer allowed her to see herself as God saw her, and it began her true healing, transforming her bruised relationships—*winning her holiness*. Alley came to see this grace as the severe yet relentless loving mercy of God. The value of her mother's suffering was an affirmation of God's glory and His power to heal us of whatever in us most needs healing, often unknown to us. Alley and her mother forgave each other for all the hurt inflicted upon each other during

Alley's childhood. Although her mother's struggles wreaked havoc on their family life, Alley no longer felt anger or bitterness. Instead, she was able to celebrate the amazing woman her mother was and to see her with renewed compassion and love. Though she was young, Alley maturely realized that we are all complicated people trying to do the best we can.

While in Lourdes, it was arranged for Alley's parents to renew their Sacrament of Marriage with the pilgrimage priest in the Grotto. When a healthy young couple exchange wedding vows, they promise to love their spouse all the days of their life, "to have and to hold, for better or worse, for richer or poorer, in sickness or in health, in good times and in bad." Although they mean what they say, most couples cannot have the full knowledge of what it is to endure being married in serious sickness. For Alley's parents, the words of their renewed vows had a deeper meaning. They again promised, from that day in the Grotto forward, to have and to hold, for worse, in sickness, in bad times, to love and honor each other until death, which would soon part them. Their children looked on the holy example of their parents before them, united and fortified for their time remaining together. The family pilgrimage to Lourdes brought them all closer to one another. Alley's mom described the pilgrimage as the true miracle they needed. She gave her children to the Immaculate Conception in the Grotto before returning home, knowing their perfect Heavenly Mother would always keep them under her protective maternal care. The full-circle moment for Alley, her siblings, and their parents came on that pilgrimage to Lourdes, a final healing visit that left them with fortitude and great peace.

After returning home, Alley decided with her fiancé to move up their wedding date to be sure the mother-of-the-bride would be there as her daughter walked down the aisle. Alley was escorted by her father, whom she had stopped calling her adoptive parent since her life-changing experiences in Lourdes. She reconnected with her biological father, learned more about her Russian heritage, and became an inspiration of faith to him. Several months after the wedding, the newlyweds discovered that they were expecting identical twin girls! They were delighted by the double blessing but midway through the pregnancy, both babies died. Although deeply grieving, Alley did not waver in her faith.

Not long after Alley's twins' death, her mother died, surrounded by her loving family. Alley and her husband persevered in faith and prayer, as her mother had shown them. A priest consoled them that Alley's mom was the first one to hold the babies in the "happiness of the other world." When Alley thinks of her mom, she remembers the tremendous faith she left her, the childlike trust she had in God, and her kind heart. Now, with four young children, Alley often wishes her mother were physically here to see her as a young mother — though she feels her mom is always spiritually with her and knows of her sweet motherhood. Becoming a mom herself has given Alley a deeper understanding of her mother, and she often wishes she could wrap her arms around her mother to tell her how loved she was, especially in those darkest moments.

Alley has stayed strong since her first pilgrimage to Lourdes, when her mother made her go to France as a troubled twelve-year-old that turbulent summer. Alley thinks every teenager should go to Lourdes, and she and her husband hope to send each of their children to the Grotto someday as youth volunteers. Perhaps while their children are in service, Alley and her husband will renew their marriage vows in the Grotto, following the holy example of her parents.

Her children rise up and bless her. (Prov. 31:28, NASB)

Daughter and Mother

Alley is living the Sacrament of Holy Marriage with a faith-filled husband. She is the mother of three young daughters and a son, along with identical twins who are with their beloved grandmother in the happiness of the other world. Alley was pleased to send her husband to serve at Lourdes while she stayed home to care for their children and their goats. Alley and her family will always be dedicated Lourdes Volunteers.

Chapter 12

A Mystery of a Holy Eucharist

Minnesota Marlow

Lourdes Volunteers was bustling with holy and hurried activity in its humble beginnings. The back room in the modest office had a conference table that doubled as a break room for working lunch meetings. Too busy to suspend ministry work for formal lunch hours, the few paid staff and office volunteers would abandon their desks midday to come together to pray, talk, eat, and meet. Registration, volunteer accommodations, airline contracts, and almost every activity were either date- or time-sensitive for the new apostolate, which was operating on the thread of a shoestring. The office manager apologized one afternoon for opening the daily mail at the end of the conference table she wiped clean after she finished eating. She was looking for something.

Among the envelopes and packages, she carefully dumped the contents of an oversize, unsealed manila envelope onto the table. She gasped. Stuck on the passport photocopy of a newly registered volunteer was a Communion Host fully covering the face of the identity picture. Shocked, everyone looked on in silence. The Host was firmly affixed to the paper. Turning the photocopy upside down or aggressively shaking it would not move or dislodge the thin wafer from the page. Was this Host consecrated? Nobody knew what to do. They stopped. They prayed together.

Catholics believe that the Holy Eucharist is the Body of Jesus Christ—truly Jesus and *not* a symbol of Him (see 1 Cor. 11:23–25; Mark 14:22–25; Luke 22:19). When the ordained priest prays the words of Consecration at Mass, transubstantiation occurs, changing the bread held in the hands of the Catholic priest into the Body of Christ. Each person in the office thoughtfully examined the paper with the attached Host. How did this come about? Was it a hoax? An accident? *Was this truly Jesus in an unexpected, extraordinary visit to the office team?*

The office called the passport holder to ask about the mysterious presence of the Host stuck onto his photo. No answer. The next call was to the Association's Spiritual Director, a Franciscan priest. Certainly, he would know what to do. Again, no answer. Messages were left for both of them in hopes of a quick response with a practical explanation and a solution.

Still stunned and unsure of what to do with this mysterious Host (consecrated or not), those in the office began a sincere discussion, and everyone had a different opinion. The local newspaper had recently featured an article about what to do if you have a consecrated Host in your possession. The nearly full-page article was written in response to a rash of postings on eBay offering holy relics for sale. A Sacred Host consecrated at a Papal Mass by the recently deceased and beloved Pope John Paul II had been listed for auction with frenzied bidding. After considerable public protest, eBay relented and returned the Sacred Host to the Catholic Church. The Holy Eucharist should never be removed from Mass or a church, except for proper distribution to the sick or the homebound or for a Eucharistic Procession. However, the newspaper listed options for those in possession of a Host: give the Host to a priest or a religious sister; return the Host to a Catholic church; or anonymously get the Host to a trustworthy Catholic who would know how to dispose of it properly.

Employees of Lourdes Volunteers were known as the "Holy Water Girls" at the post office regional center. The postal workers respected the busy apostolate and their good work, having come to know them through their frequent and excessive mailing of Lourdes Water. It was possible that a local person read the newspaper article and decided to slip their "I-don't-know-what-to-do-with-this-Host" inside the opened envelope for safe disposition by the trustworthy Lourdes Water ladies. At Catholic weddings or funerals, as Catholics receive Holy Communion, non-Catholics might follow along and accept a Host because they are unsure of what they are supposed to do. Perplexed or at a loss about what to do next, they might pocket the sacred Host. Although this rarely occurs, it has been known to have innocently, ignorantly, or unintentionally happened. Maybe someone was trying to return the Host they had pocketed at a Catholic Mass and never knew what to do with it afterward.

One office employee noted that her grandson was preparing for his First Holy Communion in the Philadelphia archdiocese. Each of the children had been given an unconsecrated Host to teach them how to receive the Holy Eucharist reverently. This practice was intended to help awkward first communicants on their special day in a crowded church full of family and parish onlookers with cameras capturing the significant moment. Perhaps this volunteer applicant had grandchildren. If so, was that applicant anxiously looking for the lost practice Host?

A pyx is a small, metal, compact-like case, about the size of a compass or a pocket watch. When a bedridden, homebound, or hospitalized parishioner is unable to attend Mass, a consecrated Host can be placed in a blessed pyx at Mass and entrusted to someone to bring the Holy Eucharist for the faithful to receive. Another employee wondered if the applicant had opened his pyx, shocked to find it empty.

Each person had a different idea of how this mystery Host could have ended up in their office, stuck to a passport photocopy—except the office manager. *She was in awe.* Erika was certain that Jesus had come to honor the humble office with His Real Presence. Beyond that, she did not try to imagine how or why this had all come about that day. As they were unable to remove the Host sealed to the letter-size photocopy paper, where to place the mysterious paper became their immediate and serious concern. If this was indeed a Sacred Host, leaving it in the mail pile would be disrespectful and unacceptable. In a nearby room was a Mass kit, a portable case containing all the components needed for a priest to offer Mass while traveling. Trying to fold the paper with the unyielding, affixed Host to a size suitable to fit inside the small case without fracturing the wafer proved a delicate challenge.

A volunteer knelt and offered an impromptu, heartfelt prayer:

> *Lord, if this is truly You, please know that we honestly desire only to honor You and Your Real Presence in our little office, to honor You always, everywhere, and forever. Fr. Jeffrey has not yet directed us how to honor or protect You, if this is truly You in this Holy Eucharist. As none of your bones were broken [John 19:36], we kindly ask that You please await Father here, safely, unbroken. Jesus, we honor You at Lourdes Volunteers by beholding Your Mother, as you told us [John 19:25–27]. You know we are all about Your Mother's business for You—and she keeps us really busy! We kindly request that You repose in this respectful place, if this is truly You, to honor our obligations in our work in this humble apostolate for You. Amen.*

The un-removable Host gently slipped off the paper—*immediately*—onto the Mass kit's paten, the small plate upon which the Host is placed during Mass. The corporal, the small white cloth used on the altar at Mass, was carefully placed around the Host, replicating a biblical burial shroud within a makeshift, temporary tabernacle.

Fr. Jeffrey called later. As a priest and a practicing psychologist, he was gravely concerned that a new volunteer applicant might have been careless with the Holy Eucharist—or worse. He decided to contact the priest who had written the letter of recommendation. A personal recommendation from a pastor is required for all volunteers to serve. Priest to priest, they would discuss the suitability of this applicant to volunteer at Lourdes.

Finally, the hopeful volunteer called. Marlow was a cheerful, kind, friendly, straightforward Minnesotan with a unique voice that matched his distinctive name. He was not only dismayed but puzzled and aghast that a Host had arrived in his registration packet. His voice shaking in distress, he was fearful and then tearful at the thought that Our Lord might have been pressed through a crushing postage machine. It was apparent that Marlow had a strong belief in the Real Presence as well as a deep, respectful love for the Holy Eucharist. He said that it was absolutely impossible that a Host could have come from his home into his registration packet envelope. He was certain of this—adamant.

An abbot vouched for Marlow, confident that he would have had nothing wrongful to do with a Host—especially a consecrated one. He also strongly insisted that Marlow be accepted as a volunteer. Friar Jeffrey relented and directed that the Host be consumed reverently in the office at once. Throughout those summer months, the office team kept a promise they had made at the lunch table. Anyone who worked on Marlow's file was to pray for him to Jesus in the Holy Eucharist, and they did—*often*.

That September, a large number of first-time volunteers came to Lourdes in response to an EWTN Catholic Television appearance appealing for English-speaking volunteers. At the opening gathering meeting in the Sanctuary, everyone in the group explained how they came to volunteer and why they decided to spend their money and sacrifice their time in demanding service instead of relaxing on a vacation. It is always fascinating to hear how someone finds his or her way to being a Lourdes Volunteer. Marlow said he was a simple factory worker and farm handyman who often tinkered alone in his work shed with only a small television to keep him company. One day, he advanced the remote to change the channel. It suddenly stopped on EWTN, a station he did not choose nor ever knew existed. Lourdes Volunteers was making an appeal for volunteers, in which Marlow had no interest. He tried to advance past the channel, but the remote was strangely stuck. He tried to change the station manually, but it stubbornly remained frozen. In frustration, he tried to lower the volume and then turn off the television, but even the sound and power buttons were jammed! Annoyed, he threw the remote across the small workshop. Forced to continue listening, Marlow was soon struck by the need for volunteers and felt deeply that volunteering was something he must do. He knew without question that he had to leave the complacency of his workshop and travel to Lourdes.

To be a volunteer in service to the universal Church in the Sanctuary at Lourdes was a surprise to Marlow. There was much to learn, coupled with a language barrier and the inexperience of a newly founded hospitality. Since its beginning, Lourdes Volunteers has included a priest in each group to offer daily Mass in English as well as spiritual direction and Confession for everyone in the group. Marlow's group became a close family and quickly noticed that everyone came to the altar for Holy Communion—*except Marlow.*

He was the only one who remained kneeling. Interestingly, the one volunteer the office had been specifically praying for to the Holy Eucharist was the only volunteer *not* receiving the Holy Eucharist in Lourdes!

On Thursdays, after hours, the group was allowed to have Mass privately in the Cachot, the small, condemned-jailhouse home of the Soubirous family at the time of the apparitions. The Cachot was formerly not a respectable place, as the home of thieves and prisoners, but afterward it became a holy place because a holy girl had lived there. The building continues to be preserved as a special place of prayer in Lourdes. It was in this humble room where Bernadette lived that Marlow received Holy Communion for the first time on the pilgrimage. It was impossible not to rejoice!

Afterward, Marlow explained that he was faithful to Mass but had not received the Holy Eucharist *for more than twenty years.* He never felt worthy. It was torture to be separated from Our Lord in His Sacramental Presence by not receiving Him. So many times over the years, priests had offered Marlow absolution and pleaded with him to return to Holy Communion. He could never bring himself to believe he was good enough. Then he came to Lourdes. He learned that Bernadette had said that the Mother of God could not find anyone less than her. Through the example of Bernadette's humility, he came to understand that, despite her unworthiness to meet with the Mother of God, she made a promise to return to the Grotto. He began to realize that although none of us is deserving, each of us is called by God. Marlow understood that through the Sacrament of Reconciliation, unworthy but absolved sinners become worthy enough to receive the Holy Eucharist. After so many years, this was the time for his prodigal-son-like, joyful return.

Not long after Marlow returned home from Lourdes, he was helping out on a nearby farm when he missed his grip while climbing a ladder that was mounted to a sixty-thousand-bushel corn-drying and storage bin. Marlow fell from the thirty-foot rung. His back was excruciatingly broken, rendering him bedridden. As soon as he was able, Marlow called the office from the hospital to say that his experience at Lourdes and his return to the Holy Eucharist was sustaining him throughout his painful, difficult recovery. For Marlow, the blessing of his pilgrimage to Lourdes continued to flow long after his return home.

Lord, I am not worthy. (Matt. 8:8)

The Passport Photo

After his spinal injury, Marlow did not return to Lourdes, but he stayed in contact with his Lourdes Volunteers family and friends. Marlow retired after forty years in the automotive industry. He continues to plant a gentlemen's garden each year and rides his Harley Davidson whenever and wherever the sun is shining.

Chapter 13

Hurt to Healed to Happy

Transatlantic Theresa

Theresa lived her entire life within a three-block radius of a working-class neighborhood in northwestern Ohio. She was content among the house where she grew up, her parish church and school (where she was a student and later became a teacher), and her home with her husband and children. The small town of Lima had everything Theresa wanted or needed in her family, friends, and church. She never expected to leave her secure comfort zone to cross the Atlantic for a surprising series of miraculous moments that would forever change her life. She never thought she would need the grace of Lourdes. Yet this is how Theresa was to become one of the first to serve with the recently founded Our Lady of Lourdes Hospitality North American Volunteers.

Life was good in 1978, when Theresa married Bruce. He was the eighth of thirteen children and was only eight years old when his father abruptly died of a heart attack, leaving his wife a shocked widow with six children at home. She was stretched thin as the sole surviving provider for her family. Understandably, there was no time or opportunity for Bruce to tighten his bond with his overworked mother. Bruce grew closer to his siblings, remaining close to them into adulthood. Nobody noticed when Bruce began to drink in his early teens, for reasons he never questioned or understood.

Turning a new decade, the newlyweds found happiness together and in the joyful arrival of two babies. Life was not perfect. It seldom is. Theresa knew Bruce drank, but that was not unusual in their world of family and friends. A few beers after work and drinks at weekend parties and on holidays were typical for everyone back then. In the years that followed, Bruce denied that he had a problem as he continued to drink more and more. For over twenty-three years, Theresa hardly noticed that his drinking had increasingly become the accepted norm. She kept her fears mostly to herself, confiding in only a few trusted friends. She worried about the effects of Bruce's drinking on their children but didn't know how to seek help for her family without betraying her husband. Things slowly got worse and then suddenly became unmanageable.

Bruce finally admitted his growing dependence on alcohol. He cycled through detox, recovery, twelve-step programs, and relapses: quit, dry out, AA, and repeat. Bruce struggled and tried medications, counseling, and hospitalizations. The man Theresa married would surface as her loving husband in between the tumultuous ups and downs of his addiction.

Theresa turned to praying, in private, but few knew the destructive hidden problem the family faced at home. Theresa was a dedicated wife who tried, by the grace of God, to live out First Corinthians in loving patience, kindness, trust, hope, and perseverance (see 1 Cor. 13:4–13). She stood by Bruce, helpless to fix a ferociously progressing disease. No one can comprehend how bad an addiction will be—*until it is*.

Around the fall of 2002, thoughts and talk of suicide regularly entered into Bruce's mind and conversations. He was double-diagnosed and treated for depression and addiction. Bruce would say that Theresa and the kids would be better off without him. They suffered individually and together until that Christmas Eve. Weary and worn out, Bruce took his life to end his earthly suffering. At the hospital, Theresa whispered to her husband, "I love you. I forgive you." But somehow, she couldn't forgive herself.

The next morning began with a phone call from their pastor, Fr. Chris. Theresa had only one question: "Could Bruce go to Heaven or be in Heaven?" The absolute assurance from a trusted priest brought her relief through a momentary peace. Theresa entrusted Bruce to the infinite love and mercy of God. It didn't come easily.

The suicide of a loved one is both heartbreaking and gut-wrenching. Suicide seems to be an earthly relief to an incomparable internal pain most of us will never know or comprehend. Likewise, we cannot imagine God's infinite love and unlimited paternal mercy for each of us as His precious beloved children. No matter how much we love a person or how close we are to someone, we can never know a soul as God does. He divinely knows the heart and mind of each one of us, totally and eternally loving us.

Sadly, there was a time when depression, suicide, and mental illness were hidden away—rarely admitted and seldom discussed. For centuries, due to misconceptions and fear, mental illness was considered outside matters of faith. Today, mental culpability is balanced with psychological capability for those who die by suicide.

Although the certitude of condemnation for the souls of those who die by their own hand is not explicitly expressed in Sacred Scripture, history reveals that the final eternal outcome of despair came into spiritual debate around the fifth century. Tragically, there was a time when some did not have a better understanding of the depths of God's mercy and denied funeral and burial services to those who had taken their lives. Thankfully, this changed many years ago. "Grave psychological disturbances, anguish, or grave fear of hardship, suffering, or torture can diminish the responsibility of the one committing suicide. We should not despair of the eternal salvation of persons who have taken their own lives. By ways known to him alone, God can provide the opportunity for salutary repentance" (*CCC* 2282–2283). These Church teachings and consolations do not condone suicide or presume upon the mercy of God. Rather, this compassionate consideration brings light into the darkness of our limited understanding of the infinite wisdom, endless love, and immeasurable mercy of God.

There is an old story of a beloved Catholic saint consoling a widow after the suicide of her beloved spouse. St. Jean-Marie Vianney was a nineteenth-century pastor in the tiny town of Ars, near Lyon, France. He heard a woman weeping loudly and disturbing others waiting in line for the Sacrament of Confession in his little parish church. The humble priest, small in stature yet large in his renown for Heavenly favor and holy insight, approached the widow to kindly request that she stop crying out loud. St. Jean Vianney was given the grace to know that, through the intercession of the Mother of God, the woman's husband had been saved at his dying moment. When her husband was a child, he had made a crown of wildflowers and placed them upon the head of a statue of the Blessed Virgin Mary. The Mother of God never forgot this sweet honor and came to his aid just as he jumped from the bridge to his intended death. The Blessed Virgin Mary helped the widow's husband reconcile himself to God just before he entered the water to end his life. Our Blessed Mother prayed with him *at the hour of his death*.

Catholics are known for their love of Mary, the Mother of Our Lord. The most favored and widely known Marian prayer begins, "Hail Mary, full of grace; the Lord is with you" (Luke 1:28). It is a plea to someone in Scripture whom we know is close to God and can intercede on our behalf (see John 2:1–12). We do the same when we ask friends to pray for us and our offering to pray for others. When we ask the Blessed Mother, we are asking a Heavenly friend who is known to be favored by God to pray for us. This beloved prayer concludes: "Holy Mary, Mother of God, pray for us sinners, now and *at the hour of our death*. Amen." Just imagine: in the last moments of our passing from this world to the other, it would be the Mother of Jesus assisting us in our final hour—in response to our repeated pleas throughout our lifetime for her to be with us at that time!

The trauma and intense grief of losing the father of her children and her husband of twenty-four years deeply wounded Theresa. She unintentionally left her children to their individual grief while she helplessly hoarded her own deep bereavement. Their personal suffering eclipsed the possibility of finding a way to express the full impact of their profoundly tragic loss to one another. Theresa was emotionally exhausted and spiritually spent. Her children held her together, literally supporting her to hold her upright during Christmas Mass. Because she was a strong woman of faith, she amazingly continued on with her obligations to family and school, while many in her situation would have understandably stayed in bed with the covers pulled over their heads. Even a discussion of suicide with seventh graders did not break her (and anyone who has been around a seventh grader long enough can imagine how else this might have gone).

Family and friends sustained Theresa through the darker moments, helping her persevere while praying for her for strength to get through each day. At times, an unending well of deep grief within her would spill over. Tears would suddenly slip out and cascade down her face in places she and Bruce used to go together or at any unexpected reminder of him. She cried alone at home every night. The Mass was one of the few occasions when Theresa publicly showed her sorrow. She would softly cry during a song, a Scripture verse, or prayer to reveal her suppressed emotions. Theresa thought her prayers were holding her together. Much later, she realized that it was the constant prayers of others that had surely gotten her through that extended time of grieving.

Before Theresa knew she would need the healing grace of Lourdes, God had a plan for a way to get her there. While Theresa stayed in her comfort zone in Lima, her younger sister, Lauren, moved often and far away. Around this time, Lauren belonged to a small Catholic parish community in northern England. Months before her brother-in-law would take his life half a world away, Lauren had registered to serve the following year at the Lourdes Sanctuary. After Bruce's funeral, she invited Theresa to come with her to the holy place of healing. Theresa thought she could never feel joy in her life ever again. The two siblings decided to join the group as a respite of sisterly love and support, hopeful for healing.

Groups of volunteers with different backgrounds from all over the Americas joined together for a week of service at Lourdes with the newly formed Lourdes Volunteers. Coordinating volunteer service roles with the limited volunteer accommodations was a challenge. Names and beds had to be pieced together by gender and service to fit into the limited rooming configurations of separate male and female housing, somewhat like a complex accommodations puzzle. Putting together people who had never met before was done with careful and prayerful consideration in the hopes that they would become friends while sharing tight European rooms during an intense and demanding service. Theresa roomed with her sister and Carolyn, a lovely, recently retired schoolteacher.

A few days after the arrival at Lourdes, Carolyn approached the group leader and asked how she had been put in a room with Theresa and Lauren. The leader responded, "If it's really good, it's the Holy Spirit! If there is a problem, it's our fault and we can make a rooming change." Soft-spoken Carolyn continued, "You know Charlie and me, we have been married for nineteen years." She continued, "What you could not possibly have known is that I was married before—and my first husband died by suicide. Putting Theresa and me together is a double blessing you cannot begin to imagine! Only a woman who has been widowed like me can understand what Theresa needs to know: all the doubting 'could have-would have-should have' wishes that perished with him, as well as the endless second-guessing that haunts a surviving spouse to stall grief and keep us stuck in perpetual remorse. By rooming with Theresa, I can help her take years off her suffering through what I have learned. After two decades, I now also realize that if Theresa should not hold herself responsible for some things, I likewise can no longer be held accountable, myself, all these years later."

Theresa was blessed to be healed, and so was Carolyn. There was crying—lots of crying. Both secular and religious experts agree that tears are the beginning of the healing process. It seemed that somehow their tears were yet another liquid grace of Lourdes.

The volunteer group went together to the Baths, prayed in the Grotto, and attended the processions. In the Piscines, Theresa received peace for her grief. She went to Confession, spent time in Adoration, and prayed the Rosary. As the week progressed, Theresa's tears lessened and recovery began—from forgiveness, to acceptance and understanding, to peace. Although there still was a lot to work through ahead, she had entered into a trustful surrender in the spiritual maternal embrace of Our Lady in the Grotto that would see her through to healing. Theresa asked the Mother of God to cover her children with her Heavenly mantle. She returned home hopeful, renewed in peace and refreshed in faith. She was healed to allow healthier grieving.

Theresa wanted others to be able to have what she found at Lourdes. She was compelled to make that happen and was surprised by the new inner strength she felt. On the flight home, she interiorly knew she had to make a meaningful commitment to help the fledgling apostolate. Theresa asked her pastor for a one-year leave of absence from her teaching position. The entire parish community had witnessed a Lourdes "miracle" through Theresa. They had watched her family in pain, attended Bruce's funeral, and witnessed the aftermath of her devastating loss. They now witnessed Theresa's newfound peace—her grief transformed into a healing through her renewed faith. Fr. Chris granted the leave, giving his full support and his blessing to Theresa for one year of missionary service with Lourdes Volunteers while her young-adult children were living and working in Cincinnati.

Theresa sold her house and moved to Syracuse, New York, the home office of Lourdes Volunteers. It made perfect sense to her. It was what she was sure she was supposed to do. It was sudden and unpredictable to others, who weren't at all sure about what Theresa was doing. Still, she moved into a combination office-apartment as a full-time volunteer. She made a lasting contribution to the survival and growth of the first Lourdes Hospitality outside Europe. There was much to learn as a new Public Association in the Catholic Church and for the small office team. Theresa was there to help in any way she could: to learn, teach, guide, lead, develop, type, copy, plan, pray, and more.

Theresa missed Bruce, but with a manageable grief that was softened and alleviated by prayer and work. She returned regularly to Ohio, the place she never dreamed she would leave. Growing in faith with total abandon, she entrusted her future and her children to God's will. At the conclusion of her year-long commitment in New York and before moving back to Ohio, Theresa returned to Lourdes to offer her second official annual service, this time in thanksgiving.

Accueils are specialized hospital-bed facilities unique to Lourdes, where the sick and the disabled stay comfortably in handicapped-accessible accommodations with their hospitalities on pilgrimage.

Volunteers offer service in helping the pilgrimages during meals in the kitchens and with housekeeping duties. Without Accueils, it would be impossible for those with serious illnesses and mobility needs to spend a week on pilgrimage in Lourdes. Likewise, these Accueils could not afford to function or house the pilgrims without these faithful, unpaid, generously selfless volunteers.

Lourdes Volunteers encouraged Accueil volunteers to assist with other services when possible. Theresa sometimes spent her free time leading the Rosary outside the Piscines, where she herself had found profound healing just the year before. The exterior of the Baths is overseen by the St. Joseph Brancardiers (stretcher-bearers). These traditionally male volunteers assist the sick onto stretchers and maintain an orderly flow of pilgrims outside as they wait to enter within. A prayerful presence at the entry to the Baths helps pilgrims anticipate a holy experience instead of enduring an anxious or nervous wait to plunge into the cold mystical spring water. The men are grateful for women volunteers to help at the microphone by singing and praying with and for anxious pilgrims. If there are only men visible outside, it could create a concern that men might also be inside where the women enter the water unclothed. Gracious women visibly present on the exterior create a calming confidence, assuring women of the same feminine welcome inside. It was especially noticeable when a rare American volunteer (there weren't many American volunteers yet in Lourdes) forfeited precious, coveted free time to offer this additional service.

By herself and lonely for the first time in Lourdes, Theresa went to the Baths to lead the Rosary. She was welcomed by the "Piscine Chef de Plateau," the man responsible for the exterior of the Baths. He greatly appreciated her extra help. The next day, when Theresa lost her room key, he offered to help her. Theresa somehow failed to notice his friend standing nearby. George was an experienced brancardier who had been coming to Lourdes for more than a dozen years. He offered up to three weeks of service every year in memory of a close friend and to honor his father, a prayerful man of deep faith who loved Our Lady of Lourdes. As he cared for his dying father back in County Kildare, George wondered if he might be of help to the sick at Lourdes someday. He signed up for service during his allotted vacation time and continued to do so every year thereafter. Exceptionally, in 2003, the Hospitalité Notre-Dame de Lourdes asked George if he could change his scheduled service dates to April. George graciously agreed to do so.

A few days after leading the Rosary at the Piscines, and the lost-key fiasco, Theresa entered the crowded volunteer cafeteria alone. The Chef de Plateau kindly invited her to join his table of English-speakers for lunch. She sat in the only open chair—next to George—as the group engaged in lively discussion. Theresa plunged into the conversation in a very American way that most Europeans would perceive as forward. The gentle Irishman turned to find the source of this unexpected American voice. He was shocked to discover that the attractive lady who had not noticed him during two conversations with his friend the previous days was now seated directly next to him. Theresa was immediately struck by his beautiful blue eyes and delighted by his Irish brogue.

George and Theresa chatted away until they were ushered out at closing time. They were so absorbed in conversation and with each other that they failed to notice the clanging of chairs being placed atop the sea of dining tables surrounding them. Outside, Theresa introduced George to her daughter and son through their pictures. When he noted what a beautiful family she had, Theresa began to cry. George tenderly wiped away her tears. They agreed to meet for the Candlelight Rosary Procession, the favorite for each of them in the daily holy happenings of the Sanctuary.

Soon after, Theresa realized she had a schedule conflict. She wrote George a note and tracked him down to deliver her regrets. The smart Irishman promptly invited her to a meal and the Rosary Procession the next night. They had dinner together and prayed. An unexpected international romance flourished between a woman who never dreamed of being in Lourdes and a man originally scheduled to be in Lourdes at a completely different time. They met in God's time, in a favored place of His Mother. They dated long-distance and exchanged visits across the Atlantic for the rest of the year. They both fell in love with Lourdes—to later fall in love *in* Lourdes.

In July, George proposed to Theresa in a proper English garden filled with yellow roses. They were married in December at St. Rose of Lima Church, with Fr. Chris officiating. They lived in England for ten years, until George retired. The couple then moved to Ohio to live *holy* ever after.

Blessed are those who mourn, for they shall be comforted. (Matt. 5:4)

Holy Ever After

Theresa and George devote their time to caring for their four beloved grandchildren and enjoying time with extended family living nearby in Ohio. They travel to Lourdes for annual service together, whenever possible.

Chapter 14

Ordinary Saints Heaven-Bound

Greatest-Generation Gene

Only saints are in Heaven. New arrivals must be surprised, at their entry, to find most of the holy citizens of eternity to be ordinary souls, just like them. Purged and purified, everyday saints make up most of the Communion of Saints. We often limit our idea of saints to those found in the litany of the formally canonized (those who are capital-*S* saints, such as St. Bernadette). The heroic, biblical saints will surely be outstanding in Heaven, and more notable than the regular, everyday saints, but comparatively fewer. Each of us was created for sainthood and for eternity in Heaven, our intended unique crown awaiting our arrival. Even if we jump out of our baptismal font and try to run away from every grace, Our Lord is always wooing us back to Himself with even more graces. And God generously sends us Heavenly help. Each of us has our own Guardian Angel, dedicated exclusively to us, solely for our soul. Additionally, if and when they are needed, God sends extra helpers for immediate or sustained intervention or assistance. Moreover, some of us choose a lifelong helpmate in a wedded spouse.

The Sacrament of Matrimony elevates the married relationship to a holy covenant, anointing a partnership ordered toward the good of the spouses and eternity in Heaven. In the Old Testament, the value of a good wife is lovingly expressed in Proverbs: "She is far more precious than jewels. The heart of her husband trusts in her, and he will have no lack of gain" (31:10–11). Helpmates have an intimate knowledge of the prominent virtues and vices of their spouses, allowing them to better orient or redirect their spouses toward Heaven. Like a personal North Star, a good marriage partner can guide his or her spouse to Our Lord and, equally, can put them both on their knees before Him. Anyone who has been married knows that a husband or wife would ideally qualify as an accurate measure of the sanctity of his or her spouse. A marriage partner can bring out the saint and the sinner in the best of us. Given enough time and situations, every married couple will eventually see it all.

After more than a half century of marriage, Gene still consistently pronounced his beloved wife, Helen, to be a saint. Gene knew he had married a worthy wife, a holy helpmate who would assist him on his earthly journey, ultimately directing him toward the goal of Heaven.

Gene and Helen retired. In their elder years, they moved in with one of their daughters. For an entire year, Helen daily asked their daughter if it would be possible for them to go to Lourdes. Helen wanted to take Gene all the way to France. Where did this new and insistent desire for Lourdes suddenly come from so late in their golden years? It didn't matter because it was impossible, as far as Helen knew. Two seniors in their eighties traveling internationally was impractical, almost dangerous. Still, every day, the couple would pray the Rosary together, with Helen kindly asking afterward about going to Lourdes. Pray, then ask. It became their routine. Then Helen died peacefully, surrounded by her cherished and loving family.

Gene and Helen had been married for sixty-five years. They met when he was in boot camp. At only seventeen years old, Gene joined the Navy and the Greatest Generation. He signed up to fight the good fight and found the love of his life while training on the East Coast. Gene married Helen before shipping out, eventually returning home to his bride after his wartime deployment. They made a few career moves before settling in the wholesome Midwest to raise thirteen children. Gene and Helen lived a life of family and prayer. They were faithful Catholics dedicated to living the Gospel, often helping others in quiet ways with unknown impact, like the hidden, humble lives of so many ordinary saints. They served both their Church and their community, but family always came first.

Helen was a faithful wife, a devoted mother, and a good cook. Gene considered himself blessed, often adding that being married to a saint was the biggest blessing of his life. After Helen died, he moved from one daughter's home to live with another daughter, Margie. Gene continued to pray the Rosary daily. Afterward, sometimes holding back tears, he would ask if he could go to Lourdes. The mysterious request, again, continued daily. Lourdes is a beloved Catholic sanctuary, but Gene and Helen never had any particular connection to Our Lady of Lourdes or to St. Bernadette. How Lourdes had become a consistent request escalating into a habitual, heartfelt plea was puzzling. Older people can be repetitive, but this seemed different. The petition was sincere and significant, every time.

As if in answer to a prayer, Margie happened upon a popular Catholic television talk show featuring Lourdes Volunteers bringing pilgrimages to France with medical volunteers. It suddenly seemed possible for her father to go to the Grotto. The next pilgrimage was specifically for wounded service members, veterans, and military families. Her father was able to join as a veteran, although Margie made no connection between the Grotto and his long-ago military service. She was just pleased to honor the year-long wish of her recently deceased mother and the ongoing wish of her father.

Europe was ravaged at the bitter end of World War II. How could nations that had recently been brutal opponents forgive each other to live so nearby in peace? After the First World War, Lourdes was the holy healing place. For the second time, the Grotto could possibly become the intersection of peace and healing between recent enemies. United prayer proved to be the holy balm for the wounds of war. Veterans poured in on pilgrimages to the southwest corner of France, carrying their disabled on stretchers into the Sanctuary. Pèlerinage Militaire International (PMI), or International Military Pilgrimage, brought together service members in need of respite and reconciliation. Five decades later, the pilgrimage continued annually, swelling to tens of thousands of service members and veterans coming together from different countries. Nobody prays more for peace than active military service members and war veterans. As the years passed, the participants included fewer war veterans and more fit-for-duty active military personnel.

Five decades later, the Grotto would prove to be a holy healing place for the lingering wounds of brutal wars. A small Lourdes Volunteers pilgrimage of recently wounded American veterans and service members was blessed with a profound experience during the fiftieth PMI in 2008, the Jubilee Year honoring the 150th anniversary of the Marian apparitions. Witnessing the fruitfulness of this unique pilgrimage dedicated exclusively to the extended military family, a larger group, including Gene, made the journey the following year. For the military men, women, and families, being in each other's company proved to be a trustful comfort, helping to facilitate the healing of inner wounds from conflicts both recent and long ago.

Traveling with his daughter and granddaughter, Gene quickly became "Grandpa Gene" to everyone in the Lourdes Volunteers pilgrimage family. Even faster, Gene became known as the American WWII vet present in Lourdes. It seemed everyone wanted to meet and honor him. The French military, veterans, and citizens all cherish the visits of American WWII veterans, especially in Normandy and during the PMI in Lourdes each May. Military patch exchanges, photographs, hugs, and salutes suddenly become common as thousands of troops descend on the Sanctuary of Lourdes in thanksgiving for the end of war and, after war, for prayer, healing, and peace. It is an extraordinary and unique experience that is lively, loud, and crowded.

Accueils are specialized hospital-bed facilities unique to Lourdes. A holy cross between a hotel and a hospital, an Accueil is ideally designed to welcome pilgrims with physical needs. The Marie Saint-Frai is the first and oldest Accueil in Lourdes. The Saint-Frai Sisters are known to be particular about prayer, cleanliness, and respect for privacy. Their volunteers are dedicated and devoted, maintaining the example of the sisters in the care of pilgrims in their house of welcome. Marietta was a faithful lifetime volunteer with the sisters. She knew the house and the rules well. She would no more walk onto the floor above or beneath her assignment than she would wander around into a local private hospital ward. Marietta was also a friend to the recently founded Lourdes Volunteers leadership ladies, often helping the new hospitality with her multilingual skills.

When Marietta heard about the arrival of the veterans, she made an exception and ventured to the floor above to find the pilgrimage director. She pleaded to meet the WWII veteran. She was from

Holland, and it was extremely important for her to see him, she explained. Military or history buffs or those who remember the movie *A Bridge Too Far* know of the brutal Battle of Arnhem. The director could not refuse her genuine, urgent plea and agreed to arrange a brief meeting.

Marietta's parents were caught hiding Jews in their home. Her father was sent away to a concentration camp, leaving his wife and young children. American soldiers rescued him at the end of the war. Her father returned home to his family, and Marietta was born soon afterward. The indebted thankfulness for those in uniform who rescued her father, her family, her town, and her country was instilled in Marietta throughout her upbringing.

The entire town celebrated Liberation Day, as all of Holland did and still does. Every year Marietta and her sister would place flowers on the graves of the heroic American young men who died for them. Mariette grew up, married a French doctor, and moved to France. From time to time, she hoped to meet an American veteran to whom she could express the heartfelt gratefulness of her family. She wanted to personally thank an American. Sixty years later, Gene arrived in Lourdes while Marietta was just a floor away. It was her opportunity finally to verbalize her genuine sentiments.

Marietta joined a small gathering around Gene and was introduced to him. She shared the concentration-camp horror her father had suffered and the trauma to her mother, the childhood suffering of her siblings in her war-torn country, and her lifelong desire to meet him in thanksgiving for rescuing them. It did not matter to Marietta whether Gene was at the battle in Arnhem or whether he was one of the Allied military who liberated her dad. To her, Gene was every courageous American serviceman, to whom every free European was indebted for their freedom. She thanked him for rescuing her father, her family, her city, and her country. She cried,

"You saved my life. I was able to be born and to grow up. I've lived a good and happy life. I have two beautiful children. I lived—thanks to you! *I lived!* Thank you, thank you, *thank you!*"

Gene cried. Everybody cried. Marietta's heart's desire was fulfilled, her heart overflowing.

The inner wounds of war are unseen. The effects might be visible or might surface from time to time, but the actual experiences are rarely openly talked about by older veterans. Fellow veterans have a profound, unspoken insight into this silent reality. The pilgrimage Medical Director, a United States Army medical department officer and recent war veteran, swiftly ordered everybody out of the area so that Gene could compose himself. In the privacy of his room, Gene tearfully explained that he was busy when he returned from the war, as everybody was. With family, work, church, and friends, there was no time to dwell on the war pains of the past. Over the years, life quickly sped by, and as if in an orchestrated crescendo, just as fast, life slowed down. Suddenly, without the distractions of a full, busy life, there was nothing but time, time to remember. Awake and asleep, whenever his mind was empty, it would fill with the realization of the horror of war and its casualties. Teenagers died in uniforms they were not big enough to fit into or old enough to wear. Many young boys tragically died. They never grew up or had a family. How could Gene, who somehow survived all of this, possibly go to Heaven?

As sure as he was that Helen was in Heaven, Gene became increasingly certain that he could not get into Heaven or be with her and God for eternity. For the few years before going to the Grotto, Gene said he could only think of one young boy in an enemy uniform who had died. He never thought of a little girl who lived—*until he met Marietta in Lourdes*. She was living proof of the good gained by many from the ultimate sacrifice of so many others.

Gene now knew he could one day go to Heaven to be with Helen, knowing he was forgiven by that one boy through the thanks of this one girl. Helen had been right all along. She knew that coming to holy Lourdes was what Gene needed.

The weight of war weighs heavily on veterans. Theologians and therapists can defend or debate just-war principles and theories and try to explain or understand trauma, but ultimately, it is healing that is needed. Our loving, all-merciful God wants to heal all wounds. Only Helen knew the turmoil within Gene. As his "helpmate to Heaven" long entrusted with his heart, she knew he needed holy healing and would find it in Lourdes. Our Heavenly Mother knew the needs of both Gene and Marietta. A practical mom, Our Lady brought them together from across the world to help them both find healing through a grace of the Grotto. Once again, Lourdes proved to be the holy intersection of healing and peace for those suffering the devastating effects of war.

As only another war veteran can understand, the medical officer helped Gene through the minefield of his internal battle long after the war ended. The Army priest chaplain provided the spiritual understanding Gene desperately needed. Gene was finally at peace, knowing that he could join his beloved Helen and be among the saints in Heaven in the presence of God for eternity.

Six years after going to Lourdes, Gene died, surrounded by his loving family. His memorial stated, "In his last days he found comfort in the hope that he would be remembered as a good man who worked hard and was faithful to his beliefs. He lived his life as a reflection of being a part of the Greatest Generation."

Eternal rest grant unto them, O Lord, and let perpetual light shine upon them. May the souls of the faithful departed, through the mercy of God, rest in peace.

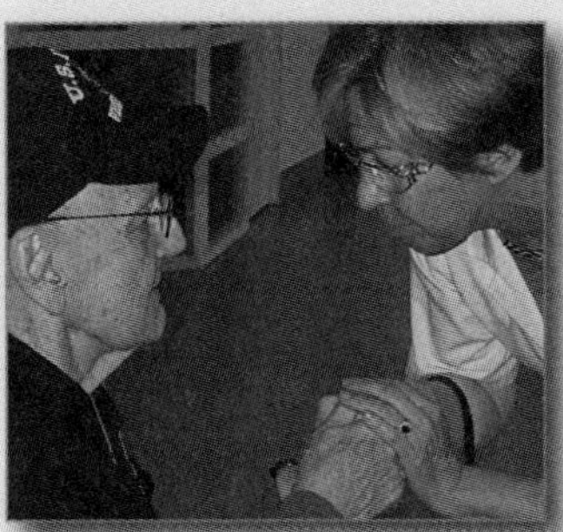

Two Grateful Hearts

Gene was a man of faith and prayer who served his country and lived a good life, loving his wife, children, and family. Marietta continues to serve with the Hospitalité Notre-Dame de Lourdes. She remains grateful to have met Gene and finally to have had the opportunity to thank him.

Chapter 15

Fostering Love

Teddy-Jeremy

Theresa was a cradle Catholic, and Kevin became a convert. They fell in love, both growing in their Faith. After marriage and four babies, they made a prayerful and conscientious decision to nurture their children in the treasure of their Catholic Faith, the foundation of their marriage and family. Together, they discerned that Theresa should give up her full-time career as a physical therapist to stay home to educate their four children, sacrificing the luxury of a comfortable second income. A homeschooling parent is a combination of a dedicated teacher, a watchful principal, a creative room mother, an expert guidance counselor, and an excitable field-trip supervisor—all rolled together in a school situated within or all around the family home. Kevin enrolled their children in a nearby respected martial arts program with the intent to instill discipline and to develop athletic skills while providing social development and interaction with students of similar ages.

Sarah, the youngest daughter, had loved the Blessed Mother since she was a little girl, but her Marian devotion slowly and unnoticeably slipped away in her early teens. Kevin and Theresa were shocked to realize that her respect for the Mother of God had eroded in less than two years under the undetected influence of their non-Catholic martial arts dojo leaders. They were so upset that they immediately removed all the children from the martial arts program. The kids were unhappy, but they accepted the decision.

Soon afterward, at Mass one Sunday, the family heard a homily about the Miraculous Medal apparitions of 1830 in Paris, and Sarah turned to her mother and whispered, "I am supposed to go to Lourdes!" Sarah felt an inspiration, like a calling that was urging her to go to the Grotto. Theresa was delighted but had no idea how a teen trip to France could be possible. And why Lourdes? On the way out of Mass, they stopped to grab the weekly national Catholic newspaper, *Our Sunday Visitor*. In the center was a full-color two-page spread celebrating youth volunteering in Lourdes, along with the story of the recently founded Lourdes Volunteers and their teen catechesis-service program. This seemed a providential grace of affirmation, like an unmistakable signpost pointing them in the direction of Lourdes.

Theresa called the office of Lourdes Volunteers and spoke at length about the opportunity for teens to serve the sick at the Sanctuary. It seemed financially impractical—actually impossible. Kindly, Theresa was assured that Our Lady would find a way. She was told, "Pay attention! If the exact amount of money needed comes to you in a way you don't expect—it is sent from Heaven for a volunteer pilgrimage to Lourdes!" Sure enough, Theresa received a call with an offer for the exact amount of money needed for the trip. A fellow physical therapist (PT) was taking a limited maternity leave and needed another PT to take over her short-term assignments temporarily. The commitment was part-time, with flexible hours and scheduling. It was a perfect fit with Theresa's homeschooling commitments and without a full-time or long-term obligation—and exactly the right amount of money to pay for the mother-and-daughter volunteer duo to go to France.

During the past century, physical therapy has become increasingly specialized. Clients can choose or can be referred to a specific therapist for various reasons. Sometimes, it comes down to logical or logistical practicalities. Like real estate, it could be narrowed down to three things: location, location, location. Some therapists are specific in their area of expertise, restricting their therapy to the bodily location of the therapeutic need, such as the hand, shoulder, or knee. If the patient requires inpatient therapy or post-surgical outpatient therapy, the physical therapy practice or health insurance provider can dictate that the location be either at a facility or at the patient's home. If the PT is traveling to the patient, the location of both the therapist and the patient can determine who will be assigned. Among her list of temporary clients, Theresa was assigned to a ten-month-old baby. She was thrilled. Theresa had always enjoyed working with children.

Teddy was placed at birth in foster care with multiple serious disabilities from excessive debilitating seizures. His mother was incapable of caring for a profoundly disabled baby. Soon after he was born, she quickly surrendered her parental rights in the hope that he would receive the needed care she was unable to provide for him. His prognosis was bleak. Teddy was blind with quadriplegia and was autistic and nonverbal. The doctors said he would never see, sit, stand, walk, or talk. Most babies like Teddy linger in foster care and institutions, remaining in the custody of governmental agencies throughout their anticipated limited lifetime. Adoption is unlikely for a baby or child requiring total dependent care. As a ward of the state in foster care, without a parental guardian, Teddy was not able to be baptized, perpetually stuck in a governmental spiritual limbo. He was placed with a temporary foster mother who was a registered nurse. She was attentive to his needs, both physically and medically. It was a good temporary fit but was not intended to be forever.

Theresa arrived for a prescribed PT assignment just south of the Great Lakes in the colorful splendor of October's vivid foliage. On paper, her temporary patient was a profoundly disabled, blind baby boy. Without warning, somehow, as soon as she held Teddy, her heart instantly and deeply knew that she was his mother. With all of her maternal instincts, she knew that he belonged at home with her family. Teddy had been unknown to her a moment before—yet he was surely, somehow, one of her family. Inexplicably, Theresa suddenly recognized that Teddy was always meant to be a part of her family. It was as if he had been lost, and now he had been found (Luke 15:24). Intrinsically, Theresa knew this was real and unmistakable. She tenderly treated his therapy needs and prayed. How could this be possible, and what should she do? What should her family do? Theresa prayed some more. She prayed a lot, and often.

Being the practical sole provider and responsible head of household, Kevin was not immediately or easily convinced. There was a lot to think through and even more to learn. Expanding their family to include a profoundly disabled baby was a serious consideration for the entire family. He wondered if he was able to handle being the father of a child with such great needs for his entire lifetime. Teddy came for visits with his foster mother. Sarah and her sister were hooked! Like Theresa, they also wanted Teddy to be at home permanently with them. Together with their mother, they made Holy Hours of dedicated prayer before the Blessed Sacrament, asking God to make a way for this beautiful boy to be with them as a forever family. It was decided that each family member would need to agree, personally and independently, to take in this baby as a full-fledged family member, forever.

Theresa had accepted the assignments to earn the pilgrimage funds. She called with excitement to Lourdes Volunteers, this time to register for the first volunteer pilgrimage of the new year. Theresa explained that she had been paying attention when the money unexpectedly came. She carefully watched the airfares online and noticed they were less expensive in the early spring. But that pilgrimage was exclusively for students at Franciscan University. The director didn't mention this, unable to refuse them or the obvious signal grace of the exact amount of funds. An exception was made that allowed the teenager and her mother to join the young-adult student group. It was providential.

Sarah was only sixteen but was mature for her age. The university students immediately and lovingly took her in like a familiar junior sister, as they were only a few years older. The passionate faith of young adults is contagious. It didn't take long for their genuine love, honor, and respect for Jesus and His Mother to rekindle Sarah's remnant of Marian devotion. After one week in the Grotto and in service with the faithful students, amid the tussle and fun of such a vivacious group of young Catholics, Sarah's faith had deepened, and her preteen Marian connection had been renewed.

Sarah also came to realize that she wanted to go to that university. The seeds of her nursing vocation were planted in Lourdes. She loved baby Teddy and looked forward to caring for him with his medical needs. Theresa and Sarah prayed in the Grotto for Mary's intercession to help bring Teddy into their family and thanked Our Lady of Lourdes for bringing Teddy to them—for without the desire to go to Lourdes and the temporary PT assignment, they could not imagine how else Teddy would have found them—or the other way around.

Throughout their time in Lourdes, Theresa and Sarah were gushing on and on about how Teddy had captured their hearts. They enlisted everyone to pray for the family to be able to adopt him. While Theresa and Sarah were in Lourdes, Kevin completed his first foster-to-adopt class. By spending time with Teddy, and through the thoughtful process of the series of classes, Kevin gradually and prayerfully came to realize what Theresa instantly knew. Teddy must be theirs. The family continued to host Teddy for limited visits. *That was it!* Teddy won the hearts of the entire family, one by one and then all at once, in a united family decision. Over time and on their own, each family member had come to agree that it was time for Teddy to come for an extended visit in consideration of a final legal adoption.

In June, eighteen-month-old Teddy was placed with the family long-term. Right away, they noticed small improvements, and not just in his physical therapy mobility. They knew it was due to consistent love and attention. Interaction with a family of parent-age adults and sibling-age children made a significant difference in both his reactions and expressions. By the end of the year, Teddy was legally adopted and his name was officially changed to Jeremy. He was baptized on New Year's Eve, his second birthday. In one day, he was blessed to become a child of God and the youngest of five children, with two loving parents, two older doting sisters, and two older protective brothers.

Caring for Jeremy inspired Sarah to become a nurse. She entered the School of Nursing at Franciscan University. In her sophomore year during the study-abroad program, Sarah returned to Lourdes to serve in the Baths in thanksgiving for Jeremy's adoption and Baptism. Sarah graduated and entered the United States Air Force. After her four-year military service commitment concluded, she married, and within a few years, Jeremy became an uncle, twice over! Sarah continued to have a strong faith, including Marian devotion. She lovingly helped with the care of her youngest brother whenever she was back at her family home.

Jeremy's seizures continued, sometimes uncontrollably. Theresa and Kevin were told a few times that he might not survive his severe prolonged seizure episodes. Some lasted seven excruciating minutes or more. The medical professionals disclosed that, from the beginning of the adoption process, they thought that Theresa and her family were intended to provide only short-term hospice care for Jeremy. They admitted that they had not expected Jeremy to survive. The family's consolation was knowing that their youngest son was baptized and loved in a family outside of governmental institutional care. Amazingly, Jeremy pulled through each scare, every time.

With the love and attention of his family, Jeremy learned to sit and eventually to take a few steps with some assistance—much to the surprise of his physicians and the delight of his family. His smile and laugh were sure indicators that he knew when his sisters, brothers, or nephews were nearby or that he wanted something. Jeremy attended a specialized school program for autistic children, with classes for the blind, and developed awareness beyond medical predictions and all previous prognoses. He was finally ready to make the journey to Lourdes. Jeremy went to the Grotto with his parents and his big brother. With the permission of his pastor back home, Jeremy received his First Holy Communion near where Bernadette knelt under the gaze of Our Lady during the apparitions.

Through family love and competent professional services, he thrived, continuing to amaze and bring joy to everyone. Beyond any medical expectations, Jeremy learned to walk short distances on his own. He cannot speak, but he expresses himself, especially with his laughter. With his brothers and sisters grown and on their own, his parents found the perfect house to accommodate their needs for Jeremy as a young adult.

Lourdes Volunteers has an expression: "We love it when Our Lady introduces us to her friends!" In this situation, she introduced

Jeremy to his family. Jeremy's parents, brothers, and sisters believe that Our Lady of Lourdes had a plan for him to be with them from the beginning. She just needed to provide the inspiration and introduction to make that possible.

> *In love he destined us for adoption to himself through Jesus Christ, in accord with the favor of his will.* (Eph. 1:4–5, NABRE)

First Christmas Photo

The family hopes to return to Lourdes someday for a pilgrimage to combine both volunteer service and prayer as pilgrims. They want to repay the debt in some small way to the Lady in the Grotto for sending them Jeremy.

Chapter 16

Revenge Reversal

Southern Cynthia

Slouched down to hunch over in an airport wheelchair, Cynthia failed in her distressed attempt to go unnoticed. She was barely hidden behind a pillar in the bustling Washington International Airport. An observant passerby would have surely noticed she was desperate to disappear. Cynthia was dismayed at her visibility in the brightly lit baggage-claim area of the crowded major airport. She was unable to make eye contact with anyone. She was culturally polite and sweet-spoken. It was evident she was not belligerent or hostile but just too out of place for small talk or, more accurately, any talk at all. The medical team was prepared, having surmounted consistent obstacles to make her international travel possible. Feeling at ease was a far stretch beyond Cynthia and had been for a very long time. She threw off any thoughts of "comfortable" on her way out the door to try to get anywhere, one pain-filled struggle at a time. Going to Lourdes was frightening for Cynthia, but she was on her way, despite herself and her crippling fear.

Cynthia had a sugary Southern drawl, the thick kind of accent ingrained with deep roots planted by generations far back in her

Alabama family tree. Her Granddaddy graduated from Harvard and brought his charming drawl safely back down south along with his prestigious medical degree.

Even in her worst distress, Cynthia remained a lovely lady. Yet she was obviously a deeply wounded woman, the type who flinches at every noise or jerks tautly in a startled response to every action. That was completely understandable considering what she had endured to survive.

The pilgrimage started out like any other. Several of the group required wheelchair assistance, including Cynthia. She was noticeable at excursion head counts because her head was literally always down for the count. Every day held a different blessing in the thoughtfully planned pilgrimage program. Everything seemed wonderful until the "winter vomiting bug" invaded Europe just before the scheduled departure back to the United States. In the fall of 2008, Cynthia and the others had embarked unknowingly on what would become infamously known to Lourdes Volunteers as "The Puke Pilgrimage." Nearing the end of the overly crowded Jubilee pilgrimage season, a norovirus steamrolled across the continent, menacing its way into France. A gastrointestinal disaster descended upon Lourdes for several days as the pilgrimage was concluding.

Despite extra sanitary precautions, some volunteers and pilgrims came down with the virus just in time for return-travel mayhem to ensue. Rushing through the lobby, the pilgrimage leader was greeted with a joyful hello, a surprise amid such stomach woes. Slowing down, she smiled in reply to the attractive woman seated a distance across the way. She looked familiar but not enough for the pilgrimage leader to recall how they knew each other. Several minutes later, as she ran through the lobby a second time, the same lady called out to her, this time by her name. They definitely knew each other. The woman was attractive with classic style, sophisticated but not stuffy.

"Cynthia!" the pilgrimage leader exclaimed. Shocked, she added, "Cynthia! I didn't recognize you! HOLY WOW! You look like a million bucks! You look like you just won the lottery!"

Cynthia replied, "Yes, ma'am! I did! I won the spiritual lottery yesterday afternoon in the Baths!"

These two women had traveled over the ocean together and had just spent every day of the past week together in Lourdes. Yet such a life-changing impact was noticeable in Cynthia's appearance that the pilgrimage leader did not recognize her! An astounding transformation was noticeable in Cynthia's appearance. She radically and visibly looked like a new woman. Cynthia had been remade, refreshed, and renewed through a liquid grace.

Getting any supportive needs pilgrimage group from France back to the United States required detailed planning, with a little luck and a lot of grace. Lourdes Volunteers learned over time that after spending a week together in the Grotto, individuals bond as a tight-knit family in the charism of hospitality. This makes return travel somewhat easier, despite inevitable delays or misconnections.

Even amid such nasty stomach upset, there was joy. Several who contracted the norovirus were unable to travel home. They were forced to stay in Lourdes with a small medical team, volunteer caregivers, and experienced leaders. Spending a few extra days in Lourdes did not seem like a burden to anyone, despite the unpleasant reason for the surprise bonus time. Almost nobody ever really wants to leave Lourdes. For those departing as scheduled, some adjustments had to be made to adapt and reconfigure the manifests.

The New York JKF Airport overnight rooming assignments were reorganized. The medical team decided that Cynthia no longer needed a nurse with her. The nonmedical pilgrimage leader, who initially did not recognize Cynthia earlier in the lobby that very morning at Lourdes, was now reassigned as her roommate that night after the international flight. This was the first time the two ladies had an opportunity to spend private or uninterrupted time together. Although the leader had heard about Cynthia's tragic life in the office when she registered to join the pilgrimage, Cynthia didn't know that, so she shared her story from the very beginning.

As a child, Cynthia was schooled by nuns who told her the stories of Lourdes and Bernadette. She and her husband both came from established and respected Southern families. Cynthia married young, knowing nothing about alcoholism, substance abuse, or PTSD in Vietnam veterans. She had two beautiful babies in a few short years. It quickly became apparent that Cynthia needed to provide for her little family. Her husband proved himself unable to work consistently. As his addictions spiraled out of control, so did his rage—in tandem with brutal escalating spousal abuse. She desperately tried to stay married. Divorce was unknown in her family. "If you made yourself a hard bed, you had to sleep on it," she said. For generations, it was just the way it was where she came from, she explained.

While working full-time to support her family, Cynthia put herself through school. She earned an advanced degree in microbiology and began her doctoral studies. Desperate to shield her young daughters from the trauma of their daddy's ongoing violent outbursts, she reluctantly accepted divorce as their safest future. To protect her and her girls then living alone, she did what any good Southern gal would do, sayin', "I got myself a dog and a gun."

One night, the dog didn't come in. Cynthia opened the door to call for their protector pet and was stunned to be confronted by her ex-husband lunging up onto the porch from his hiding place in the bushes. Brutally, he beat her, she said. He threw her around like a rag doll, with fierce force. He dragged her into the bedroom and after a particularly heavy blow, and she fell limp onto the bed.

"This is going from bad to worse," was her last conscious thought. It was worse than the worst she could have imagined. Cynthia did not realize that her loaded shotgun, intended to protect her, had slipped out from under her bed and into his grasp—to be used against her. He shoved the double barrels into her gut and pulled the trigger. He ran, leaving her for dead. Cynthia fell from the bed onto the floor in a large pool of her own blood. She has no idea how she dragged herself to the phone or how she was able to call for help, other than that she had begged God to let her live long enough to raise her little girls. She pleaded with a mother's love for her daughters. God heard her, she said. Against all medical odds, Cynthia survived. The surgeon told her that the reason all those cowboys in the old western movies grab their bellies and bleed out on screen to a dramatic death is that most gunshot wounds to the gut do just that—they kill you dead. Ugly, gruesome dead, he said.

Cynthia spent the better part of a year hospitalized. Her ex-husband was convicted and sentenced for attempted manslaughter instead of attempted murder. He hadn't brought the loaded gun with him; he just happened upon it. Therefore, the courts deemed it was not premeditated, Cynthia explained in frustration. She said she knew he had come to kill her. He had threatened to kill her many times before and had beaten her many more times before that. She and many others thought that his conviction and sentencing were far too lenient. She said that everyone thought the courts failed her and defied honest justice.

Thirty-three surgeries over eleven years, including three failed extensive skin-graft attempts, did not close the open wound in her abdomen. Constant infections plagued any possibility of healing the tissue or closing the open, disfigured abdominal hole. A gregarious, fun-loving lady was shot down to a worrisome woman, a withered introverted version of her former self. Cynthia lived smaller.

She described her life as being drastically reduced since the violent shooting. The impact on her as a victim of brutal domestic violence cascaded onto her daughters. The girls had lost the successful, independent, resilient mother they had always known. Their Momma was a debilitated and dysfunctional shell of her former self.

Cynthia was increasingly afraid of the impending release of her ex-husband from prison. In her opinion, he was rightfully convicted of shooting her, but wrongfully given too short a prison sentence for trying to kill her. She knew that her suffering would unfairly continue long after he had served his too lenient sentence and had returned to living his life as a free man. Cynthia also had fearful concerns about her daughters being around their father after his release. She was always worried or scared, most often both. Her mounting fear became terror, and her escalating resentment turned into seething hatred. Cynthia simply needed her ex-husband gone for good. She confided that she promised God, "If I did not have to scoop out pus from this wound every day, I would not have to get rid of that evil man."

Often bed-bound, Cynthia happened upon a nun on television in her Alabama birth state. Just outside Birmingham, Mother Angelica founded EWTN, the largest Catholic network in the world. This particular show was hosted by a priest and featured pilgrimages to Lourdes for the sick and the suffering. Exasperated by the continuing failed surgical attempts to close her wound and her increasing concern over the impending release of her ex-husband from prison, Cynthia needed a miracle. She faintly yet fondly recalled what the nuns from her childhood told her about the miraculous Lourdes legends of healings and miracles.

Cynthia contacted Lourdes Volunteers, never expecting to go, but more out of a desire for healing from some of "that-there miracle water" from the spring in France. The Head Nurse called Cynthia several times; they spoke at length and in detail in ongoing conversations. Cynthia had damaged muscles that compromised abdominal support and reduced blood flow to her lower body. Walking more than short distances was not possible for her. She had limited stamina and seldom ventured out in public. A wheelchair would be needed for her to travel and during her stay in Lourdes. Worse, she dreaded the thought of being in public—and in a wheelchair. Worst of all, she was frightened of being away from home for a whole week. Cynthia suffered terribly and feared that her daughters were suffering more. She persisted in her thoughts against travel and refused to go. It was simply impossible for her to make a pilgrimage. She settled on receiving Lourdes Water mailed to the self-imposed, safe cloister of her private home.

The Lourdes Volunteers nurse arranged for the office to mail Cynthia a bottle of Lourdes Water. Cynthia explained that, as a microbiologist, she knew that pouring unsterilized liquid into an open wound highly susceptible to infection was not just unadvisable or unacceptable—it was unthinkable! Cynthia was a woman of science, but she was also raised in faith. She lay in bed with the little bottle in her hand. The wound opening was about the size of a small egg and regularly filled with an unending oozing substance that she was forced to clean out every day. She said a prayer, made the Sign of the Cross, and dumped the contents of the little bottle into the gaping hole. If she woke up in the morning with a massive infection yet again—God's will be done. She would return to the hospital for yet another round of extended intravenous treatments.

Cynthia awoke in the morning—stunned! The gaping wound had healed closed! After eleven long years and thirty-three unsuccessful surgeries, the gunshot hole in her abdomen had inexplicably closed and had completely grown over while she slept! She no longer needed to scoop out the drainage or pus every day. Cynthia had made a desperate deal with God—and He kept His end of *her* bargain! Only one other person knew about her deadly plan for her convicted shooter, but that person did not know about her deal with God. Cynthia was too deeply entrenched in vengeance to let it go. She decided to cling to her vendetta, despite the miraculous healing of her wound with Lourdes Water. Her vicious hatred was greater than the hopeful promise she had made to God. Besides, only God and that one person knew. *But God knew.* In His mercy, God knew.

"Then that Lourdes Volunteers nurse kept calling me, insistin' that I had to go." Cynthia continued, "Good ol' fashioned Catholic schoolgirl guilt put upon me by that dang redheaded nurse guilted me into going on that pilgrimage." Ultimately, because the physical wound had healed, she felt obligated to go with the people who gave her the Lourdes Water for her healing. She reluctantly acquiesced. It was only after returning from the pilgrimage that she more fully understood why she really needed to go to holy Lourdes. The true reason, she whispered secretively, was something only God and one other person knew.

The bath experience in Lourdes involves both a spiritual and a physical ritual. Unclothing can be a symbolic stripping of ourselves, of who we are, alone before God. Although the actual process is modest and bathers are not exposed before others, most come to understand intrinsically a vulnerable reality. Entering into the water with an awareness of interior imperfections can allow a submerged cleansing in a supernatural grace. In the Baths, Cynthia's hidden revenge was washed out, replacing the darkness within her with the light of Christ. Her appearance was shining and her countenance so transformed that she emerged almost unrecognizable!

Cynthia was wholly sorry and genuinely repentant. She deeply regretted her intended plan against her former husband. She left the Baths to pray in the Grotto on her way to the Chapel of Reconciliation.

Through the ministry and help of a priest, and the generosity of the Sacrament of Mercy, she reconciled herself to God. As she heard the words of Christ through the priest, "Your sins are forgiven. Go in peace," she knew that her sinful intent had been wiped clean during her contrite confession. Cynthia returned home transformed and peaceful. She canceled her hateful plan against her ex-husband.

Confiding her tragic story to her pilgrimage leader, Cynthia lifted her pajama top to show the discolored indentation in her abdomen. New purplish-pinkish skin seemingly stretched across to cover the awkwardly deep indentation. Her discolored skin was fresh looking, like newborn baby skin. Cynthia continued her story, explaining how she came to Lourdes, right up to her walking out of the Baths like a new woman, surprised to be healed in an unexpected spiritual grace. The two ladies talked late into the night. They joked that they could sleep on their connecting flights home the next day, which they did.

Free from all bitterness and resentment, Cynthia returned home a changed woman. She eventually learned to trust again. A few years later, she met and married a wonderful man. With the hatred gone, there was room for love and good things in life. Cynthia came to think of her former husband as the father of her daughters and not just the man who tried to kill her. She found joy yet again. Her daughters were grown, becoming accomplished women. Her life was better than she could have possibly expected or dreamed possible during her darkest days of pain.

After her family and home were settled, Cynthia wanted to give back in some way for what she received. She returned to Lourdes as a volunteer in July 2011. The rooming situation was cramped. The same leader from her first pilgrimage was unexpectedly again assigned as her roommate, this time for ten full days. It was a joyful reunion. As before, they stayed up too late in their pajamas talking and laughing, like schoolgirls at a pj party. The exhausted volunteers in the next room pounded on the thin walls, signaling that nightly outbursts of belly laughter were too loud for their neighbors attempting to sleep after long hours of service! So they adjusted their voices to giggles and whispers treasured late into pleasantly warm summer nights of shushed sisterly sessions.

Raised as a Southern belle, Cynthia was gracious and oozed genteel hospitality. It was the traditional way of life across the southern United States. She was organized, forward-thinking, compassionate, quick-witted, and passionate about Lourdes. Her lovely way, charming Southern accent, fun sense of humor, and innate leadership skills made her a perfect pilgrimage leader for Lourdes Volunteers. Cynthia agreed to lead groups. A three-year training would require her to return to learn in tandem with an experienced leader. Cynthia committed to helping bring others to the same grace that saved her from a tragic downfall, rebuilding her up to the happy, grace-filled life she was so blessed to be living.

During one of the intimate chats with her roommate, Cynthia showed her scar again. It was no longer as deeply indented as just after the holy healing. The coloration lessened, but the scar remained as a visible call to prayer for Cynthia. She said her body held a constant reminder for her to pray for the father of her daughters.

At the conclusion of the service pilgrimage in Lourdes, Cynthia made an official Declaration of Cure at the Medical Bureau. She noticed that the Medical Director listened intently and continually took notes as he asked specific questions. After consideration of the skin being the largest organ in the human body, he found her description of her open wound that was incurable for over a decade, being spontaneously cured with Lourdes Water, to be worthy of consideration. An official dossier was opened. Cynthia said the Medical Director requested that she write down what happened to her, and he invited her to return the following year with her medical records to begin the investigation for the process of scientific scrutiny. She said that he told her that the healing of her soul in forgiveness seemed to be a miraculously blessed gift to her that he and many others might consider to be profound, possibly more meaningful than her physical cure.

Five weeks after returning home from her volunteer pilgrimage, Cynthia died in a car accident. Reconciled to God through the sacraments, Cynthia was prepared, in a significant grace of Lourdes, to meet Our Lord. The healing of her soul was then and forever surely more significant than the closing overnight of her open wound after eleven years. Cynthia was cured, blessed, and healed—physically, mentally, and spiritually—in preparation to meet God through a gift of the Grotto.

> *All bitterness, fury, anger, shouting, and reviling must be removed from you, along with all malice. [And] be kind to one another, compassionate, forgiving one another as God has forgiven you in Christ.* (Eph. 4:31–32, NABRE)

Sweet Southerner

Cynthia was a devoted mother, dedicated medical and science professional, talented pianist, fabulous Southern cook, and a passionate volunteer. She had a gracious flare, an ingenious wit, and a generous laugh—and all with a twinkle in her eyes! Cynthia was blessed to live her life grace-filled and in the sacraments after Lourdes.

Chapter 17

Broken to Blessed

Bereaved Brian

Bereavement knows no boundaries. Grief is not an equal-opportunity suffering. The death of a daughter or a son is said to be the worst of losses. If mourning a child were a planet, it would be its own private solar system. It is a universe of penetrating hurt unto itself that is completely incomparable to other losses. We don't think about it, but somewhere deep within us, we expect to grow old and someday bury our parents. We might need to bury a sibling, or a sibling might need to bury us, but it is against the natural order of life—and the human heart—to bury our child. *It just is.*

Grieving a son or a daughter never ends. Bereaving such a debilitating loss is an unbearable tragedy that often breaks parents, marriages, families, friendships, and more. Mom or Dad will never "get over it." And it *never* gets easier, although well-meaning friends or relatives might try to console suffering parents with that hurtful misconception. Hopefully, they will someday, somehow, find small ways to manage their response to living without their son or daughter in this world. But they will never stop longing. This incomparable heart-wrenching grief will truly end only when the parent dies. Faith provides a small consolation because it assures the bereaved that their greatest family reunion awaits them in Heaven.

The first small group of wounded veterans and warriors was coming together with Lourdes Volunteers to join the annual Pèlerinage Militaire International (PMI), the International Military Pilgrimage at Lourdes. It was a unique group, and it quickly became apparent that a military priest and a military medical practitioner would be best suited to assist the military pilgrims and families. Wounded warriors and veterans had different needs from those of civilians; their comfort seemed to be in the trusted company of one another. All Lourdes Volunteers Supportive Needs Pilgrimages include a volunteer medical team and one priest chaplain for every twenty-five pilgrims. Never before had there been the added requirement to be a military service member or veteran to volunteer. A deployed military priest had written a request to come to Lourdes, inspiring this particular pilgrimage. Finding a military medical professional willing to come could prove to be a difficult challenge.

Brian's name and number were given with a compassionate plea. His only son had died in a car accident the year before. Brian was deployed to Afghanistan one month later, returning home a year after having left the Church. Quite honestly, he was "pissed off" at God, he said, military style. He was a devastated dad, further bruised and broken by the damage of a long deployment to a consistently and heavily hit hot spot of conflict with intense medical demands. Military medical practitioners see the worst of what we can do to each other. Anyone in a medical command (officer or enlisted) can save or fix only so much. That's a lot of compounded death and loss for any one soul to witness—and to remember and live with every day thereafter. Everybody knew Brian was among the walking wounded. Although he was hurting, he was able to function. Medically, he was fulfilling his command duties and his obligations to his private family practice at home. But he was vacant inside. His angry grief was fueled in the war zone, which was a frenzied feeding ground for a soldier with an endless supply of personal pained angst.

When Lourdes Volunteers contacted Brian, the conversation was curt and short. He was a busy officer accustomed to being in command. The initial appeal sounded like some stupid civilian was wasting his time. Given an explanation of the types of wounds some of the military pilgrims had, Brian listened, but only because there were service members involved. He was told that if he did not come as the pilgrimage Medical Director, they probably could not go to Lourdes for the hopeful healings. That grabbed his attention, along with something his VA counselor had said a few days earlier: "If you lose your faith, *you are lost*." His counselor had recommended a pilgrimage, and now this woman on the phone was calling to ask him to join a *pilgrimage*—a word not spoken or heard every day. As Brian had learned on the battlefield and in medical practice, there are rarely coincidences. His commander signed off, in case Brian needed to help any wounded coming to France from Landstuhl Regional Medical Center, the U.S. military hospital in Germany where American wounded were medevacked from Iraq and Afghanistan. In the end, he did not need to do that, but his medical mission permission remained granted.

In 2008, Brian agreed to be the Medical Director for the first Our Lady of Lourdes Hospitality North American Volunteers Wounded Warriors, Veterans, Service Members, and Military Families Pilgrimage. It started as a small group. Brian thought it sounded as if there were more words in the program title than there were seriously wounded pilgrims. But the number of pilgrims grew quickly. Brian's plan was to tell everybody to take two aspirins and call their primary care provider at their local VA facility when they returned home. His thinking was that Lourdes was not a war zone. He wouldn't have to handle any real medical emergencies. This one-week pilgrimage would be a piece-of-cake tour wrapped up as a sweet, free trip to Europe. Besides, he was required to do an annual out-of-country military medical mission. This would qualify. "Check that off the list," he thought. It was not until the pilgrimage was over that he would reveal the real reason he agreed to come: to sip good Belgian beer in France at an outdoor café. He Googled *Lourdes* while the woman was pitching the idea to him on the phone and saw that trout were plentiful in the river that runs through the holy Sanctuary. He decided then that he would go to Lourdes and bring his fishing pole in his luggage, which he packed into his elongated duffel bag. Brian had no idea that he was invited because those who knew him knew that he needed to go to Lourdes for healing for himself. It frequently happens this way. A person comes as a volunteer to help others (or to drink beer or wine in bistros) and is blindsided by an unexpected grace in the form of conversion or inner healing.

Leisurely traveling to Lourdes on a Supportive Needs Pilgrimage is an oxymoron. Bringing disabled, sick, and dying people to France is arduous, difficult, and usually quite complicated. Brian seemed unapproachable. He was a gruff, stern, dismissive, and monosyllabic military officer. He refused to wear a white lab coat. Lourdes Volunteers had quickly figured out that the fastest way to bring a group of volunteers together as a team was to easily identify who was who, clearly and up front—leaders in navy blue suits, medical professionals in white, and priests in collars. That made it easier for the leadership team to spot a needed doc on the clock or nurse on the spot or a priest from across a crowded airport or packed plane. Most volunteers see each other for the first time at the airport, never meeting one another before departure. It was also easier for pilgrims who needed to know whom to ask for help with drainage bags, ex-fixators, pain medications, or oxygen levels. An additional and unexpected benefit was that airline personnel were also able to easily identify who was responsible for the supportive-care passengers aboard their flight. It was a visual, color-coded, simple system that worked effectively. There was just one problem: nobody wanted to wear white lab coats, nurse dresses, or scrubs in public or on an airplane.

Brian had completely disregarded everything the civilian know-nothing had said on the phone anyway. He didn't bring his lab coat. Then, while the group was struggling to get through airport security with a turtle-shell brace for a broken back, medical devices, bags of medications, wheelchairs, and more, Brian realized that not a single person in the group was looking to him for direction. He was an Army Major. He knew how to command, but nobody was listening to him because they could not *see* that he was the pilgrimage Medical Director. His leadership and rank were invisible because he was not wearing his white lab coat "uniform" or his military uniform. He was dressed like the pilgrims, in casual clothes. And he didn't realize he was brooding. Sadly, he looked exactly like the other suffering veterans—because he was one.

The white coat would have helped; the color-coded dress system really was effective, similar to military dress code. Brian understood. But his lab coats with his name embroidered on them were back at home. While changing planes in Paris, the leader asked him if he happened to bring his lab coat. "No," he smirked, adding that it was too bad she wasn't fully prepared with a size 44 for him to throw on when he needed it. Much to his surprise, she reached into her briefcase and pulled out a lab coat in that exact size, brand new, still in its plastic covering. She knew he would need it, and she would need him to wear it. Who just happens to carry the right-size lab coat? It wasn't until a few years later that Brian figured out that it was not by happenstance. It had been purchased just for him, anticipating that he would not bring his own from home, and that it would be needed. There are few coincidences when it comes to Lourdes. Everything is either well planned or totally full of grace, or both. The experienced pilgrimage leaders attest to it, saying Lourdes is absolutely grace upon grace and has proven so over and again.

A sailor was in the group, and getting off the last plane, the leader noticed blood running out of one of his ears and down his neck. She asked if he had a problem hearing during the flight. Immediately, but kindly, he dismissed her. It was just a ruptured ear drum; it was nothing compared with the broken back of the soldier in front of him. Brian was discreetly summoned to observe the situation and take care of him. He did. Brian was again summoned to listen to the deep cough of another veteran. The cough turned out to be untreated bronchitis, which developed into pneumonia by the time they landed in Pau, the last stop on the way to Lourdes. With a local VA medical facility and military benefits accessible to him back home, the vet was asked why he had not been prescribed an antibiotic before flying out. He replied, "Because, ma'am, nobody was shooting at me. It's just a cold." He didn't think a serious chest cold was worth bothering his VA primary care provider.

"Busy Brian" had no time for trout fishing or beer drinking. The hidden wounds of war quickly surfaced to be seen as the most serious needs. It seemed that sometimes the body stubbornly does not heal outside when harboring brokenness inside. Each person on the pilgrimage was suffering from within. Their supportive-care physical needs were swiftly reduced to secondary issues. The real hurting ones were the wounded of soul, and Brian was one with them.

On the first full day of the pilgrimage, Brian waited in line at the Grotto, doing whatever required assignments were expected of him and others, practical or spiritual, to "get 'er done on schedule in Lourdes."

Brian was surprised to hear the sweet voice of the Blessed Mother in the Grotto. She told him, "I know what it is to lose your only son. I am holding your son here, as I held mine there." Brian thought of the *Pietà*—the famous sculpture by Michelangelo in St. Peter's in the Vatican that depicts the Blessed Mother tenderly holding her Son after He was taken down from the Holy Cross. Standing in the Grotto, Brian *knew* Our Lady was holding his son—and that she understood. Brian was changed right then and there. All of the anger drained out of him, making room for holy consolation and healing. His only son, his fishing and hunting buddy, his best friend, was not coming back to this world. He knew that. But now Brian was consoled in the comfort that the Mother of God was tenderly holding his son in her loving arms until they would be united together again in the happiness of the other world.

Brian was still bereaved, but his grieving was transformed into holy grieving. He came back to his lifelong Catholic Faith. The Sacraments of Reconciliation and the Holy Eucharist fortified a suffering father to endure grieving for his son and the traumatic impact of his war-zone deployment so soon afterward.

The pilgrimage was an astounding combination of veterans who understood one another and had come together in a holy place of healing. They somehow became the needed strength to help each other accept grace and healing. The priest was an active-duty colonel who was only days out of the field, with sand still in the creases of his uniform, fresh from his Operation Iraqi Freedom deployment. He truly knew what they were suffering. Father was on duty on behalf of the Divine Physician with the sacraments. Many of the wounded veterans had been away from the Church since their deployments. Many were deployed multiple times, and for extended periods. After consciously disconnecting from family to be able to separate from them in the first place, reconnecting back home with them post-deployment created stressed marriages and distanced relationships. The chaplain was as busy as the medical practitioner, and they worked well together, in synchronized tandem. Brian tended to medical supportive-care needs and listened to interior wounds and then made referrals to Father for spiritual needs. The priest did the same, but the other way around. One at a time, each veteran found interior healing and peace—*every single one*. It was amazing—miraculous graces abounded!

Boarding the plane to go back home, Brian promised he would return the following year to help more veterans have a holy experience of healing in the Grotto. Once in Paris, he called the pilgrimage director, who had stayed back in Lourdes with the volunteers to clean out after the pilgrimage departed. Brian's voice was so pleasant and the conversation so friendly that she did not immediately realize that it was Brian, the brisk officer, calling. When she asked who it was, he replied, "Brian!" She asked, "Brian who?" His voice and temperament were completely unrecognizable! That is how profound a change had taken place in Brian in just one week in Lourdes. When he returned to his medical command, his sergeant, the medic with whom he was deployed to Afghanistan, suggested that the command send more wounded warriors to France. As a Muslim, he had never heard of Lourdes and did not know the Lady there. All he knew was that Brian was broken and that they couldn't fix him, but that the Lady in Lourdes sent him back from France fixed. The Protestant Army General did not know about Lourdes or the Lady either, but seeing Brian restored, he encouraged the wounded to make the journey the following year. The Lourdes Volunteers Supportive Needs Military Pilgrimage became known as the "proven-effective program" to offset suicide and for healing the stubborn interior wounds of war.

Brian made a commitment to return and to invite more military medical volunteers to help. In doing so, he made going on pilgrimage possible for hundreds of wounded warriors, veterans, service members, and military families. Brian especially took veterans suffering with PTSD to the Grotto—night or day—to find peace and healing, just as he himself had found. His faith restored at Lourdes, Brian helped many of his brother and sister veterans find healing recovery and restored faith in the Grotto, under the loving gaze of the Mother of God.

> *We are not promised the happiness of this world but of the other world.* (The Immaculate Conception to Bernadette in the Grotto)

Brian without Lab Coat

Brian has kept his promise to be a Medical Director for Supportive Care Needs Pilgrimages and continues to make it possible for anyone who needs a healing pilgrimage to Lourdes to go there.

Chapter 18

Frightened to Fearless

Jenna's Family

Members of the United States Navy Explosive Ordnance Disposal (EOD) Teams don't scare easily. It truly can be said that deep-sea divers work well under pressure. In fact, with an increase of ten atmospheres at one hundred meters of water depth, compared with the surface, special-operations scuba divers can rightfully boast that they can handle ten times more pressure than landlubbers. If that isn't enough for sailor bragging rights, add being a petite woman. Words such as *gutsy*, *amazing*, and *heroic* surface to describe Kathy, one of only a handful of the first female EOD officers in the United States Navy. To be exact, at the time, she was one of only five women out of 180 officers.

Growing up mostly barefoot as a girl in the Florida Keys, Kathy was as comfortable in the water with her flippers as she was on land with her flip-flops. Most people escape to the barrier islands to put the farthest distance possible between themselves and their past or, ideally, to disappear far away from others. If they tried to get any farther away, they would fall into the ocean. That is why Kathy's mom moved them to the southern tip of Florida—to get away from that past and to start a future anew. As a baby, Kathy and her brother spent several months in the care of trustworthy nuns while her mother relocated and stabilized their transition to southern Florida. The kindly sisters agreed to keep the two children, but only if they were first baptized Catholic. Kathy's mother consented but never found a reason while they were growing up to mention to them anything about their Baptism, or religion, or God. As a result of this flip-flop island upbringing, when Kathy enlisted as a sailor and went to a Boot Camp Sunday event, she was the only sailor who did not know the words of the Lord's Prayer.

A naval career seemed like a natural progression to guarantee that Kathy would always be near sea or shore. Military life is disciplined and structured, something she craved as the child of a mother drawn to a carefree lifestyle. This dichotomous desire and combination made Kathy an ideal sailor and a future naval officer, eventually rising to the rank of commander. She had a perfect balance of orderly consistency and comfortableness with the unpredictable chaos at sea. Despite the stability and force of a naval military, there is no controlling, commanding, or taming a wild ocean. Navy life proved to reflect her adult stability superimposed upon her bohemian childhood. Kathy knew how to roll with whatever waves swelled before her, big or small. Anyone who meets Kathy is surprised by how genuinely sweet and gentle she is as they try to imagine her expertly dismantling a ticking explosive device underwater, under pressure. In addition to her unique skills and impressive accomplishments, Kathy is surprisingly modest, sincerely humble, and noticeably attractive.

While stationed in Texas on the Gulf of Mexico, the seafaring gal met a grounded geologist and genius guitar guy, Rob. As his true first passion, he brought his music with him to college as he was picking up a degree in geology in between guitar-playing gigs. Geologists are scientists, exacting diagnosticians who study landslides, earthquakes, floods, and volcanic activity. Most people who study the solid, liquid, and gaseous matter that makes up our planet are also strong environmentalists with keen insight into the delicate balance and dependency that exists between the earth and its creatures, especially us humans. It is much the same with ocean goers' inherent love for the water and all its inhabitants. Rob was drawn to both sea and shore, specifically to the impact of oil spills on coastlines. He honed his career with a desire to preserve the shoreline and the entire environment, hoping to protect the delicate balance of nature with the needs of mankind.

Rob was perfect for Kathy. He was a cool guitar player who was grounded by land and science, with the added attraction of having deep faith. It was no wonder Rob was captivated with Kathy when they met. She was equally charmed by him: the sea-loving gal was instantly smitten with the land-loving geologist, exactly in the way they say opposites attract. Rob loved the earth's vast surfaces and studying them as much as Kathy equally loved the oceans and exploring them. They were the perfect complement to each other—an ideal surf-and-turf couple!

From a gulf apart, Rob and Kathy met when, years into her career, she was stationed on the coast of Texas. She attended a social activity for singles: a nondenominational church service with impressive music. Rob had agreed to play guitar for his brother in the congregational band. Rob and Kathy met at dinner afterward and started dating immediately. They were both in their late thirties, knew what they wanted in a marriage partner, and were quickly convinced they had found it in each other. Rob played guitar at his parish for the youth Mass, and he invited Kathy to hear him play. Kathy was instantly drawn to the holiness of the Catholic Mass and to Rob, with his deep faith. As soon as they became serious about their future together, the new couple met with Rob's parish priest. The pastor inquired whether Kathy had been baptized. That is when Kathy spoke to her mother and was surprised to learn that she had been baptized as a baby while with the nuns—*and baptized Catholic*!

The wedding was planned. Rob and Kathy agreed it was worth the years of waiting to have found each other as they were nearing forty. They took their vows seriously and felt extremely blessed. They were both happy to be married in the Catholic Church. Not long after leaving the altar, they were thrilled to discover that Kathy was pregnant. During their first year as husband and wife, Kathy entered RCIA, the study in preparation to enter the Church, growing in her new Faith and her first pregnancy. She received the Sacraments of Holy Communion and Confirmation at the Easter Vigil Mass, holding their precious one-week-old daughter, Jenna.

Three weeks later, Kathy surprisingly spent her first Mother's Day in the hospital with her beautiful baby girl. At just four weeks old, Jenna suffered a serious seizure. There is absolutely no way an unsuspecting parent can be prepared for an unexpected first-ever seizure. It is a total shock, and totally unnerving. For anyone who has never witnessed someone having a seizure, it is frightening to stand by, initially not realizing what is happening and helpless to intervene. To see your own precious infant seizing is terrifying, especially the first time it happens. It's heart-stopping. It's as if, on a sunny day without a cloud in the sky, and without warning, lightning were to strike a sweetly innocent baby.

Jenna was eventually diagnosed with idiopathic seizures. Rob and Kathy explored how best to care for her. They decided that Rob would become a full-time dad, sacrificing his career. In just a few short years, Kathy would conclude her twentieth year of military service and retire with full benefits at the full rank of commander. They would then swap roles: Kathy would stay home with Jenna while Rob would return to his professional geological career. But, before completing her twenty-year hitch, Kathy was deployed to Kabul, Afghanistan. Kathy cried— not because she was being deployed to a Middle East war zone but because of the painful six-month separation from her precious, fragile, firstborn baby. Military service members are admirably tough, indestructible, and duty-ready, but they are also beloved family members with deep ties and attachments. Their sacrifices are incomprehensible and unimaginable to most people who will never experience prolonged time apart from family and home, much less lengthy separations under extremely dangerous conditions or harsh circumstances, with the added worry of family turmoil at home. Because they had strong faith and a marriage built upon a mature and stable foundation, Kathy and Rob endured their heavyhearted half year apart as well as any young family with a seriously ill child.

Jenna's seizures increased relentlessly in frequency and intensity. Upon completion of Kathy's overseas assignment, the Navy compassionately transferred her back to Texas to be near their family support. Their parish priest adamantly said, "Go to Lourdes!" Then Rob's father, a lifelong faithful Catholic, insisted that they take little Jenna to Lourdes, offering to send the family as his gift to them. They went through the process of obtaining a baby passport for Jenna. They were packed and ready to fly the next day when Jenna aspirated fluid into her lungs. She was admitted to the hospital the night before departure, abruptly canceling their dream trip to the holy shrine in France.

In the years that followed, two more babies quickly arrived, both seizure-free. Kathy retired honorably after two decades of distinguished service. For their growing family with a medically fragile child, travel seemed too difficult, and a trip to Lourdes was eventually deemed impossible. Jenna developed multiple health issues. She was diagnosed as a quadriplegic, nonverbal juvenile with a severe seizure disorder. She would never walk or talk or grow up the way her brother and sister would. She required twenty-four-hour total care. Most days, it took both Rob and Kathy together to properly provide care for all three children. Nurses were brought in to help with Jenna, but sometimes constantly rotating nurses seemed more like work than help. At that time, private-duty and home-care nurses were becoming increasingly difficult to find.

Life became stressful and often downright scary. Jenna was susceptible to choking and could easily aspirate at any time. Bedridden, she was at risk of pneumonia. Her condition was scarier than underwater demolitions for her commander mom or environmentally catastrophic oil spills for her geologist dad. Having a child like Jenna is not for fainthearted parents. Their faith had taught Rob and Kathy intellectually that God never allows us to encounter more than we can handle, but they often felt as though they were dangling precariously just at the precise edge of what they could manage. Sometimes something can make us so fearful that we can forget we are always in God's loving, providential hands. "Jesus, I trust in You!" may become the only soothing mantra for frantic, frazzled parents and family members. We may also need the additional support of our Heavenly Mother to gently build up our weakening trust, *through her perfect trust.*

Years went by for Rob and Kathy and the children. Everyday life became as routine as could be expected with unpredictable life-threatening seizures as a reality for them. Most days were filled with medical appointments for Jenna in heroic attempts to gain some type of management over her seizure disorder. And a disorder does just that: it disorders any semblance of routine or orderly family life. The ongoing threat of seizure and the seizures themselves literally seize the normalcy from the development of the child along with normal family expectations.

The two younger children entered Catholic school, and the family struggled on, but Lourdes was always in the back of their minds. They never stopped longing to go to the Grotto. Then, one day a pilgrimage became a possibility. Our Lady of Lourdes Hospitality North American Volunteers offers Supportive Needs Pilgrimages with medical volunteers who provide supportive care throughout the international travel and the stay in France. Extensive planning of every detail is carefully and thoughtfully addressed. Even so, the idea of traveling anywhere, especially out of the country, was daunting for Kathy and Rob. But, encouraged by relatives, friends, and priests, the entire family finally left home for Lourdes.

Rob and Kathy found the medical volunteers to be amazingly helpful. The care they provided for Jenna was a loving gift of their skills, talents, and years of experience assisting the sick and the suffering to Lourdes. This allowed Rob and Kathy the gift of spending time with each other and with each of their children. The week unfolded in a series of graces that strengthened and renewed their faith. Both parents became confident in God's will for each of them and for all of their children, especially Jenna. The family returned home rested, relaxed, and peaceful, filled with joy.

The family felt called to return to the Grotto again the following year, despite the financial sacrifice. They were not disappointed. Our Lady always has a grace waiting for everyone who comes to visit her in the Grotto, each and every time. Sure enough, the graces continued to flow for the parents and the children, for a second time. They were a different family returning to Lourdes—less stressed, happier, quicker to smile, and faster to laugh. It hadn't become easier to be the parents of a child with intense care needs; it was simply easier to carry their responsibilities lightened by the power of faith and the grace of God. There will always be risks for a child with intense medical needs, like Jenna. Parents like Rob and Kathy will always be justifiably concerned. But after Lourdes, it was as if their constant fear became more manageable as their faith strengthened into a profound trust of being totally in God's hands.

For Rob and Kathy, entrusting Jenna to the Mother of God and her Son in the Grotto removed some of the excessive weight of responsibility by replacing weary worry with trustful surrender. Faith and fear are the flip sides of the same coin. At any moment, only one face of the coin can be seen from a single, straightforward angle. Focusing on faith and flipping fear behind sounds noble, like a quick or easy spin, but it is hard for parents of young children facing dangerous or severe life-threatening health issues. In Lourdes, Rob and Kathy were able to focus on their faith, diminishing their fears. They were changed as parents and transformed as a family.

A year after returning home, Rob, Kathy, and their three children were invited to speak in Rome at the Vatican to share their experiences in Lourdes. Their son was asked by a Vatican official what had happened to their family in Lourdes. He was articulate for his age, explaining, "Before Lourdes, my parents were always afraid for Jenna, and that made me and my little sister always scared. After Lourdes, my parents weren't afraid all the time, so me and my sister are not so scared anymore. We are happy at home; we laugh and do more things and go more places." When his little sister was asked what the difference was before and after Lourdes, she said, "We have lots of statues of Mary everywhere in our house now, little and BIG statues, all kinds of statues of Our Lady of Lourdes—*she is everywhere*! And we are happy because she is with us always and watches over us all the time, so we don't have to worry anymore." The Monseigneur in the Vatican said he understood and reminded them that they are always safe with Mary.

Fear not, for I am with you, be not dismayed, for I am your God; I will strengthen you, I will help you, I will uphold you with my victorious right hand. (Isa. 41:10)

Fearless Family of Faith

The family continues to grow in faith. Rob has returned to work as a geologist while Kathy cares for their children at home. Kathy became the Chairwoman of the Supportive Needs Advisory Committee for Our Lady of Lourdes Hospitality North American Volunteers. The family plans to return to Lourdes someday.

Chapter 19

Mother Knows Best

Colleen and Maris

Colleen became a social worker because she loved helping people. It was not just what she did; it was who she was. After she was diagnosed with breast cancer, she continued helping others by listening to the worries and woes of the women she met while undergoing her own treatment. She officially retired with her cancer metastasis diagnosis, but Colleen continued her unofficial job of helping others, because she was always doing something good for someone else. She had been sober for thirty years, and this personal struggle had helped to hone her perseverance and steely determination, as well as her compassion for those who faced addictive challenges. When balanced with her considerate kindness, her gutsy resolve made Colleen the ideal advocate and adviser to many. Countless people benefited from her professional and personal care.

As her body surrendered to her advancing disease, Colleen became increasingly aware of her spiritual well-being. One day after Mass, a friend offered to go to Lourdes with her. Colleen and this friend, Louise (everybody called her Lou), both believed that our Heavenly Mother knew best what Colleen needed—because moms most often do. Colleen discussed the international travel and spiritual journey with her oncologist and was encouraged by her physicians to go to Lourdes. Colleen was ready for a trip in June, until her next round of test results arrived. Her doctor said June was no longer possible and advised her to move up her trip to May. Later, additional scans revealed that May was no longer feasible. By March, her physician said April was her only option. Time was running out for a pilgrimage to France, and for Colleen.

Most people who are ill or disabled think they cannot travel internationally or domestically, especially if they use a ventilator or oxygen, receive infusion therapy or kidney dialysis, or are immobile. Following the guidelines given by primary care providers, dedicated volunteer medical teams of Lourdes Volunteers create detailed plans to ensure that what is needed can be available for transatlantic travel and throughout a person's stay in France. Despite her implanted port and medications that greatly weakened her, Colleen wanted to go to Lourdes. A mini pilgrimage was already in quick planning, specially created for a large family with two children recently diagnosed with a debilitating incurable terminal disease. That type of pilgrimage can never be arranged far in advance. Our Lady reveals whom she wishes to bring together in the Grotto—just in time. In God's time, graces arrive precisely as plans come together. Colleen was able to join an impromptu April Easter family pilgrimage.

Her volunteer nurse was a recently retired full-bird colonel who was still adjusting to walking into a room without everyone jumping to attention. The Mother of God was gently weaving together a few particular ladies to meet for an exceptional week through an extraordinary little girl, her sweet brother, and their amazing family. Our Lady of Lourdes has proven time and again to be expertly adept at this type of gracious, intricate manifest handiwork. She masterfully threads together people from afar onto her Lourdes travel roster to receive the blessings from her Son awaiting them at Lourdes, in a delicate list of sweet graces.

Traveling to Lourdes is tiring, even for a person who is healthy. Domestic flights to the pilgrimage gateway city for international departure preload fatigue long before the draining transatlantic flight. For the seriously ill, this travel is beyond exhausting. And, as Colleen said with a smile, "Cancer seizes and squeezes every ounce of energy out of you!" Drifting off to sleep on the last flight in the smaller aircraft from Paris to Pau (the airport not far from Lourdes), Colleen sensed the same exhaustion in a woman nearby. They were both weak, and they smiled knowingly at each other whenever their eyes met.

Passengers in wheelchairs are the last to deplane flights because it is easier for people in transfer chairs to exit an empty aircraft. As they waited for wheelchair assistance, Colleen felt bad for the woman near her. Colleen was accompanied by a friend, a nurse, and a pilgrimage leader dedicated to helping just her. The other woman was by herself. The two women were immediately linked by a heightened spiritual awareness perceived only by those who have intimately known serious illness and physical suffering firsthand. Although unplanned, Maris was pleased to be stopping by Lourdes on her way home to Nigeria. She was just too exhausted to be excited. Colleen reverted into her helping professional self as the two women waited together. She introduced herself, and Maris responded with a musical accent. Both ladies, weak in their airline wheelchairs, were going to the Grotto for the first time. Left unsaid, but understood, was that it would also be their only time. The conversation faded as Maris did, depleted from her long travels and treatments. Colleen immediately enlisted the pilgrimage leader to assist Maris. "Would it be possible to give my new friend a lift to Lourdes?" Colleen's smile was impossible to refuse.

Once seated inside the private ground transport to Lourdes, Maris produced a scrap of paper with the scribbled address where she had been referred to stay. It was so far from the Sanctuary that it was obvious to the pilgrimage leader that Maris should not go or stay there. Besides, she didn't have a wheelchair. The chair she was using had been lent to Lourdes Volunteers for her by the airport staff and was for use only in the terminal. How was she going to find a wheelchair in France and make her way to the Grotto from such a long distance away, by herself and without speaking French? If the family with the young children was uncomfortable having someone unknown join the small group at the last minute, Lourdes Volunteers would arrange to room Maris on another floor with a few volunteers dedicated exclusively to care for her. The young parents could see that Maris needed help. It was as if God and Our Lady had placed Maris in their midst. They quickly prayed to discern that she should join the pilgrimage. It was similar to the way Colleen and Louise had signed on, just without any advance notice or planning.

Maris was invited to join the small pilgrimage family. She was humbled by the offer and, truthfully, too tired to resist. The Advance Volunteer Team waiting in Lourdes was asked to prepare a room for Maris while the little family pilgrimage made its way from the airport to the Accueil Notre-Dame. The volunteers knew that Lourdes Volunteers did not have the funds to pay for Maris. There was no time to make appeals for donations—and there was no time to hesitate to help her. Lourdes Volunteers trusted in God's providential care. If God had sent someone in need, He would surely send all that was needed too.

After Maris rested, the volunteer nurse made a Supportive Care Plan with her. Maris revealed that she was the oldest known adult survivor of childhood sickle cell anemia. Maris's mother had instilled indebtedness to the Blessed Mother in her as thanksgiving for her novel and miraculous survival. Maris had received two bone marrow transplants at a prestigious American hospital. She had just left the

United States after another lengthy hospitalization. She said she felt that Lourdes was a good place to go on her way home. Maris had only a small bag. She was without luggage or complaint. The volunteers pulled together all Maris would need for her time in Lourdes. Maris was too tired to eat, so she slept from her arrival through the next morning. She believed that all she needed was provided to her by the grace of God, through His Mother's intercession. And she was moved to tears by God's generosity and His Mother's graciousness, which she was receiving through the volunteers in Lourdes.

Colleen wanted to rest, but she could not keep anything down. She asked to be hydrated through her port, refusing hospitalization. She insisted that she had not traveled that far to stay in a French hospital room. She was in a hospital bed in the same building overlooking the Grotto where Pope John Paul II (since canonized, St. John Paul II) stayed when he was in his wheelchair at Lourdes. She said if it was good enough for him, it was all good for her. Colleen was relieved to finally be there, just annoyed to be throwing up the only French food she had been able to eat thus far. Finally, she was able to sleep after she received a port infusion of intravenous fluids.

Every pilgrimage truly is special, made unique by each person and moment encountered. This pilgrimage turned out to be extraordinarily special. Maris was delightful, and Colleen was thrilled to be surrounded by wonderful, faithful people who blended into a little holy family pilgrimage. After praying in the Grotto, with the encouragement of her pilgrimage nurse, Colleen decided she should prepare her soul in this holy place to be ready to meet God whenever He called her, which would be soon, according to her doctors back home. She had not been to the Sacrament of Reconciliation in years. She began to prepare a list of her sins but deemed her list insufficient and incomplete to take into the confessional. She said she needed to be fully wiped clean before her nearing beatific encounter. She felt that a thorough list was required, but preparing such a detailed litany consistently became overwhelming. A priest would be helpful. But Colleen had to first get to a priest.

Colleen confided in her assigned pilgrimage nurse. She had every justification for delaying her Confession from morning until afternoon, or until the next day, or the day after, until she would likely run out of days. Colleen painstakingly prepared and redid her never-ending imperfect lists but could not complete the task. There was a kind Franciscan friar on the pilgrimage, but Colleen wanted an anonymous "hit-and-run" Confession to offload the sins of her entire life. She was worried that she was dying trying. Her faithful nurse insisted on helping Colleen to the Chapel of Reconciliation, where numerous "unknown" priests were ready and waiting to absolve contrite souls they would never see again. In the Sanctuary, priests who speak different languages are stacked in a saintly lineup row for an anonymous holy "hit-and-run" sacramental encounter. It was ideal, if only she could get there.

Weary and fatigued, Colleen had made the journey all the way to Lourdes. She wanted the consolation that everyone she loved would be all right when she was no longer in this world to care for them. She wanted to put everything in order, especially her eternal soul. St. Bernadette went to Confession after going to the Grotto, and so did Colleen, eventually. First, she went to the Baths, where she emerged refreshed and peaceful. She was then ready for the Sacrament of Reconciliation, which is what she needed eternally for the other world, more than a physical cure, limited to this brief lifetime. Through this generous sacrament, Colleen was given the gift of peace, a true peace that penetrates radiated bones and failing bodies, filling the soul to eternal capacity.

The pilgrimage seemed to go quickly, like a dream. Maris had to depart one day earlier than Colleen and the rest of the group.

Maris said she was loved beyond measure, just as St. Bernadette was quoted as saying about how best to love. At first, she was sad to be spending Easter without her family back home in Africa. Now, she was joyful to have spent Easter with her newfound family in Lourdes.

While checking in at the airport, the leader again noticed that Maris had only a passport and a very small carry-on bag. Strangely, she had no checked luggage. She had a series of mismatched individually ticketed one-way flights. Obviously, something had gone wrong with both her travel reservation and her luggage before she had arrived in Lourdes.

Maris explained what had happened. She was exhausted from her American hospitalization and had fallen asleep in the Paris airport while waiting to check her bags on a different airline for her return flight to Africa. She had missed her flight. When she woke up, all her belongings were gone—absolutely everything! Her luggage, her carry-on, and her briefcase with her phone, her laptop, her medical records, and her bank card were nowhere in sight. The only things she had left were the clothes she was wearing and her passport, her medications, and a little cash that was in the small bag she had fallen asleep clutching as a makeshift pillow under her travel-weary head. In her other hand, she held her rosary beads, her only remaining earthly possession. Airport security doubted that her belongings would be recovered. Besides, she did not want to accuse anyone of stealing her things or send someone to jail in France. With extraordinary charity and forgiveness, Maris said that whoever took her things must have needed them more than she did.

The airline personnel in Paris were moved with compassion and tried to help her make the best of her unfortunate situation. All flights to Abuja were sold out for days. It was the busy Easter holiday week with European school breaks. Without access to more money at home, it would be a challenge for her to stay in Paris. The agent behind the counter tried to help:

"Do you know anyone in France?" the agent asked Maris. "Only Our Lady of Lourdes. I have never been there, but I know her!" Maris said.

"We have just one seat left on the flight to Pau. Would you like to go to Lourdes?" the agent asked.

In a single moment, Maris considered whether she should stay in Paris and go to her embassy in an attempt to find or replace her belongings or accept the offer of the kind agent to fly to Lourdes. The round-trip ticket was exactly the only amount of cash she had left.

"You must decide quickly—that plane is about to board!" the agent added hastily. "I think you should take this ticket, *and go*," the agent whispered, smiling, urging Maris.

In faith, Maris decided to get on that plane without a plan, money, or luggage.

"Yes! I will wait in holy Lourdes for my return to Nigeria," Maris answered.

On the Internet, the agent found a place for her to stay and hurriedly wrote down the address on a slip of paper. That is how Maris had flown tearfully to the South of France, trusting that her Heavenly Mother would be waiting for her, anticipating her arrival, like a good mom who knows her every child's needs before the child knows them. On that flight, Maris met her new friend, Colleen, and was treated like a princess in Lourdes, which she called the home of her Heavenly Mother, the Queen of Heaven. Maris was wheeled, fed, loved, and cared for as a beloved daughter would be tended to by her holy mother on a surprise visit home. Maris cried, saying, "Lourdes truly is Heaven on Earth!"

Colleen returned home with the sins of her life forgiven, surrendered in peace. The Mother of God really did know what she needed. Colleen was hospitalized the day after returning home from France. Lou, her friend and traveling companion, remained true to her to the end. Colleen died two weeks later, her soul having been well prepared in Lourdes.

The colonel nurse who helped get Colleen to Confession eventually grew to like entering a room without everyone standing at attention for her. She humbly returned home and followed the example of St. Bernadette by making the Sign of the Cross thoughtfully and reverently as an act of faith and a genuine prayer in and of itself. The little family with two sick children received a special grace, especially the parents. The volunteers, especially the university students, said that they felt as though they received more than they gave. Maris experienced love without measure, as St. Bernadette would say.

After returning home, Maris sent a gift to cover the pilgrimage expenses for someone like her who might unexpectedly show up anywhere along the way on a Lourdes pilgrimage, to ensure that the graces continually flow. And they do.

I was sick and you took care of me. (Matt. 25:36, NRSVCE)

Holy Travelers

Through Our Lady of the Grotto, in God's time, Colleen and Maris became close friends as forever Lourdes sisters in Christ. Colleen and Maris were both eternally grateful for their holy experiences in Lourdes.

Chapter 20
Holy Hurricane Rescue
Mister Earl

The Ninth Ward has been known as the epicenter of the African American community for half a century in New Orleans (NO), Louisiana (LA), affectionately called "NOLA" by locals. The neighborhood once flourished but sadly descended, over time, into an area of intense and continuous struggle against poverty and crime. Still, the community maintained the familiarity of a tight-knit neighborhood. Despite the statistics supporting its bad reputation, longtime residents bristled against outside criticism of their beloved historical Ninth Ward.

Five miles away, in the nearby Seventh Ward, is a highly regarded all-boys school everybody calls "St. Aug." St. Augustine Preparatory School was founded in 1951 to provide a classical education to black students from local Catholic families. The school was known to be strict and scholarly from its very beginnings. Students and graduates were revered as intelligent, disciplined, and well-rounded young gentlemen, each respectfully called "Mister." Ninety percent of St. Aug graduates were accepted into the most elite private higher-education institutions in the United States, headed for professional success.

In 1969, one year after the tragic assassination of Martin Luther King Jr., the prestigious Harvard University actively recruited and accepted one hundred black students for the incoming class, including a few bright young men from St. Aug. Ivy League schools soon discovered that the brilliant New Orleans students were ideal collegiate candidates who excelled academically.

Earl was lured away to study at Harvard as one of the one hundred among more than twelve hundred freshmen arriving on the esteemed Cambridge campus, near Boston. Earl earned his degree in English. He was and still is a lover of words, writing, literature, and books. Later in life, he chose to pursue his other life's passion and began a second career as a chef. More than thirty years later, Earl moved back to the Ninth Ward to teach English at his alma mater, to cook, and to be closer to his aging mother and his extended family.

A humble man of faith, Earl is a big guy who could easily be mistaken for a professional football player. His personality is as sweet and gentle as his physique is large. Nearing middle age, he noticed his knees bothering him. Standing for long hours at a stove or in a classroom or walking long distances became painfully difficult. In June 2005, Earl made a pilgrimage to Lourdes with his St. Aug classmate and his wife. The three of them were at Harvard together and had remained good friends since graduation.

Walking during the pilgrimage became so painful that by the end of the week, Earl reluctantly ended up riding in a *voiture,* one of the blue rickshaw-like vehicles unique to Lourdes, designed to transport pilgrims in need of assistance around the vast hundred-plus-acre Sanctuary. One week in Lourdes and one day in a voiture earned Earl a glimpse of the humility and struggles St. Bernadette lived through in Lourdes and afterward as a religious sister in Nevers. He was especially drawn to St. Bernadette. It could have been her illiteracy, her poverty, or her humble simplicity that drew him in. It was possibly the French connection between Lourdes and New Orleans or simply a grace gifted to Earl. For whatever reason, he latched onto petite St. Bernadette as his patroness. Big Earl and little St. Bernadette were spiritually bonded in the Grotto. Harvard graduate and educator Earl had found his unlikely role model in a holy new Heavenly friend, the formally uneducated St. Bernadette Soubirous.

Earl carried around a good-size book touted to be the most accurate writings of St. Bernadette and the Lourdes apparitions. Originally an eight-volume set available only in French, a sizable condensed single volume was eventually published and translated into English. *Bernadette Speaks*, written by the late priest Père René Laurentin, is revered as the most widely respected work about Lourdes and St. Bernadette. Earl was continually reading the hefty book and never seemed to tire of learning more about his newfound spiritual sister. He returned home from France filled with Lourdes and St. Bernadette.

Earl, along with everybody else, had no idea that Hurricane Katrina was about to drastically change his world and the Ninth Ward forever.

That week, a neighbor asked Earl to keep an eye on his elderly mother over the weekend. It was just in case she needed something, and he was told that the independent lady seldom did. Earl's neighbor would be gone for only a few days. He felt better knowing someone would be close to his *Mam.* That's truly how the Ninth Ward traditionally was from within. Longtime neighborly residents had a willingness to lend a helping hand to each other, especially someone senior. Although Earl did not know the neighbor or his mother, he agreed to check in on her, in keeping with centuries of cultural respect for elders and the long-standing ward loyalty in the NOLA African American community.

Practically speaking, there are more warnings of hurricanes than there are actual hurricanes coming ashore. After all, hurricanes are wildly erratic, which is what makes them so scary. Many hurricanes divert course away from their predicted trajectory, hitting some other soon-to-be-sorry location, while some lose intensity in transitioning from water to land. Just as unexpectedly, other storms blow off their projected course or abruptly turn back out to sea. When a major hurricane does make landfall, mayhem frequently wreaks havoc that is unimaginable to anyone who has never before seen the devastating aftermath of a destructive storm. Earl decided to leave when the evacuation warnings initially flashed across his television screen. He said he knew better than to sit this one out.

A man of his word, Earl went to help his neighbor's mother, just as promised. He explained that they must leave together. She was a stoic, strong-willed woman and refused to budge from her apartment. She had lived through storms and warnings before, having survived some of the deadliest hurricanes that had ravaged her beloved New Orleans hometown. Her childhood was filled with stories of the 1915 hurricane, which destroyed twenty-five thousand buildings just a few years before she was born. She knew all about the infamously treacherous NOLA "dames;" she survived Audrey, Betsy, and Category 5 Camille. The feisty lady flat-out refused to leave her lifetime of belongings and family memories. She didn't have much, but she treasured what she had. There was no convincing her to leave her apartment. A man of integrity, Earl would not abandon her, despite the apparent impending danger to both of them.

Hurricanes have plagued the Ninth Ward since long before it was settled by the French in the early nineteenth century. The ward is located on a lower indentation of former bayou land that dips six feet below sea level. The area is bordered by a system of engineered levees and is naturally subject to flood damage when water gets trapped within it, without an outlet for relief. This is how locals came to refer to New Orleans as "The Bowl." Hurricane surges can reach as high as thirty feet, easily breaching the ten-foot-high protective levees. Once submerged underwater, the pumps drown. Once failed, the pumps are unable to relieve the destructive swelling, rendered useless to dispel water. Altogether, this was one dangerous mess waiting to happen. The Ninth Ward was about to endure the worst of the worst in a perfect-storm scenario.

Hurricane Katrina crossed the southeastern Florida coast as a Category 1, intensifying, fueled with the warm waters of the Gulf of Mexico. Evacuation warnings were blasted on the Internet across the coastal states days before Katrina was feared to return inland. Most people in the Ninth Ward got their information only from television news, not the Internet, as they were typically not computer users or electronic subscribers. The warnings were widely broadcast on TV screens, but only a mere forty-eight hours before the deadly disaster was about to strike.

Despite knowing and enduring its hurricane history, New Orleans' Ninth Ward remained the preferred home for neighborhood families, surviving and persevering through storms and struggles for generations. Residents would often refuse to evacuate before a serious storm warning for different reasons: fear or lack of fear, no place to go, or no way to get out. Looting had also become a common and sorry misfortune of evacuations in recent years, adding to the rationale for staying put. Earl's neighbor said she was worried that if she did not stay home to remove storm water immediately after the influx of water had subsided, mold would quickly spread in the sweltering August heat and would ruin everything the hurricane did not destroy.

"No sir, Mister," she said kindly. She was *not* leaving.

Earl's elder was not rude or sassy, just adamant. She was convinced that she could withstand any oncoming troubles. Earl was eerily unsettled. He knew they should leave. He could have gotten her out with emergency services and rescuers who came a few times, but she downright refused. She was a dignified woman of strongly confident character. She stood firm on her increasingly wet ground.

The water was rising fast. Katrina was reported as downgraded from Category 5 to Category 4, but the winds were still slamming inland at 135 miles per hour. The opportunities to get his neighbor out were decreasing as the effects of the storm increasingly intensified within the ward. Both the National Guard and the Coast Guard were searching for stranded residents as well as any hold-out stragglers who had wrongly risked staying behind. What was likely her last hope for a safe evacuation finally came to coerce her out, in God's last minute. It took Earl's firm insistence and the heroic rescuers' frantic urging to convince her that she had no choice but to leave. Ultimately, it took the United States National Guard to budge her out of her apartment! The Coast Guard carried her out as the last person to fit into the rescue boat. There was no room for Earl. He told them he would make his way out on his own.

The rescuers had no sooner left when the levees broke loose.

Earl looked around his apartment one last time. He knew he would be able to take only what he could carry. He eyed everything he owned, realizing he would never see his home or any of his belongings again. What should he take? He decided to grab one thing: his favorite book, *Bernadette Speaks.* He left his apartment, wading in dark water over three feet deep.

The water was rising rapidly, fueled by erratic, vicious winds. Weighing over three hundred pounds and towering over six feet tall, Earl was a mighty-size man. Hurricane Katrina brought enormous swells of water, powered by great gusts of wind that dwarfed his tall stature. Earl thought of St. Bernadette arriving for the first time in the Grotto. She heard a great gust of wind, but everything was still. It was not so for Earl. Katrina was howling with gusto and whipping winds. Earl was forcibly carried wherever the gale winds took him; fighting against the torrent proved impossible. Houses were knocked off their foundations, swiftly floating or tossed about to slam into equal-size massive building debris. Cars drifted down what looked like canals, the storm water concealing the roads smothered underneath. Heartbreakingly, dead bodies floated nearby Earl, in the surges of the swift current. They were almost within his grasp. He felt helpless, being unable to reach them, although he knew he couldn't do anything for them anyway.

The water was murky with a combined mixture of Gulf saltwater and Mississippi River sludge that made it impossible to see anything beneath the surface. Dangerous broken objects lurked sharply under the swirling swells. The powerful and massive wind-propelled water displaced landmarks and strangely mismatched objects, forging them together, sprinkling deadly debris like dangerous glitter that landed precariously where it did not fit or belong. Everything was out of place.

Moving down what used to be his familiar boulevard was arduous for Earl. The water rose above his waist, reaching almost chest high. Only his height made it possible to continue toward higher ground or a hoped-for chance encounter with more rescuers searching for survivors. Earl held his St. Bernadette book above his head in a futile effort to save it or hopefully to flag down someone to help him. Then the levees broke. A wall of water with deadly force knocked him so hard that his glasses flew off his head. Earl knew he would die.

Without his glasses, Earl cannot see a thing. If he could not see where he was going or the visible dangers scattered everywhere around him, there was no way he would make it out alive. He franticly grasped under the water, groping for his glasses, hoping they were floating near enough for him to retrieve them. He knew it was an impossible and unrealistic search. Earl needed a miracle. He shouted out loud, screaming into the storm:

> *Bernadette, you lost your home, and I now lost mine. You were poor, and now I am poor. But, Bernadette, you could see! I need my glasses! HELP ME, BERNADETTE! PLEASE!*

In the swirling storm, a petite hand gently grasped his bigger hand to press his glasses into his palm, firmly closing his fingers into a protective fist, securing his glasses tightly within his grip. Crying, he knew in that moment he would survive. Earl put on his glasses. At first, he could not see anything, until his eyes came into focus. He could not see his Bernadette. But he knew it was St. Bernadette Soubirous who had heard him and came to help him. He had called out to her, and she had answered. She had found him and his glasses so that he could see his way out of a stormy death-trap. Years later, a priest told Earl it was an angel who came to save him. Earl simply knows that he cried out in faith, and a Heavenly intercessor responded.

It was exhausting to move in the increasingly high water. With his vision restored, Earl became steady and was able to persevere in the afterglow of experiencing a personal miracle. Earl found rescuers, or they found him. They waited two days on a high bridge to be evacuated. His neighbor had been safely relocated to Texas to be reunited with her son. As expected, Earl lost everything in his apartment and the apartment itself, except his treasured book, drenched and completely ruined, and his glasses.

Tragically, as a result of Hurricane Katrina, 1,833 people died. Hurricane Katrina is the costliest hurricane in the history of the

United States, with an estimated $160 billion in damages along the Gulf Coast. It destroyed 850,000 homes, 350,000 vehicles, and 2,400 sea vessels.

Hurricane Katrina and its damaging aftermath are how most people outside New Orleans came to know the Ninth Ward. Sadly, catastrophic flooding, problematic evacuations, and the death toll brought national attention to the totally destroyed neighborhood. The greatest devastation and loss will always be the tragic deaths of almost 2,000 people.

As soon as he could, Earl contacted Lourdes Volunteers from the Houston shelter to which he had been evacuated. He insisted that he had to go volunteer in Lourdes, as soon as possible. He said he had to give back. He needed to honor his beloved St. Bernadette, who rescued him in the hurricane. Although he had lost all he had, he said he had much to be thankful for. Just one month later, despite Hurricane Rita, which dumped more water to further damage New Orleans, Earl flew to France. Lourdes Volunteers brought him to serve in thanksgiving. He selflessly offered his brancardier assistance for one week in the Sanctuary with St. Joseph Service. The Hospitalité Notre-Dame de Lourdes was delighted to have him in service.

More than one million people were displaced by Katrina. Earl lived in government shelters and housing provided for victims made homeless by Katrina, including the entire population of the Ninth Ward. For months, there was no phone service, electricity, or drinkable water in the ward. As Earl's elderly neighbor feared, mold destroyed much of what the water did not. It was almost a year before Earl and others were able to return to their beloved New Orleans.

Earl silently weeps whenever he tries to tell anyone about Katrina and the miraculous saving grace of his glasses through his beloved St. Bernadette. A well-spoken yet soft-spoken lover of eloquent prose and poetic literature, Earl tears up, struggling to find words to relay the profound experience of receiving a lifesaving intercession in his moment of need.

When asked about the credibility of the apparitions at Lourdes, St. Bernadette said: "Je ne suis pas chargée de vous le faire croire mais de vous le dire," which translates to "I am not made to make you believe, but to tell you." As with St. Bernadette, it is not Earl's responsibility to try to make anyone believe him but just to tell them about his Heavenly saintly friend, Bernadette Soubirous of Lourdes.

I will forget no one. (St. Bernadette Soubirous)

NOLA Friend of Bernadette

Earl still has a special devotion to St. Bernadette and Our Lady of Lourdes. He remains in the Ninth Ward. His former neighbor died a few years after Katrina. Earl plans to return to Lourdes and to visit Nevers to honor his friend St. Bernadette Soubirous.

Chapter 21

Pandemic Prayers

Nurse Lindsey

A microscopic plague shockingly changed the entire world in 2020. Almost everyone was caught off guard or was ill prepared for what would unfold across the globe. The reality is that we should always be ready to meet God, for we never know the day or the hour (Matt. 24:36). Yet, until our individual time is up, most of us, including the older and supposedly wiser among us, will always think we have just a little more time—*until we don't.*

A worldwide pandemic brought this truth to the forefront for almost all of us, the faithful as well as nonbelievers. Hospital nurses were especially impacted by this raw reality. Probably more than any other strata of life or profession, nurses had the frightening front-row seats in the rapidly unfolding human shock drama at the beginning of the second decade of the shiny new millennium. As a registered nurse, Lindsey was unknowingly positioned front and center.

Several years before the pandemic, Lindsey embarked on her new professional career. After college graduation, she found that shift work and nursing, in combination with family and social commitments, wrongly took precedence over her Sunday obligation to attend Mass. Before she knew it, an entire decade had sneaked by without her receiving the sacraments. A graduate of a Benedictine college, Lindsey knew how to "talk Catholic" when required, such as in a circle of older church ladies or in meetings at a Catholic hospital. But it was little more than talk. She began to wonder if she was really still a Catholic. She was surely still somehow a Christian but she was not practicing her religion. Lindsey had a stable existence but was feeling mediocre, or whatever describes wondering about the purpose of life. Was there more to life than just routine daily living?

Turning thirty, Lindsey was feeling somewhat alone and longing. She liked to travel, but that could also easily lack purpose. She providentially came upon a website about volunteer service missions for nurses. Lindsey called Lourdes Volunteers, dutifully "talked Catholic" in response to the questions asked, and signed up for a feel-good service week in Europe. In her mind, the South of France sounded like the ideal place to do something meaningful while technically not being on a French vacation.

During her first week serving with Lourdes Volunteers, Lindsey had a life-changing experience after the Baths with a return to the Sacraments of Confession and Holy Communion. Once she was reconciled to God through the grace of the sacraments, her life purpose was spiritually corrected to align with both how to live in this world and what to aspire to in the other world. She also found a strong spiritual link in a maternal bond with the Mother of God. Reflecting on her childhood, she realized how much she needed this motherly relationship, especially as an adult. Forever changed, Lindsey returned home to her life and to nursing.

Following a faith-driven path anchored in the sacraments was profoundly grace-filled and rich in virtue. Although she had been living a somewhat contented existence, Lindsey never realized that her life had been so mundane and tedious. It had been lacking in authentic joy and the vibrant passion of her rediscovered Catholic Faith. Surprisingly, after Lourdes, Lindsey was *"on fire" to live her faith*—like a fanatical Evangelical, she chuckled to herself! She wanted everyone who had been away from the Catholic Church to come back to find what she had discovered at Lourdes. She could hardly contain herself from sharing her newfound treasure of faith. She felt the best way to do this was to return to Lourdes in thanksgiving and again serve as a nurse, helping others who could not travel without medical supportive care.

Her next assignment as a Lourdes Volunteer was serious, demanding, and challenging. This was not because of the severely ill supportive-care pilgrim with a ventilator she was assigned to assist but because the woman's husband had been away from Confession and Communion for more than fifty years. Lindsey understood how easy it was for someone to have ten years slip by and gradually drift away from the sacraments. She imagined how easily additional decades could fall by the wayside. She rightly deduced that the longer a person stayed away, the harder it would be for him or her to find the way back. Lindsey was discreet yet helpful in guiding the good man and dedicated husband back to the confessional—the answer to the silent prayers of his ventilator-dependent wife.

That pilgrimage was filled with many graces, as were Lindsey's first and multiple subsequent pilgrimages. Each time she traveled with Lourdes Volunteers, the hand of God was revealed in the healing of a soul or a return to faith; on every pilgrimage, a Heavenly gift was given through the gentle and tender intercession of the Mother of God at the Grotto. Lindsey was enjoying the purpose, joy, and peace she had discovered in her life.

Then suddenly, a virus struck her city, her country, and the entire planet, hitting especially close to home in her own hospital facility.

In a large metropolitan city in the northeastern United States, COVID-19 hit hard and fast with a deadly learning curve. Precautionary measures were quickly implemented, including restricting visitors. Mandatory personal protective equipment (PPE) was required in the hospital. When Lindsey suited up for work, she thought she looked like a cross between an astronaut and a zombie from a scary Hollywood B-movie. As a nurse, she worried what her patients would think or fear seeing only her in her gear and unable to see their loved ones and friends without any usual face-to-face contact. The more patients were swabbed, the more positive results were reported. The spread of the deadly virus was fast and ferocious. Lindsey was soon involved in the care of more than one hundred COVID-positive patients. More than thirty would die while in her care—*seven of her patients dying in one shift alone.*

It didn't take long for the hospital employees themselves to become infected, despite all the strict precautionary measures. They were short-staffed in every area, from housekeeping to laundry to medical and administrative personnel. Brave, courageous, and persevering, Lindsey and her co-workers amazingly cared for both their patients and one another. As a nurse living her Faith, Lindsey knew how significant the sacraments were to the deathly sick, both in this world and dying into the other world. At the onset, Lindsey knew she had to find a priest willing to suit up and come in to anoint the Catholics and bless any others who would be comforted by a spiritual or religious presence.

Franciscans have been caring for the sick during every plague since their founding in the twelfth century. One healthy young priest friar in the archdiocese had volunteered to isolate himself from his brother friars for the length of the pandemic. His only contact would be with the sick whom he would go out to anoint. He learned how to put on protective gear safely and how to enter and exit isolation, as well as how to live quarantined. The heroic young priest essentially took on the austere spirituality of a hermit. In his habit, underneath foreboding protective equipment, Father looked like the friar from Mars.

Meeting Lindsey, he discovered a nurse with faith—and Lourdes Water! They became a holy dynamic duo whenever Father was allowed to enter. Father visited any patient who identified as Catholic or who asked for a priest, either for himself or herself or through family's requests. Many of the infected dying patients were older, and it was heartbreaking for them and their families to be separated physically from their loved ones. The spiritual care that Father provided was a true comfort, physically and spiritually present to them. Father suited up individually for each patient, for every separate room visit, again and again. As a holy bonus, Lindsey and her co-workers were able to go to Confession and receive Holy Communion. She wondered if these would be her last sacraments. Nobody expected what was happening or could imagine what might transpire next.

Then, unexpectedly, Father was no longer allowed in the hospital due to restrictions as health-department efforts to slow the death toll. It was an unfortunate situation for the patients, hospital staff, and priests. Suddenly, the medical team took on the added duties of spiritual care in lieu of a priest or family members. Some patients were with the limited staff for only hours, some for days. Modern technology and social media allowed visual screen contact, but the human interaction of the physicians, nurses, and aides was crucial to the isolated patients and a comfort to the separated family members.

From her service with Lourdes Volunteers, Lindsey knew that she had to serve the sick inflicted with the virus in a way that extended beyond the limitations of the physical medical care she could provide during a novel developing pandemic. Spiritual care was needed and was crucial for the eternal souls of her patients. In her American hospital facility at home, Lindsey was living the Message of Lourdes she had learned in France. Lourdes Volunteers helped fill her holy arsenal to fight the virus with rosaries, scapulars, prayer cards, Miraculous Medals, and, of course, the liquid grace of Lourdes Water. Room by room, Lindsey offered the small holy gifts to Catholic patients and any patient who wanted a little holy treasure, inspiration, prayer, or all of the above. Each person was thrilled to receive a holy gift or to have Lindsey quietly pray with or for him or her, something that did not happen before the pandemic. People who never mentioned or thought about God were suddenly asking for prayers. Lindsey realized there was truth in the First World War expression "There are no atheists in foxholes." Ironically, that saying and that war came about a century before, around the time of the Spanish flu, the last deadly worldwide pandemic before COVID.

As death entered into the global conversation, holy thoughts and prayer of any kind became acceptable, often welcomed in the sterile clinical settings previously lacking spirituality. Catholic or nondenominational, formal or spontaneous, silent or spoken aloud, the various prayers comforted not only the sick but also their families. Their families were greatly consoled to know their loved ones were not alone but, instead, were prayed for in their dying moments with the nurse present to them.

One woman arrived to the ward unconscious. While cataloging her personal belonging at admission, Lindsey discovered rosary beads. She wrapped them securely around the hand of her silent patient, praying the prayers aloud for her. Sometimes, people pray for us or for those we love, without our knowing it. Realizing this now can be a comfort for those who were unable to be with their loved ones during the pandemic. Knowing that this one nurse prayed for her patients can be a gift of comfort to all of us. Surely many more must have prayed the same way, without our knowledge.

The medical staff wasn't called upon only to provide extra care before their patients' deaths. While postmortem care was typically performed by funeral home employees in the hospital morgue, the escalating virus-exposure risks shifted this responsibility to the hospital staff. That duty was quickly assigned to the nurses. This was something Lindsey had formerly done as a young nursing student. Early on, many of the deceased were Catholics who died unable to receive the last sacraments. Lindsey remembered "Baptism by desire" and the generosity of God's divine mercy, superseding our human limitations. Our omnipotent God was surely present among them in the hospital and everywhere the pandemic was spreading. Lindsey prayed silently as she respectfully cared for the dead. She tenderly wrapped their heads and bodies with sterilized coverings, somewhat as Christ was prepared for burial in His Holy Shroud. Lindsey's nursing work became her holy work. She cared for each person, living and deceased, as she would care for Jesus Christ in His wheelchair, on His Holy Cross, or in His tomb.

One of the nurses kept a whiteboard at home and listed on it the names of patients to pray for. Along with her patients, Lindsey's name was soon added to the somber prayer list.

After about a month of extended, grueling shifts, Lindsey found herself getting short of breath with the slightest physical exertion. She tested positive for COVID. Her month-long personal battle began against the virus she had been physically and spiritually battling as a nurse. Splitting headaches, night sweats, extreme fatigue, shortness of breath, and excruciating pain with skin sensitivity ravaged her entire body. For days, she would be in the exact same position for twelve hours or more, motionless and immovable, soaking in sweat. Lindsey received dozens of phone calls and texts but was too weak to respond, unable to lift her head to have enough breath to speak. The spiritual warrior who had prayed with and for so many now had absolutely no energy to pray for herself. She had no physical or mental energy to pray rosaries, chaplets, or litanies, the very prayers she had recited so frequently at the bedside of her COVID patients. Lindsey's pain and suffering became her prayers, as she offered them for whoever was most in need.

When St. Bernadette was sick in the infirmary, she said, "The bed became my little white chapel. Then it became my cross. Then it became my crucifix when all I could do was lie in it and suffer." Like Lindsey, Bernadette preferred to be caring for the sick as her prayer; instead, being sick became her prayer.

A nurse practitioner and trusted friend cared for Lindsey at her home, bringing her medication, food, and comfort. Like her patients, Lindsey was not allowed to see her aging parents, her brother, nieces, nephews, or friends. Day by day, she slowly improved. After a month of quarantine, isolated alone at home, she recovered and was finally able to return to work and to care for others again.

Lindsey is forever changed as a Catholic nurse in a secular world. She believes that God doesn't waste anything and that suffering can help to purify souls. God does not make us suffer. She says that, in His wisdom, He can allow suffering.

Bernadette said, "If the Good God allows it, there's something good in it for me." Although the COVID-19 pandemic was the worst experience for her, Lindsey says she learned the best gifts from this life lesson. Grateful for her time in Lourdes, which helped her and ultimately so many others, Lindsey brought the Grotto to the sick when the sick could not go to the Grotto.

For this slight momentary affliction is preparing for us an eternal weight of glory beyond all comparison. (2 Cor. 4:17)

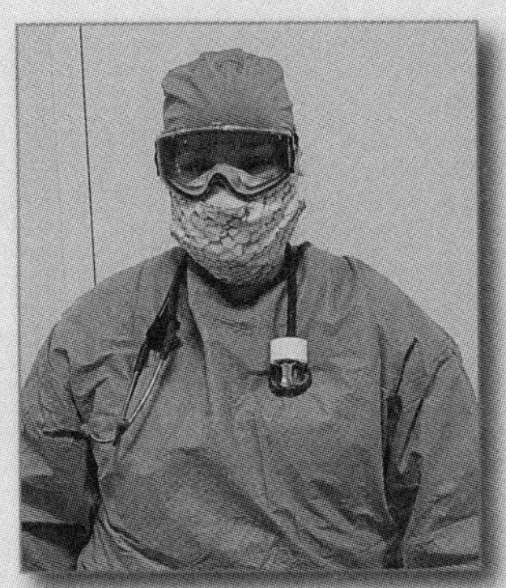

Prayerful PPE Nurse Lindsey

Lindsey recovered from COVID-19 to return to care for her patients at work, where she contracted the virus. Lindsey continues as a volunteer Head Nurse with Lourdes Volunteers to care for the sick and the suffering on pilgrimage to the holy Grotto.

Bibliography

Courtin, J. B. *Lourdes Le Domaine de Notre-Dame de 1858 à 1947*. Éditions Franciscaines Librairie-Papeterie Saint-Yves, 1947.

Diagnostic and Statistical Manual of Medical Disorders. 5th ed. Washington, DC: American Psychiatric Association, 2013.

Laurentin, René. *Bernadette Speaks: A Life of Saint Bernadette Soubirous in Her Own Words*. St. Louis, MO: Pauline Books, 2000.

Les Archives du Couvant St. Gildard, Nevers, France.

Les Archives du Sanctuaire, Lourdes, France.

Our Lady of Lourdes Hospitality North American Volunteers. https://lourdesvolunteers.org/.

Pope Francis. Message for the 54th World Communications Day. January 24, 2020.

Pope John Paul II. Encyclical Letter *Evangelium Vitae* (The Gospel of Life). March 25, 1995.

Pope Pius XI. Bull *Ineffabilis Deus*. December 8, 1854.

Sanctuaire de Notre Dame de Lourdes. https://www.lourdes-france.or.

Sanctuaire de Nevers Sainte Bernadette. Espace Bernadette Soubirous. https://www.sainte-bernadette-soubirous-nevers.com/en/.

United States Conference of Catholic Bishops. "Christian Initiation of Adults." https://www.usccb.org/beliefs-and-teachings/who-we-teach/christian-initiation-of-adults.

Glossary

AA: Acronym for Alcoholics Anonymous.

Accueil: A place of welcome; handicapped-accessible hospital-bed facility accommodations unique to Lourdes.

Accueil Marie Saint-Frai: A four-hundred-hospital-bed handicapped-accessible facility located outside St. Joseph's Gate, founded by the Congregation of the Daughters of Our Lady of Sorrows at the request of the Bishop. The facility of the Sisters of Marie St.-Frai was the first such specialized Accueil offering reasonably priced accommodations and care for those on pilgrimage.

Accueil Notre-Dame: Lourdes Sanctuary nine-hundred-hospital-bed handicapped-accessible facility overlooking the Grotto with accommodations and meals for hospitalities to bring supportive-care pilgrims on pilgrimage.

Adoration: Prayer before the Most Blessed Sacrament (the Holy Eucharist), which is usually exposed in a monstrance.

Alcoholics Anonymous: A nonprofit organization offering confidential and free daily meeting opportunities to help and support people with alcohol addiction problems or to maintain recovery, or both. The primary purpose of AA is to help alcoholics achieve and sustain sobriety.

ALS: Acronym for Amyotrophic Lateral Sclerosis, an incurable debilitating motor neuron disease (see Amyotrophic lateral sclerosis).

AMIL: Acronym for Association Médicale International de Lourdes (see further below).

Amyotrophic lateral sclerosis: Also known as ALS or Lou Gehrig's disease; an incurable debilitating nervous-system disease that affects nerve cells in the brain and the spinal cord with loss of muscle control over time (months or a few years), typically with a midlife onset.

Anointing of the Sick: The Sacrament of Sacred Anointing; a holy blessing with oils, also called Extreme Unction, administered to the faithful who are sick, dying, or in danger of death.

Apostolic Pardon: A papal blessing imparted by the Holy Father through the delegation of the bishops to priests to administer to the dying with an attached plenary indulgence for the forgiveness of temporal punishment for sins forgiven; usually, the pardon is administered with the Anointing of the Sick and the reception of Viaticum (the Last Holy Communion and last Confession with absolution).

Apostolica Penitenzieria: The oldest curial office of the Catholic Church, located at the Palazzo della Cancelleria, is known as the "tribunal of mercy," responsible for issues related to the forgiveness of sins in the Catholic Church.

Aqueró: "That" (thing) or "that one" (person) in the Bigourdan dialect of Lourdes; how Bernadette referred to the "most beautiful young lady" she saw in the Grotto.

Association: A Public Association of the Christian Faithful is a canonical Catholic entity with a purpose to be served with a specific charism, or way, to fulfill its mission.

Association Médicale International de Lourdes (AMIL): An official group of medical professionals who remain connected to the

Lourdes Sanctuary and may be called upon for consideration of cases presented as alleged or claimed cures.

Baptism: The sacrament through which "we are freed from sin and reborn as sons of God; we become members of Christ, are incorporated into the Church and made sharers in her mission: 'Baptism is the sacrament of regeneration through water in the word'" (*CCC* 1213).

Baths: Also known as the Piscines, the place in the Sanctuary where pilgrims can individually, modestly, and privately enter into a tub of slowly flowing Lourdes Water from the spring, with the assistance of volunteers.

Benediction: The solemn blessing of the faithful with the Holy Eucharist in a monstrance by a priest or deacon.

Bernadette: The French and regional-dialect female diminutive of the name Bernarde.

Bernadette Soubirous: Born Marie Bernarde Soubirous, she was the young girl favored with eighteen Heavenly visits in 1858 from the Mother of God in the Grotto in Lourdes; later professed as Sœur or Sr. Marie-Bernarde in religious life (see Bernadette Soubirous and Sœur Marie Bernarde).

Bishop: The Catholic head of a diocese as the superior responsible for the priests and the spiritual leader of the faithful, ordained by the pope as a shepherd and successor of the apostles appointed by Jesus Christ to carry on the ministries of the Church: to teach, govern, and sanctify. A bishop is formally referred to as His Excellency. In France, a bishop is called Monseigneur.

Bishop Laurence: The Most Reverend Bertrand-Sévère Mascarou Laurence, or Monseigneur Laurence, was the bishop of the Diocese of Tarbes during the time of the apparitions in 1858; as the responsible diocesan authority of the Catholic Church, he investigated the apparitions and proclaimed them as authentic Heavenly visits and pronounced seven inexplicable cures as official miracles in 1862.

Brancardier: Stretcher-bearer; St. Joseph Service male volunteers in service to lift pilgrims onto stretchers and into wheelchairs, to assist pilgrims into and out of trains and planes, to transport pilgrims on stretchers and wheelchairs, to bathe male pilgrims and children in the Baths, to guard the Grotto to maintain peace and reverent order, and to assist with the Sanctuary ceremonies, including the International Mass, the Eucharistic Procession, and the Candlelight Rosary Procession.

Bread of Angels: Holy Viaticum or the Last Holy Communion; reception of the Sacrament of the Holy Eucharist at the time of death.

Bureau des Constatations Médicales: The Medical Bureau (Office) in the Sanctuary at Lourdes where the director-physician receives pilgrims who claim to have been healed or cured; the place where the records of claims, cures, and proclaimed miracles are maintained and preserved; the place where medical professionals can join and register their presence upon arrival in Lourdes, confer about alleged claims, or consider cures as inexplicable or explainable by the strict standards imposed by the Catholic Church.

Candlelight Rosary Procession: In response to Our Lady's request during the thirteenth apparition for the "priests to tell people to come here in procession," during the pilgrimage season, from Easter to All Saints' Day and on feast days, at 9:00 p.m., thousands of pilgrims present in Lourdes gather in the Grotto with lighted candles to walk in the Procession while praying the Rosary in different languages, concluding with a priestly evening blessing from the front steps of the Rosary Basilica.

Catechesis: Religious instruction or teaching.

Catechism of the Catholic Church: *Catechismus Catholicae Ecclesiae*, known as the Catholic Catechism or the *CCC*, is a catechism of the Catholic Church for the faithful that was made available by Pope John Paul II in 1992 as a summary of concise detailed information of the form and beliefs of the Catholic Church.

Catholic: "Universal" (directly translated from Latin and Greek), most often referring to the Catholic Church or the Catholic faithful (members of the Church).

Catholic Church: The Church founded by Jesus Christ with direct succession from the apostles through to the current Holy Father in Rome.

CCC: Acronym for the *Catechism of the Catholic Church*, the compendium of the beliefs of the Catholic Faith.

Charism: A gift of the Holy Spirit for the benefit and holiness of the entire Body of Christ and the perfection of charity (*CCC* 800). As personalities are to people, charisms are to apostolates.

CMIL: Acronym for the Comité Médicale International de Lourdes.

Comité Médicale International de Lourdes (CMIL): An official group of respected physicians and scientists of varying disciplines and of different faiths, or no faith at all, that is called to examine alleged claims of cures attributed to Lourdes, the Holy Eucharist, or through the intercession of Our Lady of Lourdes or the use of Lourdes Water. Traditionally, they meet annually in Paris, under the direction and coordination of the Medical Director at Lourdes.

Communion: A sacrament instituted by Jesus Christ at the Last Supper; a consecrated Host of unleavened bread transubstantiated into the Body of Jesus Christ through the prayers of an ordained priest; also known as the Holy Eucharist.

Communion of Saints: The collective community of the faithful on Earth, the souls in Purgatory, and the saints in Heaven.

Confirmation: A sacrament increasing in us the gifts of the Holy Spirit (wisdom, understanding, knowledge, counsel, fortitude, piety, and fear of the Lord), instituted in the Upper Room, according to the Acts of the Apostles (*CCC* 1288).

Consecration: The act of setting something aside for a holy purpose with an intended commitment to God.

Convert: A person who joins a faith from no faith or a particular faith, or to join a faith or another faith or belief.

Crowned Virgin: The crowned statue of Our Lady of Lourdes in the Sanctuary of Lourdes at the Esplanade walkway, facing Rosary Square and the Rosary Basilica.

Crypt Church: *La Crypte* is the chapel consecrated in 1866, which was built at the request of Our Lady in the thirteenth apparition (March 2, 1858). It is the only church in Lourdes in which Bernadette was ever present—all other churches, chapels, and basilicas being built after she left for religious life in Nevers.

Dogma: A truth that the Catholic Church obliges as binding, revealed by God; the collective body of the teachings and doctrine of the Catholic Church (*CCC* 88).

Domain/Domaine: The Sanctuary property of Lourdes, comprising more than 100 hectares (about 250 acres) with three basilicas, twenty-five chapels, a nine-hundred-hospital-bed facility, the Medical Bureau, housing for chaplains, offices, and additional buildings to support the holy activities to welcome millions of pilgrims annually.

***Diagnostic and Statistical Manual of Mental Disorders* (*DSM* or *D.S.M.*)**: The standard classification of mental disorders used by the mental health professionals in the United States.

DSM: Acronym for the Diagnostic and Statistical Manual of Mental Disorders.

Electromyography: A diagnostic procedure to measure muscle response or electrical activity in response to a nerve's stimulation of the muscle. The test is used to help detect neuromuscular abnormalities.

EMG: Acronym for the electromyography diagnostic procedure.

Eucharist: The Holy Eucharist is the consecrated bread and wine that, by the words of Christ and the invocation of the Holy Spirit of an ordained Catholic priest, become Christ's Body and Blood (*CCC* 1333). After the Consecration, the Holy Eucharist is distributed at Mass to Catholic faithful in a state of grace. The Eucharist is also adored in a monstrance with prayer and devotions.

Eucharistic Procession: The daily solemn procession in the Sanctuary during the pilgrimage season, from Easter to All Saints' Day and on holy days throughout the winter, in which the Holy Eucharist is carried in procession under a canopy (a four-poled tent-top covering) with great honor and dignity befitting Our Lord, accompanied by music and concluding with Benediction (Eucharistic blessing).

Faithful: The followers of Jesus Christ, members of the Catholic Church.

Formation: The five-year training program of the Hospitalité Notre-Dame de Lourdes to form volunteers in service at the Lourdes Sanctuary (teaching the history of the Apparitions, the Message of Lourdes, the spirituality of the mission of service, and the practicalities of the places of the Sanctuary) to best welcome pilgrims throughout the pilgrimage season, from Easter through October, until All Saints' Day.

Grotto: (1) A grotto is a natural cave or cavern formation, usually shallow, and often in or near water. (2) The Grotto is natural cave on the outskirts of Lourdes in the southwest of France where the Mother of God appeared eighteen times to Bernadette Soubirous in 1858 and where miracles have occurred, often through the water from the spring uncovered within the Grotto by Bernadette at the direction of Our Lady of Lourdes, identifying herself as the Immaculate Conception. The Grotto was designated a holy sanctuary of the Catholic Church worthy of pilgrimage after the apparitions were approved by the local bishop of Tarbes in 1862.

Grotto replicas: Grotto recreations constructed around the world as holy places of prayer or as local or regional sites for pilgrimage, usually in the spirituality of Lourdes.

Hail Mary: The traditional Catholic prayer of the angelic acclaim and greeting of Mary in the Gospel of St. Luke (1:28) followed by a request for her intercessory prayer.

HNDL: Acronym for Hospitalité Notre-Dame de Lourdes.

Holy Communion: The Eucharist (see below) consumed by the faithful.

Holy Eucharist: The consecrated bread and wine that, by the words of Christ and the invocation of the Holy Spirit by an ordained Catholic priest, become Christ's Body and Blood (*CCC* 1333). After the Consecration, the Holy Eucharist is distributed to the faithful in a state of grace at Mass. The Eucharist is also adored in a monstrance with prayer and devotions.

Holy Mass or Mass (*Missa* in Latin): The liturgy in which the mystery of salvation is accomplished through Consecration and Transubstantiation of the Holy Eucharist, concluding with the sending forth (*missio* or mission, or commissioning) of the faithful to fulfill God's will in their daily lives (*CCC* 1332).

Holy Viaticum: The reception of Holy Communion by a sick person on his or her deathbed, usually when the Last Rites are administered.

Hospitalier (m.), Hospitalière (f.), and Hospitaller: Members of the Hospitalité Notre-Dame de Lourdes who pay their own passages and stay to offer service annually in Lourdes or members of the more than 240 diocesan, national, or religious hospitalities who bring the sick and the disabled to Lourdes.

***Hospitalité* (French) or Hospitality (English)**: (1) Catholic Public Associations of the Christian Faithful under the authority of a bishop, archbishop, or cardinal with a mission to bring the sick and disabled to Lourdes from a specific locale or with a specific charism or spirituality. (2) The gracious or generous welcome or hosting of guests, visitors, or strangers.

Hospitalité Notre-Dame de Lourdes (HNDL): A Catholic Public Association of the Christian Faithful founded in 1885, originally under the authority of the bishop of Tarbes to later become Tarbes et Lourdes. Members offer annual service in the Sanctuary of Lourdes to welcome pilgrims from around the world.

Immaculate Conception: The conception of Mary free from Original Sin in the womb of her mother (St. Anne), preserved from the stain of sin by her Son, Jesus Christ, in anticipation for her Divine Motherhood, to become the Mother of God, in a singular supernatural grace. Mary is the Immaculate Conception, this not referring to her by name or title, but who she is.

Immaculate Conception Basilica: The "Upper Church," built atop the Grotto, consecrated in 1876.

Inexplicable or unexplained cure: The scientifically proven cure of a specific illness or disease beyond (or without) medical explanation.

International Military Pilgrimage: Pèlerinage Militaire International (PMI) or Pilgrimage Military International is the annual May pilgrimage to Lourdes founded after World War II to bring peace and healing to wounded veterans, service members, military families, and war survivors.

John Paul II or Pope John Paul II or St. John Paul II: Born in Poland as Karol J. Wojtyla and later to become Pope John Paul II, he was the beloved Holy Father of the Catholic Church from 1978 until his death in 2005. He was canonized by the Catholic Church in 2014.

Last Rites: The final prayers prayed with or for a dying person in preparation for death, including the Sacraments of Anointing of the Sick, Confession or Reconciliation, and Holy Communion.

Lou Gehrig's disease: Henry Louis Gehrig is beloved as one of the greatest American baseball players. After his Yankee career was abruptly ended with his diagnosis of amyotrophic lateral sclerosis, or ALS, the disease became more commonly known as Lou Gehrig's disease (see Amyotrophic lateral sclerosis).

Lourdes: A small town of fifteen thousand inhabitants in the southwest of France in the foothills in the Département Haute Pyrénées, east of Pau and west of Tarbes and Toulouse; often referring to the Catholic Shrine and Sanctuary of Lourdes, situated at the edge of town and made famous since the 1858 apparitions of the Mother of God to a young local girl, Bernadette Soubirous, in the Grotto (cave), uncovering a spring of water resulting in cures and conversions.

Lourdes Hospitality: A Public Association of the Christian Faithful under the authority of a bishop or a religious order, with a mission to bring the sick and the suffering on pilgrimage to Lourdes, France.

Lourdes Sanctuary: *Sanctuaire Notre-Dame de Lourdes*, is the Catholic Shrine of Our Lady of Lourdes in the southwest of France, which welcomes millions of pilgrims annually, the Domain being over 100 hectares (about 250 acres) administered under the authority of the Council of the Bishops of France.

Lourdes Water: Natural undiluted spring water of the Grotto of Lourdes renowned for inexplicable healings, cures, and conversions (not the same as holy water, which is blessed water over which a priest has prayed prayers of exorcism). Lourdes Water is water from the spring of the Grotto uncovered by Bernadette at the direction of the most beautiful lady (the Immaculate Conception) in the ninth apparition, on February 25, 1858.

Mass or Holy Mass (*Missa* in Latin): The liturgy in which the mystery of salvation is accomplished through Consecration and Transubstantiation of the Holy Eucharist, concluding with the sending forth (*missio* or mission, or commissioning) of the faithful to fulfill God's will in their daily lives (*CCC* 1332).

Medical Bureau: The *Bureau des Constatations Médicales de Lourdes*, or the Office of Medical Observations of the Sanctuary of Lourdes, commonly known as the Medical Bureau by English speakers, was established in 1883 with a permanent physician in the Sanctuary to receive declarations of cures and to oversee critical examinations of alleged cures, including convening meetings to discuss the cases; the place where the extensive records of claimed cures (more than 7,800 as of the time of the publication of this book) are kept and where medical professionals can register with AMIL when present in the Sanctuary.

Military Pilgrimage: Pèlerinage Militaire International (PMI) or Pilgrimage Military International is the annual May pilgrimage to Lourdes, founded after World War II to bring peace and healing to wounded veterans.

Miracle: In Latin, *miraculum*, from *mirari*, "to wonder," a supernatural sign beyond human capability, brought about by God to signify His glory and for the salvation of mankind; a cure, healing, or restoration of life that cannot be explained other than to be attributed to God; an officially proclaimed cure or healing pronounced by a bishop of the Catholic Church.

Monseigneur: The title of a bishop (*évêque*) in France. *Monseigneur* is not to be confused with *monsignor*, pronounced the same in English. A monsignor (or *monsignori*, in Italian and French) is a priest who has been honored by the Pope for his service to the Church.

Monstrance: A metal pedestaled vessel designed to encase the Eucharistic Host to be carried in solemn processions or for exposition for prayerful devotion or ceremonies.

Mother of God: The dogma affirmed at the Council of Ephesus (AD 431) that Mary, as the Mother of Our Lord Jesus Christ, is the Mother of God in the flesh, deserving of the title and honor.

Mystagogue: From the Greek *mystagogos* and *agein*, the fourth stage in the Rite of Christian Initiation of Adults (RCIA, now OCIA: Order of Christian Initiation for Adults), in which new converts are led through the mysteries of faith as the follow-through instruction to be steadfast in living their new faith after entering the Church at Easter.

Mysteries of the Rosary: Significant moments in the lives of Jesus Christ and of Mary on which people meditate while praying the Rosary. Each set of mysteries—the Joyful, the Sorrowful, the Luminous, and the Glorious Mysteries—comprises five such moments or events.

NDL: Acronym for Notre-Dame de Lourdes, French for "Our Lady of Lourdes."

Notre-Dame de Lourdes or Notre-Dame (**NDL**): French for "Our Lady of Lourdes," referring to the Mother of God, the Immaculate

Conception, who came down from Heaven and appeared eighteen times to Bernadette in the Grotto in Lourdes in 1858.

Novena: Traditionally nine consecutive days of prayer adapted from the nine days of intense prayer of the apostles in the Upper Room after Our Lord's Ascension into Heaven, culminating in the bestowing of the gifts of the Holy Spirit.

Nun-Clean: An expression for the attentiveness to cleanliness by religious sisters and religious orders, most often associated with hospital sanitation standards.

OCIA: Acronym for the Order of Christian Initiation for Adults.

Order of Christian Initiation for Adults (OCIA): Known until 2021 as the Rite of Christian Initiation for Adults (RCIA), the process through which unbaptized men and women enter the Catholic Church.

Our Lady of Lourdes: English for the French Notre-Dame de Lourdes, referring to the Mother of God, the Immaculate Conception, who came down from Heaven to appear eighteen times to Bernadette in the Grotto in Lourdes in 1858.

Pax Christi or PiX Chapel: Built within the Sanctuary as a holy monument to commemorate peace between Germany and France after World War I by housing the relics of St. Hildegard de Bingen and St. Bernard of Clairvaux, the chapel was deconstructed after World War II to make way for the construction of the new St. Pius X Underground Basilica for the centenary of the apparitions; the chapel's precious relics were "ground together to never be separated again" and relocated within the St. Pius X Underground Basilica as the new Eucharistic Chapel renamed Pax Christi Chapel (see St. Pius X Underground Basilica).

Pèlerinage Militaire International (PMI): Pilgrimage Military International is the annual May pilgrimage to Lourdes, founded after World War II to bring peace and healing to wounded veterans, service members, military families, and war survivors.

Pilgrim: A person on a personal journey to a holy place or a place where something holy occurred in a time set aside to seek, discover, or renew faith in God and mankind.

Pilgrimage: A journey to a holy place or a place where something holy has occurred; a time set aside to seek, discover, or renew faith in God and mankind.

Pilgrimage season: From Holy Week or about March 25 until about All Saints' Day (November 1), the Sanctuary of Lourdes offers International Mass on Sundays and Wednesdays, with the Eucharist Procession at 5:00 p.m. and the Candlelight Rosary Procession at 9:00 p.m. daily. Confession is available with extended hours, and both hospital-bed handicapped facilities (Accueils) are open for pilgrimage stays with the volunteers of Hospitalité Notre-Dame de Lourdes (HNDL) and (Sanctuary) Bénévole present in service to assist pilgrims.

Piscines: The building housing separate tubs, allowing pilgrims to bathe in Lourdes Water, as interpreted from the ninth apparition on February 25, 1858, when the most beautiful lady told Bernadette to "go drink of the fountain and you wash there."

Piscinière: Hospitalité Notre-Dame de Lourdes volunteer attendant who assists pilgrims to bathe in Lourdes Water.

PiX: Abbreviation for St. Pius X, commonly referring to the Underground Basilica in Lourdes or the Pax Christi Eucharistic Chapel, now housed within the Underground Basilica (see St. Pius X Underground Basilica).

Pope: The Successor of St. Peter in an unbroken chain of apostles going back to the apostles of Jesus Christ and the founding of the Catholic Church; the pope, also called the Holy Father, is the head of the Church.

Pope John Paul II: See John Paul II.

Post-Traumatic Stress Disorder (PTSD): A mental health condition brought on by a traumatic event and causing severe anxiety.

Procession: People moving together from one location to another in an organized way as participation in a spiritual festivity or formal event. There are two holy processions each day at Lourdes during the pilgrimage season (from Holy Week through October, until All Saints' Day, November 1): the Eucharistic Procession with the Blessed Sacrament at 5:00 p.m. and the Candlelight Rosary Procession at 9:00 p.m.

Public Association of the Christian Faithful: A Catholic group of baptized persons who devote themselves together to the work of the apostolate, fostering and deepening faith.

RCIA: Acronym for Rite of Christian Initiation for Adults. The process through which unbaptized men and women enter the Catholic Church. In 2021, the process name was changed to the Order of Christian Initiation for Adults (OCIA).

Rector or *Recteur*: The Catholic priest appointed by the bishop of the Sanctuary of Lourdes as responsible for the Sanctuary, both spiritually and practically in the administration of the sacraments and the coordination of welcoming and receiving millions of pilgrims annually.

Revert: A person who has left the Catholic Church or practice of the Catholic Faith and then returns to the sacraments as a full member of the Catholic Church, or to return to the faith or the Catholic Faith.

Rosary: A series of prayers with meditations on the significant moments in the lives of Jesus Christ and of Mary, usually prayed with a set of beads to help count the prayers of petition.

Rosary Basilica: The basilica built beneath and in front of the Immaculate Conception Basilica, consecrated in 1901 with the life-size mosaics of the Mysteries of the Rosary in fifteen naves. The modern Mysteries of Light mosaics were added to the exterior for the 150th anniversary in 2008.

Sacrament: "The sacraments are efficacious signs of grace, instituted by Christ and entrusted to the Church, by which divine life is dispensed to us. The visible rites by which the sacraments are celebrated signify and make present the graces proper to each sacrament. They bear fruit in those who receive them with the required dispositions" (*CCC* 1131). There are seven sacraments: Baptism, Confirmation, the Eucharist, Reconciliation, Matrimony, Holy Orders, and Anointing of the Sick.

Saint: Proven friend of God recognized formally through canonization by the Catholic Church.

Sainte or Ste.: French title for a Catholic canonized female saint.

Sanctuaire: French for "Sanctuary."

Sanctuary: The holy ground of the Domain of Lourdes, France, or the shrine of the Catholic Church of the approved Heavenly apparitions in the Grotto in 1858.

Sanctuary or *Sanctuaire* or Shrine: A holy site or place designated as a place of pilgrimage or worship for a particular reason or a specific purpose with the approval of the local bishop for the good of the faithful (see *Code of Canon Law*, canon 1230).

***Sœur Marie Bernarde* or Sr. Marie Bernarde**: Sister or Sr. Marie Bernarde is the religious name of Bernadette Soubirous, given to her at her religious profession by her congregation, later recognized as St. Bernadette Soubirous after her canonization in 1933.

Soubirous: Family surname of St. Bernadette.

Southern belle: An expression describing an early American refined lady of genteel society in the Deep South, derived from the French word *belle*, for "beauty"; today used in reference to an American southern lady known for her polished presence, manners, and gracious hospitality.

St. John Paul II: See John Paul II

St. or Ste. Bernadette Soubirous: The visionary of Lourdes, canonized on December 8, 1933, is a patroness and intercessor for the sick, the poor, the uneducated, the marginalized, and pilgrims; her feast day on the Catholic Church calendar is April 16, the day of her death and entrance into "the happiness of the other world," as the Mother of God promised her during the third apparition, on February 18, 1858, the day her feast is celebrated in France. St. Bernadette is known as the most beautiful of the incorrupt saints. Her body rests in a glass reliquary (relic receptacle) in the chapel of the former motherhouse convent of her religious order in Nevers, now a pilgrim retreat center (see Bernadette Soubirous and Sœur Marie Bernarde).

St. Joseph's Service: Hospitalité Notre-Dame de Lourdes Service, consisting traditionally of male volunteers who offer service in assisting pilgrims at the airport and the train station and at the exterior of the Baths and in assisting men to bathe in Lourdes Water;

and to maintain peaceful order in the Grotto, at the International Mass, and in the twice-daily processions. In the 2020s, this service also guides first-year volunteers (stagiaires) in a "year of discovery" introducing each of the different services.

St. Pius X Underground Basilica or the Underground Basilica: The basilica was consecrated in 1958 for the centenary of the apparitions to seat twenty-five thousand faithful and designed with designated space for pilgrims on stretchers, in wheelchairs, and in voitures; the building is touted as an engineering feat, constructed in the subterrain rocky soil on the water table just beneath it. The Pax Christi Chapel of Peace, built for reconciliation after World War I, was deconstructed to allow the construction of the large basilica, said to be second in size only to St. Peter's in Rome. The Pax Christi Chapel is now the Eucharistic chapel at the main Sanctuary entry of the basilica.

Stage: The time of committed service in the Hospitalité Notre-Dame to Lourdes, most often one or two weeks annually.

Stagiaire: A person learning service with the Hospitalité Notre-Dame de Lourdes.

Supportive Needs Pilgrimage: Known as "Sick and Disabled Pilgrimages" by the Europeans and formerly as Special Needs Pilgrimage by Americans, these are organized pilgrimages to assist pilgrims with specialized or medical needs to travel and stay in Lourdes with the assistance of medical volunteers and lay volunteers, sometimes students and youth, accompanied by priests for a week of spiritual respite and retreat in Lourdes, France.

Tabernacle: A holy receptacle to house the Blessed Sacrament in a Catholic church or chapel.

Transubstantiation: The complete changing of the substance of unleavened bread and wine into the Body and Blood of Jesus Christ, with His Soul and Divinity (*CCC* 1413), through the words of Consecration by a Catholic priest at Mass.

Underground Basilica: See St. Pius X Underground Basilica.

Unexplained or inexplicable cure: The cure without medical or scientific explanation of a diagnosed condition or disease.

Vatican: The papal headquarters of the Catholic Church in Vatican City, within Rome, Italy.

Viaticum: The Last Holy Communion or reception of the Sacrament of the Holy Eucharist at the time of death, sometimes called "The Bread of Angels."

Chapter Annotated Summaries

Everyday Miracles of Lourdes comprises twenty-one compelling true stories of healing, love, suffering, brokenness, conversion, peace, and joy—through the grace of Lourdes. Relatable real-life experiences of differing relevant topics are woven together into a fascinating fabric of the handiwork of God, the Master Weaver of all transformative graces and miracles.

Grief, suicide, forgiveness, faith, post-abortive suffering, scrupulosity, addiction, sexual abuse, mental illness, near-death experience, the pandemic crisis, preparation for a holy death, and selfless love ultimately inspire the reader through miraculous intercessions of uniquely personal stories.

For more than a century, miraculous Lourdes stories have captivated the curious, nonbelievers, seekers, and faithful from around the world. These recent stories are sure to capture readers today.

Pope Francis about Stories

"Each of us knows different stories that have the fragrance of the Gospel, that have borne witness to the Love that transforms life. These stories cry out to be shared, recounted and brought to life in every age, in every language, in every medium" (Pope Francis, World Communications Day 2020).

Preface

A short explanation of why this book is relevant today and how it came to be written.

Introduction to Lourdes

A brief summary of the approved 1858 Apparitions at Lourdes, France; to the miracles that occurred; to inexplicable cures and the process of proclaiming an official miracle; and to Bernadette Soubirous, the saint who, as a young girl, was blessed by eighteen Heavenly visits with the Immaculate Conception.

Chapter 1. Greatest Grace Needed: Forgiving Marlene

A first-person account of descent into agoraphobia and the suffering of traumatic assaults unexpectedly healed in the Baths at Lourdes. This authentic holy experience introduces the reader to twenty chapters of amazing graces witnessed by the author in the founding of the first Lourdes Hospitality of the Americas as the grace of Lourdes continues to flow over two decades.

Chapter 2. Under Her Mantle: Changed Claudette

Suffering with bipolar disorder and addiction, a lapsed Catholic drastically changes her life as a grace and fruit of a pilgrimage to Lourdes. After receiving the Sacrament of Reconciliation in Nevers, she returns home to wear a Miraculous Medal, which becomes a significant consolation to her family when she dies unexpectedly a few years later. The grace of Lourdes changed how she lived the remainder of her life in this world and surely her journey to the "happiness of the other world."

Chapter 3. Crossing the Mary Bridge: Texas Pancho

A new convert immersed in the richness of two millennia of Catholic teachings and history deftly avoids the Blessed Mother throughout RCIA (now OCIA). Ultimately and ironically, he finds it impossible to continue to avoid the Mother of God once inside the Church. Praying in earnest, he asks Jesus to let him know if Mary is truly *that* important to Him and if He wants her to be known to him personally. Serving in Lourdes affirms that Mary is important to Jesus and to each of us.

Chapter 4. Cured to Serve: Saint-Frai Chrissy

Diagnosed with a debilitating incurable disease in the prime of life, a woman experiences an unexpected cure at Lourdes during the Papal Mass of Pope Benedict XVI for the 150th Anniversary of the Grotto apparitions in 2008. No longer needing a wheelchair or a feeding tube, the humbled woman returns to Lourdes each year for a decade to confer with the Medical Bureau about her cure and to serve the sick and suffering in thanksgiving.

Chapter 5. A Will to Live: Baby Ida-Linda

Not long after the death of her husband, a young widow discovers that she is an abortion survivor descending her into debilitating depression. A pilgrimage to Lourdes returns the broken woman from the depths of despair to her childhood Catholic faith, to fully embrace her life as worth living in the sacraments.

Chapter 6. To "Bee" in the Heavenly Procession: Floral Cora

An unsuspecting home gardener is unknowingly severely allergic to bees. She is stung in the throat and lands in a coma in the intensive care unit of a California hospital. Inexplicably, she finds herself following the Eucharistic Procession at Lourdes, France. Once awake, she is convinced that when we die, we need only to follow Jesus in the Holy Eucharist to Heaven, just as pilgrims at Lourdes follow along in the Eucharistic Procession daily in the Sanctuary in France.

Chapter 7. A Sign of the Cross: Joyful Jamie

A young-adult quadriplegic sinks into bitterness, discouraged by living in an institutional government-sponsored group home. In Lourdes, he discovers his joyful purpose, and although unable to move his arms, he becomes a catechist, teaching others to make a holy Sign of the Cross, like Bernadette and Our Lady in the Grotto.

Chapter 8. Last Obstacle to Total Love: Wishful Andrea

A beautiful young dying woman hides her discomfort around disabled people until she winds up in a wheelchair herself. Weakened after a platelet transfusion in Lourdes, avoiding people in wheelchairs proves impossible in the miraculous international city for the sick and the disabled. Surrounded by people also seated in wheelchairs, she quickly falls in love with each person she encounters and is transformed so as to overcome her last obstacle to total love.

Chapter 9. A Liquid Grace Fills the Hole: Scottish Sheena

Pregnant at fifteen in an unchurched family in which abortion is a solution and not a problem, a pregnant teen is dragged by her mother, kicking and screaming, to abort her baby. She grows up continuing to bereave the forced loss of her first child, with nothing able to fill the secret gaping void within her. Arriving to volunteer in Lourdes, she is surprised to discover that a liquid grace fills the hole within her, making her forever whole again.

Chapter 10. 'Til Death Do Us Part: Dolores and Alejandro

A prayerful elderly couple struggles as the wife, nearing her hundredth birthday, comes to fear surviving her beloved husband. Although she has lost her zest for life along with her appetite, after receiving Anointing of the Sick and the Sacrament of Reconciliation in Lourdes, her faith is strengthened, her appetite returns, and her zeal for living is restored in the confidence of God's plan for the happiness of each of us in this world and in the other, as Our Lady promised Bernadette.

Chapter 11. Blessed Daughter and Mother: Awesome Alley

Adopted at four years old and then sexually abused by a neighbor a few years later, a little girl suffers with her terrible secret while her mother battles bouts of debilitating depression. As a preteen, she slips into a rebellious angst and is sent to Lourdes to serve on a youth mission trip. There she finds faith and healing, returning to Lourdes each summer to receive a different grace awaiting her, forming her to become a faithful, holy young woman, wife, and mother.

Chapter 12. A Mystery of a Holy Eucharist: Minnesota Marlow

Mysteriously, a registration packet arrives in the Lourdes Volunteers office with the Holy Eucharist inexplicably attached to the passport photo. Unbeknownst to the office team, scrupulosity had long overtaken the faithful man with the mysterious Host covering his face. Convinced he was unworthy to receive the Holy Eucharist for decades, while serving in Lourdes, through learning the humility of Bernadette and her love of the Holy Eucharist, he returns to the sacraments.

Chapter 13. Hurt to Healed to Happy: Transatlantic Theresa

Broken in unending grief after the death of her husband by suicide, a widow finds healing and consolation in Lourdes. She discovers the compassion of the Catholic Church for those grieving the loss of loved ones who have taken their lives, often misunderstood within and outside the Church. In thanksgiving for her healing to holy grieving, she dedicates one year full-time to helping the new Lourdes Hospitality. Returning to France to serve at the conclusion of her selfless service, the widow meets a charming Irish volunteer and eventually remarries, finding happiness again.

Chapter 14. Ordinary Saints Heaven-Bound: Greatest-Generation Gene

A World War II veteran is nearing the end of his life struggles, plagued by the memory of an enemy boy dying in a uniform he was too small to fit into and too young to wear. Arriving in Lourdes during the annual International Military Pilgrimage, he meets a volunteer from Arnhem, Holland, with a lifelong desire to thank the Allied Forces for saving her city and country. Meeting together in Lourdes, the volunteer is finally able to thank an American veteran for making it possible for her to grow up and live a happy life, while the veteran comes to realize that, although many young boys died in the war, many young girls and boys were saved and survived by those losses. The meeting finally brings peace to them both.

Chapter 15. Fostering Love: Teddy-Jeremy

A profoundly disabled infant is placed in foster care at birth. His mother, unable to care for her blind, autistic, quadriplegic child, quickly relinquishes her parental rights. It is predicted that the child will linger in foster care or institutionalization to meet an early death. Taking a temporary assignment to pay for a mother-daughter volunteer pilgrimage to Lourdes, a physical therapist meets the baby and falls in love with him, and the family officially adopts him. He is baptized and years later receives Holy Communion in the Grotto at Lourdes to become a living Eucharistic tabernacle.

Chapter 16. Revenge Reversal: Southern Cynthia

A young mother is shot point-blank in the abdomen by her ex-husband and left for dead. Suffering through thirty-three life-saving surgeries, she resents that the shotgun wound never closes and is often infected. Fearful of the impending release of her abusive perpetrator, she secretly plots a final revenge. A small bottle of Lourdes Water poured into the gaping hole miraculously closes her open wound overnight. Making a pilgrimage to Lourdes in thanksgiving, she unexpectedly repents of her plan to settle the score with her ex-husband after his release from prison.

Chapter 17. Broken to Blessed: Bereaved Brian

Devastated by the death of his only son in a tragic car accident, a medical officer is deployed one month later to the war-torn Middle East. Returning home one year later, he is embittered, without faith and away from the Church. Recruited to assist American wounded and disabled service members and veterans to Lourdes for the International Military Pilgrimage, he is consoled by Our Lady of Lourdes in the Grotto, bringing him home to the sacraments and the Catholic Church.

Chapter 18. Frightened to Fearless: Jenna's Family

A fearless U.S. Navy Explosives Ordnance Disposal (EOD) officer and special-operations diver with nerves of steel becomes increasingly frightened for the life of her severely disabled daughter with an incurable, debilitating medical condition. After a family pilgrimage to Lourdes, the Navy veteran, her husband, and their two other children find confidence in God's plan for them, allowing happiness to be restored at home, with worry replaced by trust in God's will for their little holy family.

Chapter 19. Mother Knows Best: Colleen and Maris

Traveling to Lourdes, a lone woman in the airport is invited to join a small pilgrimage, which is later discovered to be the answer to her desperate prayers in Paris after losing all of her belongings in the airport while missing her flight home to Africa. Meanwhile, the dying woman who extended the impromptu invitation, with the help of her newfound friend and the nurse assigned to assist her, makes a holy Confession, reconciling herself to God in preparation for a holy death.

Chapter 20. Holy Hurricane Rescue: Mister Earl

Following a pilgrimage to Lourdes, a new devotee of Bernadette returns home to New Orleans, promising a neighbor that he will watch over his elderly mother for the weekend. Hurricane Katrina strikes the unsuspecting residents, and the man struggles to coax his neighbor to safety. Refusing to abandon her, he finally convinces her to be evacuated as the water is rising dangerously fast. Making his way out, he is overcome by the wind and the deep water, screaming out to Bernadette for her intercession: he needs a miracle to survive. She hears his plea and intercedes to save him.

Chapter 21. Pandemic Prayers: Nurse Lindsey

Assisting the sick on pilgrimage to Lourdes, a nurse returns to the sacraments after a ten-year lapse. Soon after, the worldwide pandemic strikes, with the nurse finding herself responsible for one hundred virus-stricken patients. Bolstered by her experience in Lourdes, she finds a priest to bring Anointing to her Catholic patients, caring for both their bodies and souls. Contracting the virus herself, the nurse comes to know personally the value of suffering from her Lourdes experience and St. Bernadette.

About the Author

Marlene Watkins is the founder of Our Lady of Lourdes Hospitality North American Volunteers, the first Lourdes Hospitality outside Europe and the first in the Americas.

In twenty-five years, as a volunteer, Marlene has led more than two hundred pilgrimages to Lourdes for more than seven thousand pilgrims, including the seriously ill and the profoundly disabled, with medical, adult, university, and youth volunteers. Marlene has also guided Lourdes Virtual Pilgrimage Experiences™ across North America and in Europe, Asia, South America, and Africa.

Marlene hosts the popular weekly series *My Lourdes Faith Journey* on EWTN and has appeared on CBS, EWTN, PBS, and the BBC. In 2015, Marlene was named an Our Sunday Visitor "Catholic of the Year" and is a speaker at conferences, events, on radio shows and podcasts.

Marlene is a wife, mother, grandmother, Secular Franciscan, and member of the Hospitalité Notre-Dame de Lourdes. She and her husband, Bill, live in Syracuse, New York, or in the LourdesMobile RV, traveling America the Beautiful to share the Gospel Message of Lourdes.

All proceeds from *Everyday Miracles of Lourdes* support the mission of Our Lady of Lourdes Hospitality North American Volunteers, a Public Association of the Christian Faithful and 501(c)3 non-profit charity: www.lourdesvolunteers.org.